White-Collar Deviance

White-Collar Deviance

David R. Simon
San Jose State University
University of California, Berkeley

Frank E. Hagan
Mercyhurst College

Allyn and Bacon
Boston • London • Toronto • Sydney • Tokyo • Singapore

To Judy for all the encouragement and support.
To MaryAnn and Shannon

Editor in Chief, Social Sciences: Karen Hanson
Editorial Assistant: Heather Ahlstrom
Marketing Manager: Suzy Spivey
Editorial Production Service: Chestnut Hill Enterprises, Inc.
Cover Administrator: Jennifer Hart

Copyright © 1999 by Allyn & Bacon
A Viacom Company
160 Gould Street
Needham Heights, MA 02194

Internet: www.abacon.com
America Online: keyword: College Online

Library of Congress Cataloging-in-Publication Data

Simon, David R.
    White collar deviance / by David R. Simon and Frank E. Hagan.
      p.   cm.
    Includes bibliographical references and index.
    ISBN 0-205-27508-7
    1. White collar crimes—United States. 2. Deviant behavior.
  3. Elite (Social sciences)—United States. 4. Corporations—United
States—Corrupt practices. I. Hagan, Frank E. II. Title.
HV6769.S57   1998
364.16'8—dc21   98-5771
                               CIP

Printed in the United States of America

10 9 8 7 6 5 4 3 2 1 RRD-VA 03 02 01 00 99 98

Brief Contents

Contents

Preface

Paradigm shift is a phrase that is used only infrequently in social science. However, that is what those of us who toil in the vineyards of white-collar crime studies face. For example, in June, 1996, the National White Collar Crime Center sponsored an academic workshop of white-collar crime scholars entitled, "Definitional Dilemma: Can and Should There Be a Universal Definition of White Collar Crime?" (Helmkamp, Ball, & Townsend, 1996). For three days white-collar crime experts, including the authors of this book, debated this issue. On the second day, a group of participants during lunch attempted, half in jest, to agree on a definition by passing around and revising a definition written on a napkin. This "National White Collar Crime Center definition" of white-collar crime fits the authors' definition of white-collar deviance:

> *Planned illegal* or unethical acts *of deception committed by an individual or organization,* usually *during the course of legitimate occupational activity by persons of high or respectable social status for personal or organizational gain that violates fiduciary responsibility or public trust (Helmkamp, Ball, & Townsend, 1996, p. iii).*

For the first time, a group with the sanction of the federal government has endorsed a definition of white-collar crime based on something other than violations of law. The implications of this definition are immense, and this book is an effort to explore some of the implications of this new definition.

Ethical issues have now been "officially" introduced into the study of "white-collar crime" (or more correctly, as the title of this text reflects, white-collar *deviance*). While it may seem to some that introducing an ethical dimension into the study of so-called white-collar wrongdoing is to merely touch off an endless debate, we beg to differ. As one of the authors of this book has argued for nearly twenty years (Simon, 1997; 1999), the measurable standard of harm (damage)—physical, financial, and moral—constitutes an objective, empirical standard by which the ethical dimensions of a deviant act may be assessed. (This line of reasoning is more fully explored in Chapter 1.)

White-collar wrongdoing of all types and forms will now have to be reclassified, and new typologies of wrongdoing may emerge. To this end, one of the many features of this book is an in-depth examination of both extant and proposed typologies of acts of white-collar deviance. These are explored in Chapter 1 and most other chapters throughout the book. Some of the critical thinking exercises at the end of each of the first seven chapters also reflect our typological concerns.

The new definition of white-collar deviance leads us to a basic classification scheme, one that notes the qualitative and quantitative differences between elite versus nonelite white-collar deviance. This distinction is also described in Chapter 1, which contains an explanation of the economic and political environment that shapes both the culture and nature of elite and nonelite white-collar wrongdoing.

Acts of elite deviance are of such seriousness that they constitute grounds for a separate area of study. To this end, Chapters 2 and 3 contain in-depth discussions of economic and political aspects of elite deviance.

Chapters 4 and 5 explore various dimensions of occupational and professional white-collar deviance as perpetrated by both elite and nonelite white-collar deviants. Here are explored a host of scandals and fraud schemes that contribute to so much of the financial and moral harm that haunts American life.

Chapter 6, unique among white-collar crime writings, analyzes the similarities and interrelationships between white-collar wrongdoing and the activities of organized criminal syndicates. A key argument here is that much of what the media tell us about organized crime is mythical. Gangsters, deviant businesspeople, corrupt politicians, and criminal justice system personnel are all equal and interactive players in a corrupted world.

Chapter 7 presents a multiunit theory of white-collar deviance. It argues that a comprehensive sociological theory of white-collar wrongdoing must explain causal variables on the macro, organizational, and individual levels. The chapter offers a paradigm for such an analysis, as well as hypotheses derived from the paradigm. Similarly analyzed are victimization patterns associated with white-collar deviance, as well as the various interrelationships between all types of deviant behavior.

Finally, Chapter 8 focuses on the policy issues related to topics explored in this book. The chapter discusses both extant policies, as well as those policies we believe necessary for adoption if inroads against this most serious of social problems are to be made. Finally, this chapter also contains an appendix of readings and organizations that will aid those concerned in fighting the various ills associated with white-collar deviance. We present this as an aid to both instructors and students seeking to overcome the resignation and cynicism that so often characterize the attempt to "afflict the comfortable."

White-Collar Deviance, like the authors' other works, is a volume written with passion and with the hope of changing the dangerous patterns associated with white-collar wrongdoing. We sincerely want you to enjoy this book, and to join us in the fight against the great evils it portrays.

Acknowledgments

David Simon would like to thank those who have provided various forms of inspiration in the writing of this book, especially Max Lopez-Ceperro, his pastor. Thanked as well is Judy Simon for her great love and intellectual stimulation relating to the issues raised here.

Frank Hagan would like to thank Editor-in-Chief Karen Hanson of Allyn and Bacon for her encouragement. Thanks also to MaryAnn Hagan for her support and tolerance of my life as a writer.

Chapter 1

White-Collar Deviance: An Emerging Perspective

Why White-Collar "Deviance"?

- Members of the National Security Council conduct secret, illegal foreign policy financed in part by bankrupting savings and loan organizations.
- An intelligence agency steals the commercial secrets of a private company. That same private company employs organized criminals to control labor unions. Another company forces its franchise holders to swindle customers on automobile repairs, while another rolls back odometers on "new" cars before selling them as new products.
- Chinese agents are accused of buying influence in U.S. federal elections through campaign donations.
- Prudential-Bache is convicted of swindling policyholders.
- Mexican, Japanese, and Russian officials are accused of cooperating with organized crime and drug gangs; tobacco companies admit lying about the lethal consequences of their product.
- High government officials in Albania swindle their citizens in a huge Ponzi scheme.
- The CIA is revealed to have a long history of entering into agreements with drug smugglers, even to the point of engaging in joint drug-trafficking ventures to raise funds for its various covert operations.

Scandalous episodes from the Kennedy-Johnson years to the Clinton White House have rocked virtually every recent administration:

- During the Vietnam War (1964–1975), the Pentagon Papers, investigative reporting, and leaks from within the government had the effect of turning public opinion against the war and the government. A number of governmental transgressions were revealed, including:

- The manipulation of Congress by President Johnson with the Gulf of Tonkin incident; the indictment of high-ranking officers for war crimes similar to those committed by the Germans and Japanese during World War II.
- The deliberate destruction of civilian targets by U.S. forces; intelligence agency suppression of information regarding enemy troop strength and sympathizers in South Vietnam; falsified reports by U.S. field commanders regarding the destruction of enemy targets; the spraying of more than five million acres of South Vietnam with defoliating chemicals; the execution of more than 40,000 so-called enemy agents by the Central Intelligence Agency (CIA) under the Phoenix Program (most without trial); and unauthorized bombing raids against North Vietnam.

- From early 1969 until May 1970, President Nixon assured the U.S. people that the neutrality of Cambodia was being respected. Yet Nixon had secretly ordered the bombing of so-called enemy sanctuaries in that country during that period. He was able to keep the bombings secret through the use of a double-entry bookkeeping system arranged between the White House and the Department of Defense.
- In 1975, governmental investigations revealed that the CIA had violated its charter by engaging in domestic intelligence, opening the mail of U.S. citizens and spying on congresspersons and newspaper reporters. Moreover, this organization plotted the assassinations of a number of foreign political officials. Most significant, the Senate Intelligence Committee revealed that every U.S. president from Eisenhower to Nixon had lied to the American people about the activities of the CIA. Public confidence in government was also lowered when it became known that every president since Franklin Roosevelt had used the Federal Bureau of Investigation (FBI) for political and sometimes illegal purposes. After J. Edgar Hoover's death, we found out how the FBI had been used by its longtime chief to silence his and the bureau's critics. Hoover had also involved the FBI in a number of illegal acts to defeat or neutralize those domestic groups that he thought were subversive (Simon, 1999, Chapter 6).
- The Watergate scandal, and its aftermath, 1972–1974, brought down the Nixon administration. Watergate was also the most significant contributor to low public confidence in government in the past quarter century. The litany of illegal acts by governmental officials and/or their agents in Watergate included securing illegal campaign contributions, dirty tricks to discredit political opponents, burglary, bribery, perjury, wiretapping, harassment of administration opponents with tax audits, and the like.
- The Reagan administration did virtually nothing to increase public confidence in the ethical conduct of government officials. In 1987, news broke concerning what was to be the most damaging scandal of the Reagan presidency, the so-called Iran-Contra affair. The root of the scandal involved the diversion of funds from profits on missiles sold to the Iranian government.

At first, the entire episode was blamed on U.S. Marine Lt. Col. Oliver North. Virtually all high-ranking officials of the Reagan administration claiming they were "out of the loop" concerning any knowledge of the events. Subsequent investigations and trial testimony, however, pointed to a massive cover-up by White House aides and others.

Both the illegal arms sales and illegal solicitation of funds were orchestrated by a secret group, Operation Enterprise, set up apart from the CIA and other governmental agencies to assure secrecy. It was composed of retired military and intelligence personnel, arms dealers, and drug smugglers.

A report issued in 1994 by Special Council Lawrence Walsh indicated that Reagan administration officials covered up many aspects of the scandal to insure "plausible deniability" of knowledge of the scandal by President Reagan. Walsh's report also concluded that former President George Bush had lied to the press and the American people concerning his knowledge of various aspects of Iran Contra.

The Clinton administration began suffering from the effects of scandal almost immediately upon taking office:

- Two nominees for attorney general, Zoe Baird and Judge Kimba Wood, had both employed illegal aliens in violation of a 1986 immigration law, and their nominations had to be withdrawn.
- A special prosecutor was appointed in 1994 to investigate the connection of the president and Mrs. Clinton to the failed Whitewater savings and loan in Arkansas. Soon after, the president established his own legal defense fund, hoping to raise $2 million to ward off his increasing legal costs. The president is also being sued for sexual harassment by a former employee of the state of Arkansas, and Mr. Clinton is in a position requiring constant defense of his own moral character.
- One hundred agents of the Bureau of Alcohol, Tobacco, and Firearms burned the Waco, Texas, compound of the extremist Branch Dividians cult in 1993. At least 72 cult members died in the fire and gun battle. The agents in charge significantly altered written plans for the raid after the 100 deaths, and then tried to conceal the changes from officials investigating the raid (Simon, 1996, 3–5).

The U.S. Congress has also suffered its share of scandals, and these have badly damaged its credibility.

- In 1993, the former House Postmaster Robert Rota and three House Post Office employees plead guilty to stealing cash and stamps. Rota claimed he gave two House members, Dan Rostenkowski (D-IL) and Joe Kolter (D-PA), $30,000 in Post Office funds. Rostenkowski, powerful head of the House Ways and Means Committee, was released in fall 1997 from a halfway house after serving a 15-month prison term.

The above listed acts involve various business and political organizations in the United States and throughout the world. At first glance, these episodes may seem diverse and unrelated, but what is important for our purposes is what these various acts have in common. The characteristics they share comprise what we term "white-collar deviance." Their common characteristics are as follows:

1. White-collar deviance is not restricted to just legally defined crimes, but includes many unethical acts, harmful activities, civil and regulatory violations, and the like. The term white-collar deviance or offenses is a more encompassing construct than "white-collar crime."

2. Deviant acts are so categorized because they are *harmful*. Harm is a useful criterion because it may be *objectively* defined and measured, and need not be the subject of endless philosophical debate concerning values, or whether or not a harmful act is still harmful even if has not been officially labeled as "a social problem" by the larger society.

3. There are three basic types of harm that will serve as our criteria for white-collar deviance. These include:

a. *Physical harm:* physical injury, illness, death. Many types of white-collar deviance cause physical injury and/or death. These include not telling workers they are coming into contact with dangerous chemicals, cancer-causing substances that are added to the food supply, the U.S. government's use of atomic bullets in the Gulf War, which exposed its own troops to radioactivity, and countless others discussed in depth below.

b. *Financial harm:* fraud, and various scams that are not legally defined as fraud but that nevertheless cause consumers and investors to be deprived of their funds without receiving the goods or services for which they contracted. Just to take one common example: Every drugstore in the United States features products that are termed "fat burners," yet there is no scientific evidence whatever that any substance will "burn" fat. Such products are legal, but worthless.

c. *Moral harm:* deviant behavior by elites (people who head governmental and corporate institutions) that encourages deviance, distrust, cynicism, or alienation among the rest of the population. Before Richard Nixon resigned from the presidency in 1974, for example, his administration had been involved in a broad range of deviant acts: burglarizing of the headquarters of the Democratic National Committee, attempts to rig elections, lying to Congress and the American people about the secret illegal bombing of Cambodia, bribery, and tax evasion (Simon, 1996, 3–4). After the Watergate scandal and Nixon's resignation, confidence in government fell dramatically, and it has never recovered.

4. White-collar crime and deviance fall into two basic categories. First, many examples that opened this chapter involve the largest and most wealthy global corporations and the most powerful branches of the American government. When such entities are the perpetrators, one is speaking of *elite white-collar deviance.* In general, elite white-collar deviance is more harmful because the actors involved have the most resources, and the consequences of their acts are more often national, international, or even global in scope. *Nonelite white collar deviance,* in contrast, involves businesses and governmental organizations whose actions impact more on a regional, state, or local level, and while the actions of such entities can still be devastating within their confines, they nevertheless are usually less consequential than acts of elite white-collar deviance.

5. White-collar offenders do not view themselves as criminals, and crime is not their predominant activity. This distinguishes white-collar offending from some other types of elite crime such as professional and organized crime (Hagan, 1996). There is, however, overwhelming evidence that most white-collar wrongdoing is planned, and that those engaging in it know that it is illegal (Kappeler et al., 1997, 142–144).

The concept of "white-collar crime" was first introduced by Edwin Sutherland in a 1939 address to the American Sociological Association. He defined white-collar crime as "a crime committed by a person of respectability and high social status in the course of his occupation" (Sutherland, 1940). Later, Sutherland (1949) conducted an empirical investigation of such "crimes in the suites," examining regulatory agency records on the seventy largest industrial and mercantile corporations for a 40-year period. He found that every one was a violator of regulations against false advertising, patent abuse, wartime trade violations, price-fixing, fraud, and intended manufacturing and sale of faulty goods. He also noted that even though such crimes cost far more than "crime in the streets," they were handled in a very mild manner.

Figure 1.1 provides working definitions of the various types of deviance and crime to be discussed (see Albanese, 1995; Blankenship, 1995; and Jamieson, 1995).

As recounted in the Preface, in June 1996, the National White Collar Crime Center sponsored an academic workshop of white-collar crime scholars entitled, "Definitional Dilemma: Can and Should There Be a Universal Definition of White Collar Crime?" (Helmkamp, Ball,

---

Sutherland's initial definition of "white collar crime" has been criticized for being too general; however, many of the synonyms, proposed substitutes, variations, and related terms have failed to provide any greater lexicographic precision.

White Collar Crime involves "a crime committed by a person of respectability and high social status in the course of his occupation" (Sutherland, 1949, 9).

Criminaloid is a concept introduced by E. A. Rose (1907) that preceded Sutherland. Criminaloids are "those who prospered through flagitious [grossly wicked] practices."

Avocational Crime is a crime that is deterrable by the prospect of public labeling as a criminal, committed by one who does not think of himself or herself as a criminal and whose major source of income or status is something other than crime (Geis, 1974, 273).

Corporate Crime consists of the offense committed by corporate officials for their corporations and the offenses of the corporation itself (Clinard & Quinney, 1986, 188).

Economic Crime refers to any nonviolent, illegal activity that principally involves deceit, misrepresentation, concealment, manipulation, breach of trust, subterfuge, or illegal circumvention (American Bar Association, 1952).

Elite Crime is a violation of the law committed by a person or group of persons in the course of an otherwise respected and legitimate occupation or financial activity (Coleman, 1989, 5).

Elite Deviance refers to "acts by elites and/or the organizations they head that result in any of the following types of harms": physical, financial, or moral (Simon, 1996, 35).

Occupational Crime consists of offenses committed by individuals for themselves in the course of their occupations and of offenses of employees against their employers (Clinard & Quinney, 1986, 188).

Organizational Crime involves illegal actions taken in accordance with operative organizational goals that seriously (physically or economically) harm employees, consumers, or the general public (Schrager & Short, 1978, 411–412).

Professional Crime is illegal behavior for economic gain or even for economic livelihood that involves a highly developed criminal career, considerable skill, high status among criminals, and fairly successful avoidance of detection (Clinard & Quinney, 1986, 246).

Upperworld Crime refers to laundering acts committed by those who, due to their position in the social structure, have obtained specialized kinds of occupational slots essential for the commission of these offenses (Geis, 1974, 114).

FIGURE 1.1   Definitions of White-Collar Crime/Deviance and Related Concepts

& Townsend, 1996). For three days white-collar crime experts, including the authors of this book, debated this issue. On the second day a group of participants during lunch attempted, half in jest, to agree on a definition by passing around and revising a definition written on a napkin. This "National White Collar Crime Center definition" of white-collar crime fits the authors' definition of *white-collar deviance:*

> *Planned illegal* or unethical acts *of deception committed by an individual or organization, usually during the course of legitimate occupational activity by persons of high or respectable social status for personal or organizational gain that violates fiduciary responsibility or public trust (Helmkamp, Ball, & Townsend, 1996, p. iii).*

Sutherland's (1949, 9) initial concept of white-collar crime, defined as "a crime by a person of respectability and high social status in the course of his occupation" has been criticized on a number of points mainly relating to the unclear importance attached to the status of the offender and the fact that such crime includes deviant behaviors that are not necessarily illegal (Quinney, 1964, 285). While these criticisms are on target, the importance of Sutherland's concept lies not in the scientific utility, but rather in its sensitizing quality. It alerted us to a phenomenon and, as a result, the field of criminology would never be the same.

Weisburd and Schlegel (1992, 352–353) add:

> *Indeed, the concept of white-collar crime itself has come under increasing attack. Much of this has been in the form of "soul searching" by those who want to more clearly define what the study of white-collar crime should encompass. Should we limit our concern to crimes of the upper socioeconomic classes, or to those that involve some occupational or organizational position for their commission? Should we focus on the offender or the offense, or should we see white-collar crime as the result of some special blend of interaction between them? Whatever direction the debate over definition in white-collar crime has taken, it has more often served to confuse those outside the small cadre of scholars concerned with white-collar crime than to put to rest the definitional confusions that have plagued this field of research since Sutherland coined the term.*

A widely cited attempt to delineate types of white-collar crime (defined as economic crime) was that of Herbert Edelhertz (1970), who defined four types:

1. Crimes by persons operating on an individual ad hoc basis; for example, income tax, credit card, or bankruptcy fraud.

2. Crimes in the course of their occupations by those operating inside business, government, or other establishments, in violation of their duty of loyalty and fidelity to employer or client. This category is what Clinard and Quinney (1986) and others call occupational crime. Examples include embezzlement, insider trading, commercial bribery, and kickbacks.

3. Crimes incidental to and in furtherance of business operations, but not the central purpose of the business. This is what Clinard and Quinney (1986) call corporate crime, or others refer to as organizational crime. Examples are antitrust violations, deceptive advertising, and commercial espionage.

4. White-collar crime as a business, or as a central activity. These types of crime are examples of professional crime and include scams, con artist operations, land frauds, and phony charity and religious frauds. This typology will be discussed further in Chapters 2 through 6.

Figure 1.2 attempts to capture the relationship between white-collar deviance, elite deviance, white-collar crime, and economic crime. While white-collar deviance and elite deviance are the largest categories subsuming all white-collar crime, some minor economic crime may not be included as either white-collar crime or deviance. Some might prefer to refer to lower-level economic crime committed by lower-status individuals as "blue-collar crime," although in modern society it is difficult to identify the boundary (Clarke, 1990; Croal, 1992). The debate continues regarding the proper term for this subject matter: One author of this text emphasizes "elite deviance" (Simon, 1996) and the other "white-collar crime" (Hagan, 1998). The choice of the term "white-collar deviance" attempts to combine these approaches as well as make a major point: Each of the rival concepts depicted in Figures 1.2 and 1.3 refers to similar yet separate realities; and any attempt to come up with one concept that, by consensus, covers all of these is futile. We will use these terms at times as synonyms, since this is common in the literature and does not do any vital harm to the business of describing and analyzing white-collar deviance.

Figure 1.3 illustrates the existence of five types of white-collar deviance:

1. Occupational deviance/crime
2. Organizational deviance/crime
3. Professional white-collar deviance/crime

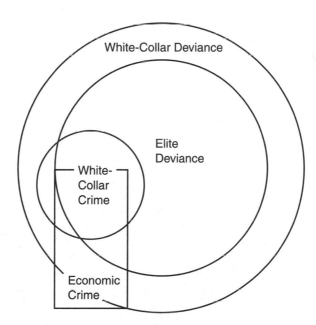

FIGURE 1.2 **Interrelationship between White-Collar Deviance, Elite Deviance, White-Collar Crime, and Economic Crime**

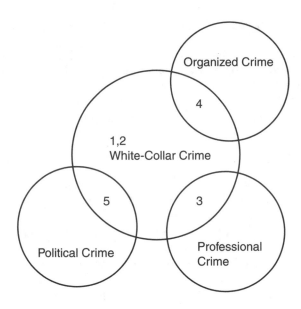

1. Occupational deviance/crime
2. Organizational deviance/crime
3. Professional white-collar deviance/crime
4. Organized white-collar deviance/crime
5. Political white-collar deviance/crime

FIGURE 1.3   Types of White-Collar Crime

   4. Organized white-collar deviance/crime
   5. Political white-collar deviance/crime

The distinction between occupational crime and organizational crime, which was first suggested by Clinard and Quinney (1986), is accepted by most criminologists. Each refers to crimes committed as part of a legitimate occupation; in the former it is for the benefit of the individual, and in the latter it is on behalf of the employing organization. In professional white-collar deviance/crime, those in legitimate occupations begin to imitate the tactics of professional criminals. The Savings and Loan scandal, the PTL scandal, and the systematic cheating of customers on automobile repairs by Sears serve as examples and will be discussed in more detail later. Organized white-collar deviance/crime will be illustrated later by the prosecution of legitimate businesses under federal RICO (Racketeer-Influenced and Corrupt Organizations) provisions. The BCCI (Bank of Credit and Commerce International) affair and Iran-Contra scandal will serve as examples of political white-collar deviance/crime.

How the System Is Structured

In his award-winning book of essays, *The United States, 1952–1992,* noted intellectual Gore Vidal satirically described the U.S. system of political economy and its workings.

Vidal insists that the nation's most powerful political leaders all work for a huge bank. The bank possesses "ownership (yes, ownership) of the United States" (Vidal, 1993, 939). In 1978, only 4 percent of Americans had a net worth of $60,000 or more, and over half the population possessed a net worth of $3,000 or less. By 1995, 1 percent of the population owned 25 percent of the nation's privately held wealth, nearly 50 percent of all corporate stock, nearly one-third of the nation's real estate, nearly two-thirds of all bonds, and 15.7 percent of all yearly income. Five percent of the nation's households now earn more money than 60 percent of middle-class households (Domhoff, 1998, 1, 105; Jensen, et al., 1997, 73). The distribution of wealth and income is now more unequal in the United States than in any other industrial democracy.

Today, just five gigantic corporations (Exxon, Ford, General Motors, IBM, and General Electric) possess 28 percent of the nation's industrial assets. The largest 100 corporate firms own nearly 75 percent of all industrial assets and account for 72 percent of all manufacturing jobs, and three-fourths of all U.S. Department of Defense contracts. Eleven banks own one-third of all banking assets, and the top 50 (out of nearly 15,000) own nearly two-thirds of all banking assets.

The structure of this corporate community encompasses the nation's 800 to 1,000 largest firms in manufacturing, banking, real estate, media, advertising, public relations, insurance, and law. These firms are thoroughly interrelated with one another through stock ownership and seats on the boards of directors of various companies. It is this network that provides a general environment within which common political and business ideologies are formed.

This distribution of wealth and ownership of corporations make it possible for corporate executives to interact in common social circles. Numerous studies (Domhoff, 1998; Mills, 1956; Olsen & Marger, eds., 1993) confirm that upper-class people often belong to the same exclusive social clubs, vacation at the same resorts, often intermarry, send their children to the same select list of private preparatory schools and elite universities, direct tax-exempt charitable foundations and policy discussion associations, and support influential policy-oriented think tanks. Thus a majority of the largest 25 corporations in every sector of the U.S. economy had at least one director who was a member of the nation's most exclusive private social clubs (e.g., Bohemain Grove in Northern California). In 1980, 30 percent of the top 800 corporations, including 23 of the top 25 largest banks, had at least one officer who belonged to Bohemian Grove (Domhoff, 1998, 88).

These super-rich corporate executives and their employees form the nation's power elite, which forms the leadership group for the nation's upper class and its political leaders. This tiny minority of wealthy Americans and their underlings together control two-thirds of the nation's economic activity, and a great deal of the activities of our supposedly democratic government.

There are no countervailing institutions in U.S. life that regularly check the power of the corporate elite and their political allies. To be sure, there are 22 million small- and medium-size businesses (employing 500 or fewer people) in the United States. Collectively, these firms make 52 percent of all sales and employ 54 percent of the private labor force. However, there are too many of these businesses, and they are too diverse in size and too lacking in financial assets "to have any collective power that could challenge the corporate community" (Domhoff, 1998, 57).

The gigantic global corporations possess the power to invest capital where and when they want to. They can move their factories and offices whenever they feel challenged by government regulations or high-priced union labor. Only 10 to 12 percent of workers belong to unions in the United States, and the American union movement has never enjoyed the political influence enjoyed by most West European labor movements. How this control is exercised forms the environment in which business crime and political corruption meet and mutually feed off each other.

The Policy-Making Process

Policy formation in the United States begins with informal social networks of corporate executives who meet and get to know one another in corporate boardrooms, exclusive social clubs, and discussion groups that identify which issues will become the focus of government action. Soon thereafter begins the flow of money and ideas. From corporate inner sanctums policy formation branches out into elite research universities and think tanks. These entities are funded by research grants from the largest charitable foundations—foundations that are owned by corporate-owning families. Policy also becomes the responsibility of governmental task forces and commissions as well as various government agencies and bureaus. A brief description of these various entities reveals much about their approach to policy and their links to the corporate elite.

Elite Policy-Making Organizations

Tax-Exempt Charitable Foundations

There are 20 gigantic tax-exempt foundations (out of over 3,000 general foundations) in the United States that have endowments of $1 billion or more. The largest 20 foundations are under the firm control of leaders of the national upper class. In all, some 862 of the largest foundations are funded by and directed by officers of the nation's largest corporations. These foundations serve two important purposes. (1) These organizations are tax exempt, established by super-rich and other corporate-owning families as a vehicle that insures that private wealth is passed directly to their heirs. Many foundation heads are children of their super-rich founders who are paid hefty salaries for serving as foundation officers. (2) Large foundations fund research and various programs in the arts, medicine, social and educational policy, and environmental protection at elite universities and private think tanks. In short, foundation monies function to set the agenda concerning which issues will be researched and what perspective that research will take. For example, studies of poverty are almost never done from the perspective of those who believe that great inequalities of wealth and income are the chief causes of poverty. Rather, poverty, and its attendant social problems, are nearly always studied with an eye on the behavior and attitudes of the poor and what they have done to bring about their own misery (see Simon, 1996, Chapters 8 to 10, for a detailed analysis).

One study of the 12 largest private foundations found that 50 percent of foundation trustees were members of the nation's upper class. These foundation trustees also occupied executive positions in the nation's 201 largest corporations (Domhoff, 1998, 129). Most of these large foundations bear the names of the upper-class families who founded them. Ford, Carnegie, Mellon, Pew, and Danforth are the most famous of these family-run entities. The large foundations are also intimately linked to the nation's most prestigious research think tanks.

Research Think Tanks and the Upper Class

Among the country's most important research think tanks are organizations such as the Brookings Institution, the American Enterprise Institute, Urban Institute, the National Bureau of Economic Research, the Rand Corporation, and Resources for the Future. Their links to the upper class and its corporate wealth are easily established. Thus 25 of the Brookings Institution's 33 directors (86 percent) also hold 50 directorships on the nation's 48 largest corporations. Likewise, 17 of the American Enterprise Institute's 26 directors hold 40 directorships in 37 of America's largest corporations (Domhoff, 1998, 134).

The story in academia is no different. Of the 55 university professors holding positions on President Clinton's National Science Advisory Committee, over half also serve on boards of firms with sales of over $100 million. Fully half of the country's largest corporations have university presidents and professors on their corporate boards of directors (Domhoff, 1998, 134). Many of these academics and business leaders are linked to each other as members of various elite policy discussion groups.

There are political extremists who seem to take delight in their belief that elite policy discussion groups are part of an international conspiracy designed to bring a socialist world government to dominate the affairs of all earthlings. The truth about such groups is far more mundane and logical.

Elite policy discussion groups serve important functions: (1) These groups provide discussion forums where corporate leaders can become aware of important policy issues via interacting with experts from academia and think tanks. (2) The groups allow elites with differing opinions to reach compromises with one another. (3) Elite discussion groups provide training for those corporate leaders who desire a career in public service. (4) Such groups provide an informal recruitment function for academics who desire positions in government as staff members or advisors in agencies of federal or state government. (5) Lastly, these groups influence the policy-making process in the United States by producing a large number of publications, including journals, magazines, books, and white (position) papers. These are public documents often furnished to policy makers in Congress and various departments in the executive branch of the federal government. Most are widely read by university professors, graduate students, and officials at various levels of government in the United States. With all the public dissemination these publications receive, conspiracies are both unnecessary and much too troublesome.

Among the leading discussion groups are:

The Council on Foreign Relations (CFR)—established after World War I to determine the United States's role in world affairs. The CFR publishes a leading foreign-policy journal, *Foreign Affairs,* and 16 of the last U.S. secretaries of state have been members of the CFR before their appointments. One of every 5 CFR members is an officer in a major corporation, including executives from 37 percent of the nation's 500 largest corporations and 16 of the largest 25 insurance companies, and 115 CFR members are on boards of 67 charitable foundations. The CFR was founded by Standard Oil fortune heir David Rockefeller, who is also the former president of the nation's largest bank, Chase Manhattan. Rockefeller is also the founder of another foreign-policy discussion group, the Trilateral Commission (TC). While the CFR is made up largely of U.S. elites, the TC consists of international experts from various developed nations in North America, Europe, and Asia (e.g., Japan).

Committee for Economic Development (CED)—established in the 1940s to undertake economic planning in the aftermath of World War II. The CED is dominated by members of the largest 200 U.S. corporations.

The Business Council (BC)—composed of presidents and chief executive officers of the largest U.S. corporations. Over 150 Business Council members are listed in *Who's Who in America.* The members hold 730 directorships in 435 of the largest banks and corporations, 49 foundation trusteeships in 36 different foundations, and 125 trusteeships in 36 different U.S. universities (Domhoff, 1998, 155).

The Business Roundtable—Founded in 1972, today it is one of the most powerful lobbies in Washington. Its members include many of the chief executive officers of the nation's largest 200 corporations (their total assets are over $1.3 trillion). In 1997, the Roundtable's 79 directors sat on the boards of 134 of the nation's largest corporations, including 32 on boards of the nation's 50 largest corporations (Domhoff, 1998, 155).

The Business Roundtable was successful in stopping tax reform, got laws passed that subject Federal Trade Commission rulings to congressional veto, supported oil and gas deregulation, and blocked creation of a consumer protection office. It also successfully opposed efforts to strengthen the nation's antitrust laws, those which prohibit unfair business competition and price fixing (Jensen, et al., 1997, 89). The 150 large corporations that make up the Business Roundtable each pay $10,000 to $35,000 in annual dues.

The institutional structure of the nation's power elite may be summarized as follows:

1. Twenty-five elite universities and colleges annually garner half of all educational endowment funds, and some 656 corporate elites sit on their boards of trustees. A mere 50 foundations (out of over 1,200) control 40 percent of all foundation assets. Foundations account for a large proportion of funds devoted to university and foundation research. Foundation executives usually have experience in either corporate America or the federal government.

2. Elite civic associations (such as the Council on Foreign Relations) bring together national (and sometimes international) elites from the corporate, educational, legal, and governmental worlds. The political scientist Thomas Dye (1990) views these associations as coordinators of national policy. They typically issue white papers on domestic and international policy matters. Membership in them is often a prerequisite for a high-ranking cabinet post. Twenty of the last twenty-one secretaries of state, for example, have been members of the Council on Foreign Relations (Simon, 1996, 21).

3. The mass media are central to the policy-making process because they set limits on the breadth of ideological views that enter the policy-making debate in the United States. The media also choose which stories to emphasize and which to ignore. The major media almost completely ignored the savings and loan scandal, for example, until the industry's losses became so overwhelming that Congress had to vote billions of dollars to bail it out. Finally, the media are merely a group of corporations that are owned by other corporations and financial institutions. Controlling shares in the three major television networks are owned by five large New York banks (Citibank, Chase, Morgan Guarantee, Bank of New York, and Banker's Trust). The 500 largest U.S. corporations account for 90 percent of all prime-time television network advertising revenues.

4. Twenty-eight large law firms do much of the legal work for corporations and the upper class. Ninety percent of all the legal work in the United States is done for a mere 10 percent of the population. These law firms are also heavily involved in the lobbying process in Washington, and many of their partners are former members of the president's cabinet.

5. The research institutes known as think tanks typically receive money from corporate and governmental sources. The Rand Corporation and the Stanford Research Institute (owned by Stanford University until 1970) are annually awarded about 5 percent of the Pentagon's research and development budget (Simon, 1996, 23).

Numerous studies have confirmed the power of elite networks in the United States and other modern democracies (Olsen & Marger, eds., 1993, 153–249; Gilbert & Kahl, 1993; Greenberg, 1985; Domhoff, 1998; Dye, 1990; Dye & Zeigler, 1996).

Elite rule has not only made the United States less democratic by converting American democracy into what Greider terms "a busy commerce in deal making" (1992, 112), it has also converted much of American society into what C. Wright Mills described as "a network of rackets" (1960, 17).

How the System Works: The "Network of Rackets"

One way the corporate rich insure that their interests are satisfied is by financing political campaigns. It is the case in the United States that only 4 percent of the population gives any money of sufficient amount—at any level of government—to be called a serious contribution. Only 0.25 of one percent of the population gives $200 or more and provides 80 percent of all monies donated to political campaigns (Domhoff, 1998, 218). Thus the richest 1 to 5 percent of the population pays for political campaigns. The resultant system is something of a corrupt gravy train that only the rich and powerful may board. There are two central sources of booty, private profit and government spending, and they are often impossible to separate. Government spending at all levels in the United States accounts for approximately 40 percent of the nation's Gross Domestic Product (GDP)—about $2.7 trillion (Gross, 1996, 60). Two-thirds of this money is spent by the federal government, and much of it is disbursed with tremendous discretion. The train is fueled by all manner of institutionalized corrupt practices, some of which are unethical, others downright illegal. Here stated are some of the system's most irritating and outrageous examples.

- Campaign financing has become something of a gigantic auction in which access to officials now goes to the highest bidder. Thus during the 1992 election campaign the Democrats published a slick brochure promising that for $100,000 contributors would receive a dinner with the president and two with the vice president; a post on a trade mission to a foreign country (transportation provided at government expense); two policy "retreats" with top American officials; and the loan of a Democratic National Committee staff member to act as gofer to fulfill any personal requests. A $50,000 donation was good for a dinner with the vice president and a reception with the president; two official briefings on the state of the union; and VIP treatment at the 1996 Convention.

- Lesser donations (as "little" as $10,000) garnered a reception with President Clinton and a dinner with Al Gore. The poverty-stricken female with only $1,000 could attend a reception with Mrs. Clinton and Mrs. Gore and the administration's female appointees.
- The Republicans offered similar "packages," including a "photo op" with President Bush, lunch with Dan Quayle, and breakfast with the Republican congressional delegation and so on.
- These pay-for-access deals are merely symbols of a much more widespread condition. At the 1992 GOP convention, for example, large corporations, such as Exxon, Shell Oil, DuPont, and AT&T, among others, donated $4 million for galas and parties.
- Atlantic Richfield hosted a reception in which a small "victory choo-choo" train entered the room with George Bush and Dan Quayle riding the caboose.

How symbolic! The political money train in America rolls on $200 million worth of "soft money"—money not donated directly to a particular candidate—each year. These come from unlimited contributions by individuals and companies to nonfederal party accounts. One non-soft money rule ("24E") allows unlimited direct donations to a presidential candidate by individuals (Gross, 1996, 45).

Moreover, there are numerous corporations that contributed $100,000 or more to both party conventions. There is a loophole in Federal Election Commission (FEC) rules that allows corporations to give goods and services directly to party conventions. The FEC rules do not view goods and services as money, which is prohibited in presidential nominating conventions. Rules adopted in 1994 permit any commercial vendor to give goods and services for "promotional considerations."

The Center for Responsive Politics investigated ten corporations giving at least $100,000 to each major party's convention, and discovered the reasons for doing so. Some of the most notorious examples include:

ABBOTT LABORATORIES. Abbott favors a bill that will make it easier for U.S. pharmaceutical companies to export drugs and medical devices that the Food and Drug Administration (FDA) has not approved for sale in the United States. Its request was granted when it was included in a spending bill that Congress passed in March 1996.

AMERICAN TELEPHONE & TELEGRAPH (AT&T). Of primary concern for AT&T is the Federal Communications Commission's new telecommunications law. AT&T won a competition with Sprint for an increased share of the multimillion-dollar federal government contract.

BANKAMERICA CORPORATION. BankAmerica wants banking reform proposals—now bogged down because of fights between banking and insurance companies. The bank favors a Federal Reserve Board proposal to ease regulations on banks like BankAmerica, which offer securities services through subsidiaries.

BAXTER INTERNATIONAL. This biotechnology firm lobbies on all issues relating to drugs and medical devices, including tort reform, patents, export laws, funding for the National Institutes of Health, and blood safety. (The firm specializes in drugs and devices relating to blood, such as blood substitutes.) With many products in the approval pipeline at the FDA, the company has an interest in several legislative proposals that would change the drug and medical device approval process.

BROWNING-FERRIS INDUSTRIES. Browning-Ferris deals in garbage: collecting, processing, and disposing it. The firm's lobbyists track the many environmental laws that can affect this type of business, including Superfund, the Clean Water Act, and solid-waste transportation rules. The company is closely watching congressional proposals on "flow control," those arrangements local governments make with specific facilities to receive only their waste.

CHRYSLER CORPORATION/UNITED AUTO WORKERS CHRYSLER NATIONAL TRAINING CENTER. Chrysler and the United Auto Workers founded the National Training Center in the 1980s as part of contract negotiations. The center provides training, job counseling, and other types of educational services for Chrysler employees.

LOCKHEED MARTIN. This defense powerhouse was formed by the federally subsidized merger of Lockheed and Martin Marietta Corporation in March 1995. The company wants compensation from the government for the restructuring costs of its merger, but some in Congress want to repeal this Defense Department policy. The House included a measure that would prohibit federal funds from being used to pay for the merger costs of defense contractors in its version of this year's defense spending bill. The company still has a chance to weigh in on the legislation, however; the House and Senate must reconcile their different versions.

TENNECO. In June, the shipbuilding firm and a fleet of five other companies managed to save shipbuilding subsidies by pushing for amendments to a bill intended to promote free trade. The House recently authorized $701 million to Newport News Shipbuilding, a subsidiary, to develop the SSN-23 nuclear submarine.

UNITED AIRLINES. Flying the friendly skies would have become even friendlier for those at United if they had won the battle they were fighting with six other airlines to change the airline ticket tax to a passenger user fee. United is still pushing for bills that would repeal a tax on aviation fuel and require government personnel to travel on strictly U.S.-owned aircraft (*Multinational Monitor,* 1996).

Finally, there are the political action committees (PACs), specialized interest groups that donate to political campaigns of members of congress and state legislators. Each PAC may give $10,000 to any politician they like. The 4,016 PACs registered in Washington, DC, gave a staggering $391,760,117 in 1994 to candidates at all levels of government. Some $131 million was from various corporate PACs—$67 million to Democrats and $64 million to Republicans. (Only $42 million came from labor unions, $40 million of which went to the Democrats) (Domhoff, 1998, 218.) The major Hollywood movie studio executives alone gave $500,000 to the Democratic National Committee. Just one corporate executive, the CEO of Archers Daniels Midland, gave $1 million to Senator Dole and $270,000 to President Clinton. Over 70 percent of this money was given to incumbents, who usually outspend their challengers and, when they do, the incumbents win 90 percent of the time (Gross, 1996, 14, 43, 50, 52).

There are also secret Democratic and Republican PACs controlled by party leaders that funnel funds to favorite candidates. Chart 1.1 lists some of the major PACs and the donations they gave during the 1995–1996 election cycle. Thus the financing of political campaigns functions to (1) keep challengers from getting elected, (2) corrupt those politicians in power, and (3) forge an alliance between corporate interests and incumbent politicians.

There are numerous secret institutions within the structure of the United States's political economy. The Federal Financing Bank makes secret loans to large corporations and to other federal agencies "off the books," which helps hide the actual size of the national debt. From 1976 to 1996, the bank made $65 billion in loans, some to the U.S. Postal Service. Another secretive structure, the National Security Agency (NSA), has an annual budget of $8 billion and over 22,000 employees. All of the NSA's activities are classified as secret. Investigative reporters have confirmed that the agency monitors every cable, satellite, telephone, and diplomatic and military message in the entire world (Jensen, et al., 1997, 90–94). It is also important to understand that white-collar deviance of all types is no longer something that happens strictly within the borders of the United States, but is very much a global problem.

The Global Environment and International White-Collar Deviance

At the center of the global economy are the world's wealthiest nations. These nations have the highest gross domestic products and highest per capita incomes on earth. These advanced countries are characterized by capitalistic economies—those based on private property ownership and nominally democratic forms of government. The International Monetary Fund classifies 28 nations as advanced, including the United States, United Kingdom, France, Germany, Canada, Italy, and Japan, all other members of the European Union (e.g., Sweden, Norway, etc.), New Zealand, Australia, Israel, and four emerging Asian nations: South Korea, Taiwan, Singapore, and Hong Kong. The most advanced of these countries—United States, United Kingdom, France, Germany, Canada, Italy, and Japan—have formed an economic alliance called the Group of Seven (G-7). The purposes of the G-7 alliance are to promote global trade and to finance economic stability in the world's so-called developing nations. Two additional organizations that aid in keeping international markets stable are the International Monetary Fund (IMF) and the World Bank.

The IMF and World Bank are specialized agencies of the United Nations. The IMF makes loans to poor nations that are having problems paying off their debts. Their indebtedness—over $1 trillion—is owed to advanced nations' governments and the largest banks in developed nations. The World Bank makes loans for long-term growth and development in poor nations.

The IMF classifies 28 nations as being in a state of economic transition. These include all of the former Soviet Bloc nations in Eastern and Central Europe and Mongolia. Finally, there are 128 developing nations in Asia, Africa, and Latin America—so-called Third World nations with incomes of under $2,000 per person. At this income level, people live in abject poverty, and there are over 17,000 deaths per day due to starvation, as well as

CHART 1.1   Selected PAC Donations, 1995–1996

Contributions from Finance, Insurance, and Real Estate PACs to Federal Candidates by Selected PACs, 1995–1996*

PAC	Amount	Dems	Repubs
American Institute of CPA's	$1,082,980	$379,255	$698,725
National Assn. of Realtors	$983,863	$306,108	$677,255
American Bankers Assn.	$804,800	$215,450	$589,350
National Assn. of Life Underwriters	$667,925	$200,100	$467,825
Ernst & Young	$570,440	$275,065	$295,375
Credit Union National Assn.	$454,692	$179,681	$274,011
Indep. Insurance Agents of America	$428,382	$125,263	$303,119
Arthur Andersen & Co.	$365,903	$168,435	$197,468
JP Morgan & Co.	$360,150	$137,650	$222,500
Deloitte & Touche	$358,337	$128,558	$229,779

Contributions from Agriculture Industry PACs to Federal Candidates, 1995–1996*

PAC	Amount	Dems	Repubs
Philip Morris	$614,986	$195,505	$418,481
RJR Nabisco	$498,450	$130,450	$368,000
American Crystal Sugar Corp.	$437,825	$211,450	$226,375
Associated Milk Producers	$386,150	$173,000	$212,650
Mid-America Dairymen	$369,350	$152,050	$217,300
Food Marketing Institute	$353,528	$57,000	$295,528
U.S. Tobacco Co.	$330,600	$74,150	$256,450
American Sugarbeet Growers Assn.	$283,479	$142,247	$141,232
National Cattlemen's Assn.	$278,645	$36,750	$241,895
Brown & Williamson Tobacco	$240,675	$50,150	$190,525

Contributions from Defense Industry PACs to Federal Candidates, 1995–1996

PAC	Amount	Dems	Repubs
Lockheed Martin	$708,975	$218,850	$490,125
Northrop Grumman Corp.	$568,975	$157,700	$411,275
Tenneco Inc.	$444,007	$125,050	$318,957
Loral Corp.	$307,025	$155,925	$151,100
McDonnell Douglas	$287,820	$99,900	$187,920
General Dynamics	$263,512	$91,950	$171,562
Textron Inc.	$246,800	$92,100	$154,700
Rockwell International	$234,400	$60,850	$173,550
Raytheon Co.	$232,200	$66,975	$165,225
Hughes Aircraft	$225,150	$78,000	$147,150

*Compiled by the Center for Responsive Politics from data released electronically by the Federal Election Commission on September 3, 1996.

NOTE: Data does not aggregate donations from firms or groups maintaining multiple PACs.

Source: *Multinational Monitor* (October, 1996).

numerous problems of disease, illiteracy, political turmoil, and instability. This group of so-called Third World nations has experienced a war or revolution on the average of one a month since the end of World War II (Wright, 1997, 506; Simon, 1999, Chapter 5).

The global economy is dominated by the multinational corporations of developed nations. For example, the number of corporations controlling more than half of the American mass media went from 50 in 1982 to 10 in 1996. Globally, however, five large corporations dominate global movies, television, and news magazines (Jensen, et al., 1997, 202).

These transitional and poor nations are the economic targets of the advanced nations, international corporations, and banks. Thus between 1990 and 1996, the amount of private capital investment flowing from advanced to poor nations rose from $44 billion to $243.8 billion. Each day some $1 trillion in finance capital electronically circles the global investment casino. Of this amount, only $300 million goes for the purchase of goods and services. The remainder is spent on speculation for profit (Wright, 1997, 506). With the rise in global investment has come the emergence of global forms of white-collar deviance. Such behavior takes a variety of forms, including:

- Exporting dangerous pharmaceuticals that are banned for sale in advanced nations.
- The dumping of imported toxic waste.
- Alliances with global crime syndicates engaged in the $850 billion yearly global narcotics trade.
- Global prostitution engaged in by vice-dealing corporations.
- The international smuggling of the bodies (or parts thereof) of endangered species.
- Government-provided foreign aid to nations that violate basic human rights.
- Bribery and other forms of corruption taking place between international corporations and governments.
- The illegal sales of weapons.

These forms of white-collar deviance are discussed throughout this book.

Discussion

In this chapter we have explored the aspects of the global economy that cause white-collar deviance. Modern life is structured by impersonal institutions:

1. A world system composed of capitalist economies and competing nation-states.
2. Advanced societies in which wealth is concentrated in the hands of elites and power is exercised through bureaucratic organizations.

The centralization of wealth and power in the hands of a fortunate few who own much of corporate America and have inordinate influence over government policy has given rise to a host of deviant behaviors. The most important of these problems is a set of institutionalized deviant and criminal practices that can be called the "higher immorality." The people most adversely affected by these acts tend to be the poorest members of their societies.

Critical Thinking Exercise 1-1: The Higher Immorality

Look up the categories having to do with corporate crime in the latest complete *New York Times* Index or the *Wall Street Journal* Index. These categories include:

1. Antitrust violations
2. Pollution law violations
3. False advertising
4. Fraud
5. Sexual harassment

Do you notice any patterns in respect to which industries have the most violations? Many violations take place in the petroleum, automobile, and drug industries. Do these firms serve as models of corporate behavior for others? Were any specific corporations involved in more than one violation?

Chapter *2*

Corporate/Organizational White-Collar Deviance and the Political Economy

The Corporate Environment of Elite White-Collar Deviance

The corporate milieu that is conducive to corporate deviance is one of power, privilege, and secrecy. Much of this structure is composed of interlocking ownership through oligopolies. An *oligopoly* occurs when fewer than four firms control at least 50 percent of a market for a given product. Oligopoly is one of the great contradictions of the capitalist economy. Oligopolies formed in the United States between 1865 and 1920.

For all the folklore about the wonders of competition, there is evidence that firms go to considerable lengths to eliminate competition at every opportunity. Table 2.1 describes the extent of oligopoly in major U.S. industries. When four or fewer firms control 50 percent or more of a given market, the magic law of supply and demand ceases to function. For example, between 1970 and 1980, demand for American automobiles reached an all-time low in the postwar United States. Yet the price of American cars doubled during this period. Prices in oligopolistic markets are determined by price leadership, wherein one giant company raises prices and the others follow suit.

Oligopolization of the economy causes numerous additional harms, not the least of which is inflation. A study by the Federal Trade Commission concluded that prices in industries where four or fewer firms control at least 50 percent of market share would fall by at least 25 percent if market share shrank to just 40 percent. A second study by economist John Blair concluded that when four or fewer firms control 70 percent or more of sales, profits are 50 percent higher than in less-concentrated industries. Thus corporate concentration enriches a relatively few people while costing the average consumer in buying power, power which has not meaningfully increased since 1969.

TABLE 2.1　Degree of Oligopolization
in Major Industries Held
by Four or Fewer Firms

Industry	Percent of Market Share
Razors and Blades	99
Light Bulbs	91
Cigarettes	90
Electric Calculators	90
Linoleum	90
Clocks and Watches	84
Refrigerators	82
Cereal	80
Roasted Coffee	66

The corporate environment with its concentrated power and wealth also breeds an arrogance conducive to deviance. Three-fourths of the American people now believe that corporate executive salaries are too high. The Securities and Exchange Commission has ruled that executive pay can come before corporate stockholders for a vote. The average salary of American corporate executives stands at around $1.4 million, over 300 times the earnings of the average American worker. In 1995 alone, executive compensation increased by 23 percent (Gross, 1996, 150). Stock options and other benefits push total average executive compensation to between $10 million and $78 million per year. Leon Hirsch, CEO of U.S. Surgical, who took home $118 million in 1991, believed that he was underpaid that year.

This "never enough" ideology has served corporate chieftains well. They frequently possess the power to reward themselves by placing people on corporate boards who are predisposed to vote them pay increases. CEOs are also likely to get raises if other CEOs are getting them, whether their companies are having profitable years or not. Aside from their enormous salaries, there are unprecedented privileges and additional forms of compensation, such as various corporate stock options—the right to purchase one's company's stock at a specific future date and price. Sometimes corporations allow executives to withdraw high-price stock options and publish new ones to reflect lower market prices. Some companies even provide low-cost or no-interest loans so additional stock options may be purchased, and the loans are sometimes forgiven if the price of the firm's stock falls. This means top corporate executives are exempt from the same market risks to which ordinary investors are subject. Other advantageous compensation plans are also available (see Simon, 1999, 70–75).

Corporate executives also usually receive numerous additional benefits, including:

- Free financial counseling, and tax assistance.
- Free legal assistance from top attorneys. (Remember O. J. Simpson's "Dream Team" of criminal attorneys? Executives charged with corporate wrongdoing often receive top legal talent paid for by their firms.)

- Company automobiles and chauffeur services (for business and sometimes for personal use).
- Company-provided private jets, boats, and apartments (for business and sometimes for personal use).
- Company-paid or subsidized travel, recreation facilities, and club memberships.
- Liberal expense accounts and personal use of business credit cards.
- Complete family medical and dental coverage, usually with no deductibles (some 40 million people in the United States have no medical insurance at all much of the time).
- College expenses for their children.
- Paid sabbaticals.
- The best and most complete forms of disability, accident, and life insurance.
- Multimillion-dollar pension plans, sometimes paid on top of the retired executive's new salary as a consultant to the old firm (Simon, 1999, 75).

An additional aspect of the corporate milieu is the legal environment itself. The corporate-owned mass media has always advanced the ideology that violent (street) crime constitutes the "real" crime problem in the United States. Never mind that white-collar criminality costs Americans over forty times what violent crime does and costs at least four times as many lives. And what are the penalties for all this illegality? Frequently they are miniscule and often do not even exist.

- Out of over 51,000 federal criminal indictments in 1994, only 250 (less than one-half of 1 percent) involved criminal charges against businesses that violated the nation's occupational, health, safety, and environmental regulations (Phillips, et al., 1997, 38).
- Clinard and Yeager (1978) found that in over 500 corporate crime cases in which a firm was found guilty, prison terms were imposed in only 2 percent of cases. The average imprisonment term was only 6 months. Compare this with street crime imprisonment. In California, a "three-strike" felon was sentenced to life in prison for stealing a pizza.

A related reality concerns media coverage of corporate scandal. Have you ever noticed that when a large corporation is charged with a crime, the press routinely conducts interviews and receives corporate press releases telling the firm's side of the story? This is standard practice in an industry whose entire existence depends on corporate advertising revenues.

When is the last time an accused violent criminal called a press conference so as to inform the press of an abusive childhood, the wounds of poverty, or a broken family? The closest incident to such a happening took place in late 1997 when then Golden State Warrior's star Latrel Sprewel called a press conference to explain why he tried to strangle his coach during a practice session.

This was a remarkable event in many ways, one that shows the triple standard of justice in America. A man (or woman) in almost any other profession would at the very least have been fired. In many work places, such acts are reported to police as assaults and prosecuted as felonies. Of course, Sprewel is no ordinary worker. He is a professional athlete, a key player in a multimillion-dollar corporation. Sprewel himself lost a multiyear $25 million contract and received a 1-year suspension from National Basketball Association (NBA) play. The suspension is currently being appealed, but that is not the end of the story.

In response to his suspension, Mr. Sprewel called a press conference. On the dais with him were a number of lawyers, one of whom, Johnny Cochran, became famous by defending another famous sports figure, O. J. Simpson. Other members of Sprewel's defense team included an attorney from the NBA players' union, his personal accountant, and several NBA players, who were present to demonstrate their "support." This means that the players felt threatened by the possibility that the NBA might make a habit of suspending the lucrative contracts of its errant players.

And what was the outcome of this media event? Sprewel addressed the gathered media expressing satisfaction for the opportunity to tell his side of the story. And what was his story? Basically, it was that he had lost his temper, which he admitted he cannot control, although he tried (more than once, it turns out). Now, since he had made this public admission (which, at the time, did not include an apology to the coach), the public was, one supposes, to extend its sympathy and support to the suspended multimillionaire.

What do you think would happen if a typical murderer wanted to explain his behavior and asked to hold a press conference after being charged with a killing (complete with the presence of several attorneys and, to explain the economic impact of being imprisoned on his family, his accountant)? Most likely, the judge in the case would place a gag order on the accused and order a psychiatric evaluation.

Press coverage, or the lack of it, is much different for rich celebrities and corporations. If the corporation happens to own a television network (as, for example, General Electric owns NBC), little airtime is likely to be devoted to such a story on its nightly news broadcast. The odds are it will never be mentioned.

How do we know this? For over 20 years, Carl Jensen, professor of journalism at California State University, has headed Project Censored, which chooses the most important and least covered news stories for a given year. In 1997, Project Censored published a summary of the 200 stories it had selected for the previous twenty years (Jensen, et al., 1997). Consider the following examples of corporate deviance:

- In 1976, it was learned that each year 500,000 people in the world's poor nations are poisoned by pesticides and pharmaceuticals that have been banned for sale in the world's advanced economies. By 1995, the United States had exported 58 million pounds of banned pesticides to developing nations between 1991 and 1994 (Jensen, et al., 1997, 37–38).
- In 1976, it was learned that members of the U.S. Department of State had collaborated with members of the Organization of Petroleum Exporting Countries and other oil producers to deliberately inflate world oil prices. Yet, by 1995, the United States imported 50 percent of its oil supplies, and domestic gasoline prices had risen to record levels in summer and fall of 1997 (Jensen, et al., 1997, 39).
- For years Mobil Oil used dummy companies to conduct business with Zimbabwe, a major violator of basic human rights that has been embargoed and condemned by "virtually every nation on earth" (Jensen, et al., 1997, 39). In 1996, Mobil Oil continued doing business with Zimbabwe, and Texaco Oil illegally sold oil to Haiti, a nation whose military leaders were involved in global drug trafficking and human-rights violations. Some of the military leaders were on the payroll of the CIA.

- In the 1970s, baby-formula makers Nestle and Bristol Myers advertised their products in Third World nations by giving free samples to mothers and promising economic modernization and increased social status, and discouraging new mothers from breast feeding. These infant formulas caused 35,000 deaths and untold cases of brain damage in part because mothers lacked facilities for boiling the clean water necessary for using them. As of 1995, despite numerous international boycotts of their products, formula makers were still advertising their products, which now cause over one million deaths per year in poor nations (Jensen, et al., 1997, 52–53).
- The savings and loan scandal remains the largest financial scandal in American history. Some $500 billion was looted, and 700 of the S&Ls failed. Sixty percent of these failures were due to fraud. The bonds sold to pay these debts will not be paid until 2030. Millions more are being wasted on arbitrary accounting procedures. The CIA and the Mafia were involved in the failure of 22 failed S&Ls, 10 in Texas alone. Much of this scandal took place with scarcely a yawn from the mainstream press (Jensen, et al., 1997, 250–251).
- Medical fraud in the United States is estimated at $100 billion per year. And medical negligence by 5 to 10 percent of the nation's doctors causes 1.3 million injuries and 80,000 deaths; it costs an estimated $50 billion annually (Jensen, et al., 1997, 300, 330). In one February, 1996 case alone, Corning Inc. was fined $6.8 million because its Bioran Medical Laboratory billed Medicare for blood tests that doctors never requested. In October, 1996, Corning paid an additional $119 million due to fraudulent billing. Corning also paid $39.8 million in 1993 and $8.6 million in 1995 in fines for Medicare fraud (Sherrill, 1997).

Aside from being neglected by establishment media outlets, these stories share some interesting commonalties. First, after 20 years, most of the harmful conditions described in the stories are not only still around, they are worse. Second, the corporate media is still neglecting these important stories, and it is this lack of media attention that impedes the formation of the public outrage necessary for their possible amelioration. Nowhere has this been more true than in the case of U.S. tobacco firms, an example that tells us much about deviance within the environment of the U.S. political economy.

Tobacco: A Symbolic Case Study

Use of tobacco is the most preventable cause of death in the United States and much of the world. Each year 420,000 Americans die from the effects of cigarette smoking, as do 3 million people in the world's poor nations. By the year 2000, an estimated 60 million people, 50 million men and 10 million women, will have died from tobacco in the last half of the twentieth century worldwide (more than all the innocents killed by Hitler, Stalin, and Chairman Mao combined) (Jensen, et al., 1997, 3). Independent economists and government agencies estimate that smoking costs Americans about $100 billion a year in medical bills, lost work productivity, increased maintenance costs, and so on. Tobacco-related medical bills alone were estimated at $50 billion in 1993 (Wright, 1997, 399).

The physical harms associated with tobacco products are numerous.

420,000 American smokers die approximately 10 years earlier than expected.

Smoking causes nearly 90 percent of all lung cancer and 30 percent of all cancer deaths. It is associated with cancer of the mouth, esophagus, stomach, pancreas, kidney, bladder, and cervix.

Tobacco is associated with many cardiovascular diseases, including heart attacks, strokes, vascular diseases, and blood clot formations.

Lung diseases—including 80,000 annual deaths from chronic bronchitis, pneumonia, and emphysema.

Birth problems—including spontaneous abortions, with women who smoke experiencing ten times more miscarriages than women who do not. Some 2,000 children under age 2 die because their mothers smoked during pregnancy. Infants of smoking mothers experience a 50 percent higher risk of Sudden Infant Death Syndrome (SIDS) and 74 percent greater incidence of low birth weight. Infants exposed to any cigarette smoke have 3.5 times the risk of dying of SIDS than infants not exposed.

Second-hand smoke is also a major health hazard. Nonsmokers exposed to the smoke of tobacco smokers account for 3,000 lung cancer deaths, 150,000 to 300,000 bronchitis and pneumonia cases in children under 18 months old, and double the risk of heart disease (Wright, 1997, 410).

Can you imagine what the government would do if an illegal drug was causing over 500,000 deaths a year in the United States? A major public health emergency would probably be declared. Nicotine, tobacco's chief addictive substance, would have been declared addictive (not just a habit), and major antismoking campaigns would warn all Americans of the dangers linked to smoking and exposure to cigarette smoke. There would even be free drug-treatment programs for addicts and smoking-prevention programs for those not yet addicted.

Instead, the nation and much of the world have paid a tragic price so that a few large tobacco firms, their stockholders, and advertising firms can make billions in profits while the unsuspecting and the addicted experience all manner of physical and financial harm. The real tragedy, perhaps, is that so much of this suffering could have been avoided decades ago.

In 1938, journalist George Seldes criticized the American press for failure to point out the link between cigarette smoking and lung cancer. In five separate studies by Dr. Raymond Perry of the Johns Hopkins University Department of Biology, it was concluded that smoking significantly decreased the human life span. Between 1940 and 1950, Seldes published over a hundred antitobacco pieces in his own private newsletter. Yet it was not until the mid-1990s that illness from smoking was publicized by the mass media. And it was not until 1996 and 1997 that:

- The Food and Drug Administration issued a regulation restricting the sale of cigarettes to teens and minor children.
- State attorneys general filed 40 lawsuits against tobacco firms along with 17 class-action suits involving the medical costs of smoking (Jensen, et al., 1997, 20).
- The tobacco firms agreed to pay over $368 billion to repay health costs, fund antismoking campaigns, and cease advertising to children via the use of "Joe Camel"-like cartoon characters.

Why did it take nearly 60 years for the United States to declare smoking a public health crisis? The answers lie in the structure and workings of the U.S. political economy.

Tobacco firms, like other large corporations, donate large sums of money to political campaigns, especially the campaigns of those politicians from tobacco producing states. Chart 1.1 covers donations made by tobacco lobbyists in the 1995–1996 election cycle. This insures cigarette makers of a set of allies in Congress and in other places in Washington (the Department of Justice and the Food and Drug Administration).

Second, tobacco companies spend about $6 billion per year on the advertisement and promotion of their products. This includes paying Hollywood studios to feature scenes in movies that depict smoking as glamorous, fun, a sign of independence, popularity, personal power, success, and sex appeal. This means having movie heroes and heroines use tobacco at every opportunity. Promotional efforts also involve conducting campaigns in which tee shirts, mugs, and other items with the logos of tobacco firms are either given away free or redeemed by smokers with cigarette pack coupons.

Third, the market research conducted by tobacco firms is done with scientific precision. Through this research the firms know that if young people do not start smoking by age 19, they probably will not ever smoke. Tobacco firms also know that every day 5,000 people either stop smoking voluntarily or die from the effects of smoking. This means that each day 5,000 new smokers must be found, and the tobacco firms try to induce young people to smoke with all manner of slick magazine ads, billboard ads aimed at youth, especially minority youths, and promotional campaigns (*Consumer Reports,* 1998).

For decades, tobacco advertisers were able to deny that they were aiming the ads at children. Finally, in early 1998, secret tobacco-company documents, discovered by government investigators, explicitly described advertising campaigns aimed at children. This falsehood was merely the tip of the tobacco industry's dirty iceberg:

- For years, tobacco groups claimed that they had never tried to develop a cigarette with higher than normal nicotine levels. In early 1998, secret documents revealed that the tobacco industry has hired a San Francisco firm to smuggle tobacco plants out of the United States so research on hyper-nicotine plants could be hidden from government regulators and the public.
- For three decades, the tobacco industry engaged in a criminal conspiracy to hide knowledge of the ill effects caused by smoking from government agencies and the public.
- In 1996, several high-ranking tobacco executives testified under oath at Congressional hearings that smoking was not addictive. The next year, memos written by tobacco-company employees were discovered that plainly described the addictive nature of smoking. In January, 1998, executives from the seven largest tobacco firms testified before Congress that they had lied during their 1996 testimony concerning the health dangers and addictive nature of smoking. Recently discovered documents also revealed that the tobacco firms had done more research on and possessed more knowledge of the addictive nature of nicotine than any government agency or any medical school or university scientists. Yet, as with most testimony by corporate executives, there were no plans to indict the tobacco executives for having lied under oath in 1996.
- Tobacco conglomerates spend millions of dollars to hire lawyers, conduct research, and make sure that information it does not want to become public is kept secret for as long as possible.

Aiding the tobacco industry as well is a heavily advertised and reinforced cultural notion of individual responsibility. This notion, taken for granted in the United States, is not believed by most of the world's cultures. Subtle messages in various speeches, ads, booklets, and media programs function to convince Americans that people's problems are caused by their own personal failures. In order for harmful conditions to be defined as social problems, the causes of such problems must be presented within this individualistic ideology. For example, Mothers Against Drunk Driving (MADD) was given credibility by mainstream media and politicians because the group fixed the responsibility for drunk driving (which is responsible for half of the deaths from vehicle accidents) at the individual level. Blame was assigned to those individuals who drive while intoxicated. Escaping any responsibility (at first, at least) were liquor companies whose advertisements openly encourage people to consume alcohol and liquor establishments that do not limit sales to customers who have become inebriated.

Tobacco firms capitalized on this individualistic ethic by claiming that they were not really encouraging people to smoke, and that smoking was strictly an individual choice. The facts that smoking is addictive and that addiction dramatically impacts people's ability to make rational consumer choices were (and are) never mentioned by the tobacco industries. When the dangers of smoking finally became public knowledge in the 1970s, tobacco firms limited their own legal liability by agreeing to place warning labels on cigarettes. Tobacco-industry spokespersons could then claim that individuals could now make an informed choice about smoking, and that their legal liability extended only to those smokers who began using cigarettes before warning labels were placed on cigarette packs. Studies demonstrated that many young people, especially lower-class minorities, could not understand some of the esoteric labels, such as "cigarette smoke contains carbon monoxide." (Cigars, which contain over ten times the tobacco-related toxins than do cigarettes, as of 1997 were still sold with no warning labels, as was chewing tobacco, a major cause of mouth and throat cancer.)

All of this is not to argue that all American corporations produce death-causing products and lie, cheat, and steal to cover their harms. The point rather is that several dimensions of the United State's institutional arrangements and cultural values greatly contributed to the tobacco industry's ability to continue to make billions in profit from a physically harmful, addictive product, whose harmful consequences were manipulatively hidden from the public and policymakers.

Corporate Deviance

As noted in Chapter 1, high-level corporate executives often possess access to those members of the power elite who govern the nation and much of the world. Indeed, sometimes they serve in such roles themselves. Another frightening consequence of concentrated corporate ownership and corporate-held political power is that corporate practices are unregulated by either government or effective political opposition by consumers and workers. This lack of control over corporations has contributed to the drastic economic changes of the United States over the last quarter-century, and to numerous other social harms.

The result is an atmosphere that breeds *corporate deviance,* acts of immense physical, financial, and moral harm committed by wealthy and powerful corporations no longer being constrained by government in their relentless pursuit of profits. These harms involve:

1. The frequent breaking of antitrust and other corporate laws.
2. Physical harm inflicted on consumers (from dangerous products) and workers (from dangerous working conditions), and pollution of the environment.
3. Financial harm stemming from monopolistic pricing practices (price-fixing).

As previously indicated, while head of the white-collar crime section of the U.S. Justice Department, Herbert Edelhertz (1970) developed a typology of white-collar crime, which consisted of:

1. Crimes by individuals on an individual or ad hoc basis. [General White-Collar Crime]
2. Crimes in the course of their occupations by those operating inside business, government, or other establishments, in violation of their duty of loyalty and fidelity to employer or client. [Occupational Crime/Deviance]
3. Crimes incidental to and in furtherance of business operations, but not the central purpose of business. [Organizational/Corporate Crime/Deviance]
4. White-collar crime as a business, or as the central activity. [Professional White-Collar Crime/Deviance]

The brackets have been added by the authors to identify where Edelhertz's types fall in our discussion. Category 3 is presented in Figure 2.1 and provides some interesting examples as well as an overview of the types of activities to be covered in this chapter.

Included under crimes in furtherance of business are tax violations, antitrust (price-fixing) violations, commercial bribery, food and drug violations, and false weights and measures. In the latter, cheating thousands of customers on a fraction of the weight of an item, for example, a pound of meat in the wholesale area, can result in huge profits. Other examples include misrepresentation of credit terms to consumers, use of phony collateral (items of value used to back a loan in case of default), "check-kiting" (writing checks for which there are insufficient funds), and Securities Act violations. Edelhertz also includes categories which we will include later in the chapter on occupational white-collar crime, such as collusion (kickbacks) between physicians and pharmacists, or the latter illegally dispensing drugs. Other violations include immigration fraud (particularly in employment), housing-code violations by landlords, and deceptive advertising. The biggest victims of crime in the United States are governments—federal, state, and local. They are victimized by a multitude of violations including false claims and statements and a variety of rip-offs related to the billions of dollars spent every year in defense, welfare, medical, and social programs. Finally, Edelhertz mentions labor violations and commercial espionage. While this laundry list of offenses is hardly exhaustive or mutually exclusive, it does serve to impress on us the variety of activities to be found under the label of organizational white-collar crime/deviance.

Few studies have been done on corporate crime rates, one indication of how powerful corporate interests have succeeded in defining the American crime problems as a "street" (i.e., lower-class) problem. Those studies that have been done indicate that the penalties for corporate criminal violations are quite meager. They provide no deterrent to corporate crime, which includes antitrust, advertising law, and pollution law violations. Studies of punishment in corporate-crime cases reveal that only about 2 percent of corporate-crime cases result in imprisonment. *Price-fixing,* a criminal act in which two or more firms con-

Crime incidental to and in furtherance of business operations, but not the central purpose of the business:

1. Tax violations.
2. Antitrust violations.
3. Commercial bribery of another's employee, officer or fiduciary (including union officers).
4. Food and drug violations.
5. False weights and measures.
6. Violations of Truth-in-Lending Act by misrepresentation of credit terms and prices.
7. Submission or publication of false financial statements to obtain credit.
8. Use of fictitious or overvalued collateral.
9. Check-kiting to obtain operating capital on short-term financing.
10. Securities Act violations, i.e., sale of nonregistered securities to obtain operating capital, false proxy statements, manipulation of market to support corporate credit or access to capital markets, etc.
11. Collusion between physicians and pharmacists to cause the writing of unnecessary prescriptions.
12. Dispensing by pharmacists in violation of law, excluding narcotics traffic.
13. Immigration fraud in support of employment-agency operations.
14. Housing-code violations by landlords.
15. Deceptive advertising.
16. Fraud against the government:

    a. False claims.
    b. False statements:

       (1) To induce contracts.
       (2) AID frauds.
       (3) Housing frauds.
       (4) SBA frauds such as SBIC bootstrapping, self-dealing, cross dealing, etc., or obtaining direct loans by use of false financial statements.

    c. Moving contracts in urban renewal.

17. Labor violations (Davis-Bacon Act).
18. Commercial espionage.

FIGURE 2.1   Edelhertz's Category Corresponding to Organizational Crimes

Source: Herbert Edelhertz. 1970. *The Nature, Impact and Prosecution of White-Collar Crime.* Washington, DC: National Institute of Law Enforcement and Criminal Justice, Government Printing Office, 73–75.

spire to rig prices, alone costs American consumers about $60 billion per year in lost purchasing power.

The largest of the most recent price-fixing scandals belongs to Archer-Daniels-Midland. ADM overcharged its lysine customers more than $170 million, and its citric-acid customers were overcharged by $400 million. The record $100 million fine levied at ADM is nothing compared to the $1 billion in overcharges in the price-fixing case, or the $13.6 billion annual income and the huge agricultural subsidies from the federal government (Sherrill, 1997).

Price-gouging, charging high prices when cheaper versions of the same product are available, is another deviant practice. Gouging is especially common in the prescription drug industry. For example, a 100-tablet amount of Abbott's erythromycin wholesales for $15.50, but the generic brand wholesales for $6.20 per 100 tablets (Simon, 1999, 100ff).

Fraud, a crime based on inducing people to part with their valuables or money via lies, deceptions, or misrepresentation, *is the most common property crime in America.* It costs American consumers tens of billions of dollars every year. Repair fraud alone costs consumers an estimated $20 billion per year (Simon, 1999, 99ff). Some of the more serious examples in recent years include the following (Sherrill, 1997):

- In 1996 it was learned that as many as 25 million consumers were overcharged $600 million between 1989 and 1994 by contact-lens giants like Bausch and Lomb, Johnson and Johnson Vision Products, and Ciba Vision Corporation, as well as several optometry trade organizations. Attorneys general in 22 states sued these entities for price conspiracy.
- The largest pharmaceuticals paid $350 million in 1996 as settlement to retail drug stores for overcharging. The Federal Trade Commission (FTC) is still investigating the case on grounds of conspiracy.
- The $3.2-billion-a-year Florida nursing-home industry was fined $2.5 million in 1996 for providing extremely poor care to residents. So far, only one firm (Ambrosia) has paid its meager $19,500 levy. The homes merely appeal the fines, and the cases take years to settle.
- The FTC requires funeral parlors to provide itemized price lists to prospective customers. However, the FTC did its own research and learned that 8,000 (out of 20,000 funeral homes) ignore the requirement. Thus far the FTC has accused only 20 funeral homes of ignoring the rule. A recent *60 Minutes* segment (January, 1998) about funeral homes revealed that large corporations are buying funeral parlors, after which prices are dramatically raised. A simple casket wholesaling for a few hundred dollars may end up costing over $1,000.

These examples also point up one of the key myths involving corporate crime. Corporate crime and other acts of the powerful are apologized for as mere oversights or accidents, lacking in the criminal intent exhibited by violent street criminals. Indeed, "the argument that corporate offenders lack criminal intent is one of a series of guilt-neutralizing myths employed by white-collar criminals to excuse their conduct" (Kappeler, et al., 1993, 105).

Moreover, the incidents described above, and many others mentioned throughout this book, indicate exactly deliberate intent. Fraud is a crime that usually requires a good deal of advanced planning, even conspiracy (a form of criminal intent), and must, therefore, be deliberate.

Another important form of fraud is fraudulent advertising. This type of advertising differs from the puffery advertising in that the claims made are demonstrably false, and, hence, illegal. Such advertising can be extremely harmful.

- In 1996, the FDA ordered Pfizer to immediately cease making misleading promotional claims for Zoloft, a popular anti-depressant (worldwide sales of $1 billion a year) concerning its lack of side effects (Sherrill, 1997).
- In 1997, numerous home-exercise equipment makers were forced to stop advertising that their products would automatically cause weight loss and abdominal size decreases when used for only a few minutes, three times per week.

- In 1976, some $3.5 billion was spent on the 500,000 nonprescription drugs sold in the United States. The drugs are heavily advertised as being effective, but half of them perform no useful function. Antihistamines are a glaring example. Each year billions of dollars are wasted by cold sufferers who buy these products. Advertised for decades as relieving cold symptoms, in the early 1990s it was learned that these substances only relieve the sneezing and itching of allergy sufferers. By 1999, the over-the-counter drug market is predicted to top $16.7 billion and contains numerous drugs that either do nothing (e.g., fat burners) or are actually harmful (Jensen, et al., 1997, 45).

Merger Mania

Between 1989 and 1996, the United States lost 3.1 million manufacturing and white-collar jobs. Many of these positions were eliminated as a result of corporate mergers, leveraged buyouts (LBOs), and so-called downsizing (Gross, 1996, 149). Corporate mergers in the 1990s have been devastating to American workers. According to the *New York Times,* "more than 43 million jobs have been erased in the United States since 1979. Increasingly the jobs that are disappearing are those of higher-paid, white-collar workers, many at large corporations, women as well as men, many at the peak of their careers."

Nearly three-quarters of all households have had a close encounter with layoffs since 1980, according to a new poll by the *New York Times.* In one-third of all households, a family member has lost a job, and nearly 40 percent more know a relative, friend, or neighbor who was laid off. About 19 million people, a number matching the adult population of New York and New Jersey combined, acknowledged that a lost job in their household had precipitated a major crisis in their lives, according to the *Times* poll (Simon, 1999, 70ff).

1. *Corporate Mergers:* In 1996 alone, over $65 billion was spent on corporate mergers (Table 2.2).

2. *Overseas Investments:* In Mexico alone, the number of plants owned by U.S. firms increased from 620 to 2,200 between 1980 and 1992, and the number of jobs held by Mexican workers in those plants increased from 119,550 to nearly 600,000 (Perot & Choate, 1993, 48–49). These firms experience gross labor costs of only $1.15 to $1.50 per hour in

TABLE 2.2 Largest Corporate Mergers, 1996–1997

Company	Acquirer	Billions of Dollars
Ciba-Geigy	Sandoz	$30.1
Lucent Technologies	Shareholders	$24.1
Grand Metropolitan	Guiness	$22.3
NYNEX	Bell Atlantic	$21.3
Capital Cities/ABC	Walt Disney	$18.9
Pacific Telesis	SBC Communications	$16.5

Source: Wright, 1997, 354.

Mexico (versus costs of $7–$10 per hour in the United States). As of 1997, the advanced nations' corporations had capital investments of $243.8 billion in developing nations (up from $44 billion in 1990). The rate of return on investments in developing nations is two-thirds more than the return on investments in advanced nations (Simon, 1999, 185ff; Wright, 1997, 506).

For all the hype about the new global economy, a mere one-tenth of 1 percent of U.S. firms make half of all profits on overseas investments, and 90 percent of all foreign tax credits. While reports underestimate the actual profits from abroad, around 30 percent of the profits made by these corporate giants stem from overseas activity (compared to 10 percent in 1950).

Foreign investment is extremely important for the largest of the multinational corporations from advanced nations, accounting for over half of all profits for 13 of the largest corporations in the late 1980s. These include: Exxon (75 percent), Gillette (63 percent), Mobil Oil (61 percent), Colgate-Palmolive (56 percent), Dow Chemical (56 percent), Coca-Cola (55 percent), and IBM (54 percent) (Braun, 1993, 102). Thus foreign investment is an increasingly important source of profitable investment for corporate America.

3. *The Militarized Economy:* From 1945 to 1992, the United States spent over $4 trillion on national defense, $2 trillion of which was spent between 1980 and 1992 (Simon, 1996, 166). In the 1980s and early 1990s, over 80 percent of U.S. research and development (R&D) was devoted to military hardware (i.e., weapons). The billions of dollars in government R&D money were accompanied by additional billions in capital investment in defense-contracting firms. Seventy-five percent of the defense weapons systems contracts annually go to the largest 100 corporations in the United States. All this money poured into defense ate away at industrial competitiveness. The per capita investment in civilian research and development in the United States has been far lower, for many years, than in Japan and Western Europe. The result: U.S. business, with the exception of perhaps space and satellite technology, is no longer leading the world as it did 20 years ago. For example, in 1975, the first 15 places on the Fortune 500 list of the world's largest companies included 11 American corporations. Now there are only 7.

In the past, huge military expenditures have resulted in massive government deficits, which contribute to inflation and a decline in purchasing power for average families. Large defense expenditures have also diverted monies that could have been spent on pressing domestic social problems, including education, health care, public infrastructure, school dropouts, drugs, and so on (Hopkins, 1993, A-11). They have also resulted in countless corporate scandals.

Corporate Deviance and the Pentagon Waste Machine

Out of 30,000 firms engaged in weapons contracting, the top 25 are awarded more than 50 percent of all defense weapons business. Among the firms garnering the lion's share of defense contracts are corporate giants like Lockheed-Martin, McDonnell Douglas, Rockwell, General Electric, Boeing, United Technologies, Raytheon, Westinghouse, IBM, RCA, Ford, General Motors, and Exxon. The weapons industry is notoriously noncompetitive. Inefficiency, cost overruns, waste, and corruption are rampant. At times, it is characterized by excessive secrecy, designed to hide mistakes and criminal behavior from Congress and the public (Simon, 1999, Chapter 5).

Pentagon procurement is also riddled with a continuing pattern of fraud and other crimes among defense contractors. Consider a few of the 1996 scandals, described by Robert Sherrill (1997):

- United Telecontrol Electronics used defective bolts to hold a 500-pound Maverick missile to the wing of a plane. UTE used falsified computer-controlled measurements to make it look like the parts had passed inspection. The crime disrupted operations at U.S. air bases and endangered the lives of military personnel. A former UTE vice president plead guilty to fraud and received a maximum 21-month prison term and paid a $40,000 fine.
- The Navy blames defective F-18 gearboxes for emergency landings, in-flight fires, and loss of one of the planes in the Gulf War. The Navy found that all 150 gearboxes it inspected were defective. The manufacturer, the $6.7-billion company Lucas Industries, paid a meager $106 million fine after pleading guilty to falsifying records.
- In 1986 two employees of Hughes Aircraft told federal officials that the company was falsifying test reports. The whistleblowers were harassed and eventually left Hughes. Then they filed suit under the False Claims Act. Ten years later they were finally awarded $891,000, $450,000 in legal fees, and $3.1 million for the Pentagon. In 1992, Hughes was fined $3.5 million for criminal failure to properly test jet-fighter equipment and other weapons. The military continues to award contracts to Hughes.
- In the 1980s, Litton Industries confessed it had defrauded the Pentagon by price inflation and other deceptive practices on dozens of Navy electronics contracts. In 1996, Litton, still doing business with the Pentagon, was raided by federal agents in Los Angeles in an investigation of overcharges during the previous decade.
- Lockheed Martin settled its influence-peddling scandal of the 1980s for a $5.3-million fine on Martin Marietta's $30 million in overcharges. The contract in question, for a supersonic low-altitude target for missile test, was cancelled. Not, however, before Martin Marietta piled up cost overruns of $92 million.
- McDonnell Douglas paid a $500,000 fine for misleading the Pentagon on its C-17 cargo jet contract of $6.6 billion. The company falsified estimates it showed the government, while its actual estimates showed a $1 billion loss, a difference paid by the taxpayers.
- According to a U.S. Senate hearing, between 1985 and 1995, $13 billion paid to weapons contractors by the Pentagon was simply "lost," and another $15 billion remains unaccounted for due to "financial management troubles."
- The most recent estimate is that military waste and fraud costs U.S. taxpayers $172 billion per year.
- A 1996 report by the Council for a Livable World, an arms-control advocacy group that has sought reductions in defense spending, says there are at least $29 billion in wasteful programs. Titled "The Pentagon Follies," the report details such things as,
  - Construction of a third golf course at Andrews Air Force Base in Maryland.
  - The Naval Academy keeps a herd of 319 cows at an annual cost of $1.2 million. The academy says it is now trying to sell the cows.

- Funds from the Pentagon's Morale, Welfare and Recreation program are used to lease part of a 287-room hotel at Disney World. The hotel loses $27.2 million each year, which is compensated for by a federal subsidy.
- A door hinge for the C-17 aircraft cost $2,187 after a subcontractor failed to provide the part. The part regularly costs $31.

- Large shipments of illegal arms are moving undetected across U.S. borders. Fewer than 500 of the Customs Service's 18,000 employees watch arms exports along U.S. borders. Each year between $2 billion and $10 billion in illegal arms are traded, often to terrorists or opposition groups seeking to overthrow legitimate governments, such as the factions attempting to overthrow the government of Trinidad and Iraqi interests seeking assault rifles. Only 21 cases for Arms Export Control violations were brought by the U.S. Department of Justice in 1992, less than 10 percent of the illegal weapons that are either exported from or imported to the United States.
- According to a 1996 General Accounting Office report, 80 percent of the Navy's purchase orders are inaccurate.
- Moreover, an Air Force purchase order of $888,000 worth of ammunition was listed as $333 million, 37,500 percent over priced. In 1992 alone, the Army Corps of Engineers misplaced $1.3 billion of its own equipment.

As of 1994, government investigations of contract abuse were initiated against 70 percent of the Pentagon's top 100 contractors, and fines for that year totaled a record $1.2 billion.

One problem with Pentagon-related waste and fraud is that there seems to be little penalty involved when it comes to the right of companies to continue to do business with the government. As William Greider (1992, 112–113) notes, "exemptions to law are granted routinely to the major defense contractors…who committed criminal fraud against the government…. Twenty-five of the one hundred largest contractors have been found guilty of…fraud in recent years…. Typically they plead guilty and pay a fine. To appease the public, the Pentagon sometimes 'suspends' contractors, but the suspensions are always lifted in time for the company to participate in the next bidding for contracts."

Another problem with Pentagon procurement is that contracts are let on a "cost-plus" basis, meaning that profit made by the company involved is always a fixed percentage (e.g., 10 percent) of the final cost of the project. If a contract is initially signed for a billion dollars, the cost will typically rise to say $3.2 billion due to alleged increases in various costs of production. The Pentagon rarely refuses such increases because it has already sunk billions into such projects. The typical cost overrun from the 1960s to the early 1990s was about 230 to 320 percent of initial costs (Simon, 1999, 170 ff).

There are additional harms associated with the United States's permanent war economy. First, the military is a major environmental polluter. It poisons ground water, air, and soil with a host of toxic and radioactive chemicals in the United States and overseas in bombing exercises and the production of nuclear, chemical, and biological weapons. Around the world, there are an estimated 21,000 contaminated sites on nuclear weapons plants and military bases (Parenti, 1995, 88).

In the United States, the military has caused environmental scandals. The U.S. military produces some 500,000 tons of toxic waste each year, more than the five largest American chemical firms combined. The military even sold some of its waste and explosive chemicals to unsuspecting civilians at a 1991 auction. It has been estimated that the cost of cleaning up the toxic mess at McClellan Air Force Base alone will exceed $700 million (Jensen, et al., 1997, 170).

- From the 1940s to the 1970s, the U.S. military and other agencies conducted radiation exposure (usually atomic bomb) tests on hundreds of unsuspecting citizens and members of the military. The Veterans Administration (VA) admitted that it had shredded thousands of files. When a group of radiation-surviving veterans pressed the VA for claims, they were rejected. The VA claimed that studies had shown its own tests did not support the survivors' claims. Later the VA admitted that the test results had been falsified (Jensen, et al., 1997, 196–197).
- In 1984, it was revealed that U.S. leaders had lied about Russian military strength by inflating estimates of the Soviet military budget. Estimates on Russian weapon system costs were based on what the costs would have been if they were made in the United States. Billions of dollars in unnecessary weapons were purchased based on the false estimates of the Russian threat.
- More recently (1996–1997) the Pentagon has actually funded mergers of defense-contracting firms. Lockheed-Martin received $60 million from the Defense Department in order to buy a subsidiary of General Dynamics.

Environmental Elite Deviance

One of the most serious forms of corporate deviance is environmental crime. These are acts of environmental destruction that often present an immediate physical and financial threat to those affected.

- In the 1970s, U.S. makers of death-causing asbestos began moving their factories to countries like Mexico and India, poor nations with more lenient environmental regulations. By 1995, the number of such plants in less-developed nations had actually increased (Jensen, et al., 1997, 66–67).
- In 1978, press reports claimed that some Occidental Petroleum workers in Lathrop, California, were being made sterile by exposure to a pesticide called DBCP. Today sperm counts among men all over the United States are almost 50 percent lower than they were 30 years ago (Jensen, et al., 1997, 69).
- It has now been determined that the United States's fatty, dyed, and artificially flavored food supply may cause mental disturbances such as depression (Jensen, et al., 1997, 72).
- In 1979, alternative press reports claimed that 100,000 U.S. workers die each year from diseases picked up at work. Some 21 million workers in the United States are exposed to hazardous chemicals, and 40 percent of cancers are linked to industrial chemicals. By 1995, the number of occupationally related deaths was on the increase (Jensen, et al., 1997, 83).
- Industrial fishing fleets routinely discard 60 billion pounds of fish per year, some endangered species. Millions of the fish are caught, thrown overboard, and left to die

because they are too small to eat. Clinton-backer Don Tyson is trying to convince the federal government to grant his $4 billion firm corporate rights to the Alaska fishery without having to pay a dime in royalties.

What all this means is that corporate violators of ecological criminal laws are part of an entire political economy, a macro environment over which they exert considerable control. Part of this environment concerns the global political economy in which such transnational corporations operate. Often, corporate violations are international in scope, and involve not just violations of hazardous waste laws, but corruption statutes as well.

The problem of environmental destruction thus represents one of the most dangerous contradictions of giving priority to the value of accumulating wealth without regard to the means of doing so. Environmental problems, however, do not effect all populations equally; they are socially patterned.

Patterns of Environmental Victimization

The victimization of nonelites by environmental harms is a global pattern, one that especially strikes people of color. *Environmental racism* is the term used to describe the victimization of people of color by corporate polluters. Various studies have established that minorities and working-class whites in the United States are at considerable risk from such victimization:

- In 1996, three Kentucky coal executives were sent to prison in the deaths of 10 workers. In 1989 methane gas exploded in a Pyro Mining Company shaft. Prior to the explosion the executives misled federal inspectors concerning the mine's hazards. For being accessories in the deaths of the miners, the executives drew sentences ranging from 5 months to 18 months and fines of $375 to $3,000 ($300 per victim) (Sherrill, 1997).
- By 1986, some two million tons of radioactive uranium tailings had been dumped on Native American lands, and cancer rates among Navajo teens have climbed to seventeen times the national average (Rosen, 1994, 225).
- African Americans are 40 percent more likely to live in neighborhoods in which toxic-waste dump sites are located than are nonminorities. In southern United States, 60 percent of neighborhoods surrounding waste-disposal sites are African American (Simon, 1997, 214–215). Nationally, 60 percent of African American communities are endangered by abandoned toxic-waste dumps and commercial hazardous-waste landfills. In the United States, the lower a family's income, the higher the lead content in children's blood (Parenti, 1995, 112).
- Some communities are repeatedly victimized by toxic hazards. When North Richmond, California, experienced a 15-mile long toxic cloud from a ruptured rail car at General Chemical's plant, it marked the fifteenth time a serious industrial accident occurred at a Contra Costa county chemical facility or refinery within the previous 5 years. Within the county itself, there are at least 38 industrial sites in which 94 million pounds of some 45 industrial chemicals are stored (Rosen, 1994, 223–224).

It is the poor and working class people of all colors who tend to live the closest to chemical factories, toxic dump sites, and incinerators, and suffer the highest rates of pollution-caused cancer (Hilts, 1993, A–1). Likewise, recent studies confirm that toxic-cleanup programs under the Superfund law take longer and are less thorough in minority areas. A related harm associated with ecological destruction can be termed "employee blackmail." This occurs when corporate polluters threaten victims living near factories where they work with job losses, should the victims continue pressing claims for environmental justice (investigations and cleanups) (Rosen, 1994, 225–226). Moreover, violations of environmental justice cause moral harm in the form of decreased public confidence in corporate and/or governmental legitimacy. There is overwhelming public-opinion data indicating that corporations which pollute the environment deepen public distrust of corporations (Simon, 1996, 5ff), especially of those citizens living near pollution sites.

Finally, the most helpless victims of environmental pollution are animals, many of whom are endangered. In the last 20 years, the U.S. Department of Interior claims, over 300 species of wildlife have become extinct, and another 850 are now considered endangered (1,100 species if plants are included) (Frank & Lynch, 1992, 84). There are a number of causes of this carnage, but toxic incidents, such as the Exxon Valdez oil spill, is one of them. Thousands of animals, fish, and birds in Alaska were killed as a result of the spill. Numerous other chemical accidents and hazardous waste incidents have collectively killed millions of fish and other wildlife the world over.

The above examples are paralleled by victimization statistics of both humans and other species in Third World nations. Populations who have suffered at the hands of polluting multinational corporations and lax, sometimes corrupt, governmental policies are overwhelmingly people of color, and among the poorest and most powerless of the world's population. From Bhopal, India (where a 1984 chemical accident from a Union Carbide plant killed 5,000 and injured 30,000) (Frank & Lynch, 1992, 73), to Mexican border towns near Maquiladora plants, the victims of hazardous toxic-waste scandals are most frequently those with the least access to sanitation, health education, and health care. Third World women and children have frequently suffered victimization from dangerous products banned for use in the United States and exported to Third World nations, including pesticides like DBC. These incidents serve to further increase the distrust and alienation experienced by people of color and by people everywhere victimized by corporate pollution.

International Environmental Deviance

A large number of toxic-waste problems are exported to foreign countries, many of which have involved the illegal bribery of officials of foreign governments. The advanced nations of the world generate about 400 million tons of toxic waste annually; 60 percent comes from the United States. A shipment of toxic waste leaves the United States every 5 minutes on every day of the year. The vast majority of this internationally exported toxic waste, 80 percent, is sent to Canada and Britain (Cass, 1994, 2). The Environmental Protection Agency (EPA) requires U.S. companies to provide onsite disposal facilities for toxic waste that cost upwards of $30 million and take years to build. However, such waste can be dumped in Third World nations for a fraction of the cost, sometimes for as little as $20 a ton (Cass, 1994, 7). In 1991, an internal memo written by one of the World Bank's chief economists advocated that the World Bank encourage "more migration of dirty industries to the Less Developed Countries" (Rosen, 1994, 226), thus giving credence to those who believe that environmental racism is an intentional policy.

At times, multinational corporations have provided handsome financial rewards to the recipient nations. For example, Guinea-Bissau, which has a gross national product of $150 million, will make $150 to $600 million over a 5-year period in a deal to accept toxic waste from three European nations.

Third World participation in the waste dumping of advanced nations has generated a host of scandals (Brooks, 1988; Cass, 1994):

- In April 1988, five top government officials in the Congo were indicted after they concluded a deal to import one million tons of chemical waste and pesticide residue, receiving $4 million in commissions from a firm specializing in hazardous-waste disposal. The total contract was worth $84 million.
- After dumping toxic waste in Nigeria and Lebanon, in 1988, Italy agreed to take back some 6,400 tons. What's more, Nigeria recalled its Italian ambassador and arrested 25 people when it discovered some of the waste was radioactive. To complicate matters, Italian dock workers in ten port cities have refused to handle the waste. Italy has pledged to ban further toxic exports to the developing world and plans to spend $7 billion a year to clean up its own toxic dumps at home. The Italian government has also sued 22 waste-producing firms to force them to turn over $75 million to pay for transporting and treating incoming waste.
- Currently, some 100 million gallons of untreated sewage are dumped into the Rio Grande River daily, 10 million gallons in El Paso alone (Kelly, 1993, 15). Rather than pay for incineration of hazardous waste at licensed U.S. facilities, some firms load wastes on trucks which are then smuggled into Mexico for illegal dumping. It is currently estimated that the pollution caused by Maquiladoras will cost over $16 billion to clean up, but, thus far, the World Bank has committed itself to just $1.8 billion in loans to Mexico for this purpose.

On both sides of the U.S.–Mexican border, there have been reports of deformed fish, human birth defects, increased cancer rates, and a doubling of typhoid and infectious hepatitis (Wolkimir, 1994, 27, 30). In towns like Matamoras, xylene levels in the drinking water behind the Stepan Chemical plant are 50,000 higher than those considered safe in the United States. Xylene levels near Matamoras' General Motors plant are 6,000 greater than those considered safe in the U.S. Moreover, 90 percent of the toxic waste generated in Matamoras is being disposed of illegally and improperly.

One result of this pollution is a drastic rise in birth defects. Between 1990 and 1992, 42 babies in Matamoras were born with underdeveloped brains. Mexico lacks the necessary financial resources to either enforce existing regulations or pay for the cleanup of toxic-waste pollution sites along its border (Kelly, 1993, 13, 16–17). Ironically, the greatest problem with toxic dumping in Third World nations is that much of the time it is perfectly legal. About all that concerned citizens in developing nations can do is publicize the dangers involved. What environmental disasters may befall such nations in the future is anyone's guess.

Third World dumping involves a series of related implications. For instance, some would suggest that deliberate racist and genocidal policies are being practiced by certain corporations and government agencies. Corporate dumping may well have such effects on the nonwhite people of the world. The same may be said concerning support by corporations and government for regimes that violate human rights. Taken collectively, all of this indicates that the waste industry is one of the most corrupt industries in the world (Jensen, et al., 1993, 57). Most disturbingly, many times the federal government has covered up, and at other times been a co-conspirator in, the violation of environmental and other laws.

Governmental Pollution

The U.S. federal government is probably the nation's chief polluter. All federal facilities discharge almost 2.5 million tons of toxic and radioactive waste without reporting it annually. The Government Accounting Office estimates that 95 percent (200 million) of U.S. government toxic pollution is exempt from the government's own reporting procedures. At Department of Defense weapons plants alone, there are 14,401 potentially contaminated dump sites.

Many of these sites have been the focus of their own scandals. For example, in 1991, it was learned that the companies that operated the Department of Energy's Savannah River nuclear reactor, Westinghouse and Bechtel subsidiaries, hid huge cost overruns by illegally transferring tens of millions of dollars in and out of construction accounts. The illegal transfers also went to pay Bechtel's expensive management fees, to construct unauthorized new projects, and to hide other cost increases from both Congress and the Department of Energy.

The scandal followed news by the General Accounting Office that the cleanup of the Department of Energy's radioactive poisons would cost $200 billion or more and would take up to fifty years. The department has spent $3 billion trying to repair three nuclear reactors at its Savannah River plant, only one of which will be reopened. Moreover, it has shut down its plutonium-machining and -processing plant in Colorado and a nuclear repository in New Mexico because of safety and environmental problems.

Various agencies of the U.S. government are named as PRPs (Primary Responsible Parties) at 8 percent of the Superfund sites, but this estimate is considered very conservative because the federal government is exempt in over 90 percent of cases from EPA regulations. Likewise, more than half of the 10.5 billion pounds of toxic chemicals released into the air, soil, and water are not covered by EPA regulations (Caldicott, 1992, 7). The environmental crime violations by corporations and government are also symbolic of a deeper harm, the relationship between alienation and mass consumption as a way of life.

Corporate Deviance and Alienation: "Affluenza"

In 1997, "Affluenza," a PBS special (September 15), gave the nation a disturbing look at the more alienating consequences of its mass consumption economy. The symptoms include:

- Shopping fever—the shopping mall has replaced the neighborhood in many U.S. suburban locations. People in U.S. societies sometimes use shopping as a substitute for unmet emotional needs for relationships and recognition. In fact, the average U.S. parent shops 6 hours a week and spends 40 minutes with their children. There was a time in the United States when consumption had a very negative connotation. It was a synonym for tuberculosis. Now the self-esteem of many individuals, especially teens, is tied to the ability to consume.

- Chronic stress—Nearly one-third of U.S. families are over their heads in credit-card debt, work long hours, and try to juggle their work and family lives. The percentage of Americans describing themselves as "very happy" hit its high point in 1957 and has been declining ever since.

- Bankruptcies—chronic credit-card debt and other expenses often lead to bankruptcy. More Americans declared bankruptcy in 1997 than graduated from college.

- Fractured couples and families—not only do parents spend less time with children, but relationship problems—divorce, risky remarriage, and disillusioned children and step-children—contribute substantially to feelings of alienation. The documentary pointed out that because so much economic activity revolves around buying things that have to be replaced, Americans have come to view relationships as just another commodity which can always be "traded in" for "newer models." Even right-wing fundamentalist Christian organizations complain of the social dislocations caused by consumerism. Advertising that pits children against their parents is going too far because it trans-forms kids into manipulative consumers. During the program, advertising executives in a conference at Disneyworld were shown discussing how to encourage antisocial behavior among children.

- Crime—the documentary notes that some of the poorest of the United States's teens have committed crimes to obtain the latest gold chains and Nike sneakers. Peer pressure and the ever-present reality of corporate advertising create much envy among the world's have-nots. Much white-collar deviance, as we have seen, comes from this "more is never enough mentality."

- Global harm—mass-consumption economies deplete the earth's supply of precious resources, extinguish many animal species, and cause massive pollution, global warm-ing, and other dangers. The great contradiction of mass consumption is that it uses up resources at an alarming rate, and in doing so, generates pollution on a global scale. The child born into the typical middle-class American home will go through 28,627 alumi-num cans and 12,000 grocery bags, burn out 750 light bulbs, eat 8,486 pounds of red meat and 17,591 eggs (equal to the lifetime production of 35 chickens), and wear and discard 250 shirts and 115 pairs of shoes. The United States contains only 5 percent of the world's population but consumes 25 percent of the fossil fuels used annually and a disproportional amount of other raw materials as well. The average American's energy use is equivalent to the consumption of 3 Japanese, 6 Mexicans, 12 Chinese, 33 Indians, 147 Bangladeshis, 281 Tanzanians, or 422 Ethiopians. There is considerable doubt as to whether the world can survive more mass-consumption societies.

Another alienation issue is that people are frequently dehumanized (viewed in less than human terms) by government and corporations.

- The Ford Motor Company asked the National Highway Traffic and Safety Administra-tion to estimate the monetary worth of a human life. What, Ford wanted to know, was the average wrongful death claim in a vehicle accident? About $200,000 was the gov-ernment's reply. Ford used this figure in an internal company memo that argued it would be more profitable to produce a car that Ford knew would kill and seriously disfigure an estimated 360 people than it would be to spend $11.80 per vehicle to correct a defective gas tank. The result: Ford let the Pinto roll off the assembly line, and hundreds of people were victims of a crime Indiana prosecutors tried to label "corporate homicide" (Simon, 1999, 123ff).

- The Federal Aviation Administration estimates the cost of human life lost in airplane crashes at about $650,000. The Occupational Health & Safety Administration claims dead construction workers are worth $3.5 million, but the Office of Management and Budget claims dead construction workers are only worth about $1 million. The deception associated with these estimates is that they appear "rational," (i.e., efficient), but they really are not. Human beings are reduced to mere producers of income (economic actors) and their worth is simply calculated based on their expected earnings over a lifetime. This makes some people's lives worth a great deal more than others (Greider, 1992, 54).
- The Clean Air Act of 1990 permits chemical, steel, and petroleum firms discharging poisonous materials into the atmosphere to kill as many as 10 people in 100,000 in the neighborhoods surrounding their plants. Moreover, the act gives companies 20 years to achieve these standards (Greider, 1992, 56). All of these examples point to yet another related problem; namely, the failure of government to control corporate crime.

Discussion

Multinational oligopolistic conglomerates now dominate the United States and the global economy. Oligopoly is a structure in which four or fewer firms control at least 50 percent of a given product's market. The existence of oligopoly also increases the likelihood of a host of harmful economic practices including

Price-fixing.

Fraud.

Price-gouging.

False advertising.

Mergers and acquisitions at the expense of job expansion.

Transfer of plants to foreign (Third World) nations, such as Mexico, where labor costs are a fraction of their U.S. counterparts, and many costly regulations can be easily evaded.

Undemocractic influence within the federal government, resulting in all manner of corporate subsidies and tax breaks at the expense of the average taxpayer.

Conventional wisdom is demonstrably false concerning the realities of corporate crime. Crimes by corporations are more harmful than street crime by any objective measure. Corporate crime takes at least five times as many lives as street crime, costs at least six times more money, and, along with other forms of elite deviance, contributes greatly to the mass distrust of the institutions of political economy. Many of these practices, as well as the militarization of the economy after World War II, have made the manufacturing sector of the U.S. economy uncompetitive with products from such nations as Germany and Japan.

The government, far from being a neutral party in economic matters, is deeply involved in all aspects of economic life. The government hosts numerous subsidy, tax-relief, and loan-guarantee programs, all designed to aid in the accumulation of corporate profits. These programs are largely paid for by the heavily taxed American middle class.

These examples, together with the other facts examined in this chapter, point to the dangerousness of America's persistent myths about its economic and political systems. The relative lack of free market mechanisms, the harmful nature of corporate crime, and the undemocratic influence of wealthy individuals and corporations speak volumes about the most harmful macro problems facing the nation. The same is true for the harms committed by government, the subject of our next chapter.

Critical Thinking Exercise 2-1: Business Crime and Punishment in the United States

The *Wall Street Journal* calls itself "the daily diary of the American Dream." As argued in Chapter 2, the values connected with the American Dream, as well as a lack of opportunity, encourage a great deal of criminal behavior, including crimes among corporations. Using 50 recent issues of the *Wall Street Journal*, do a content analysis of the amount of corporate and employee crime. In your analysis, answer the following questions,

    I. What is the most common crime committed by corporations?
    II. What percentage of the articles mention prison as part of the sentence imposed on convicted executives and employees?
    III. What is the average fine imposed on corporations? On employees?
    IV. Who are the most frequent victims of corporate criminals? The public? The government? Women? Children? Minorities?

What do the results of your study indicate about the way corporate and white-collar employees are treated by the criminal justice system?

Political White-Collar Deviance, The Politics of Corruption

The Roots of Corruption: The Political Milieu

A major contributor to political corruption in the United States concerns all manner of privileges and perks that politicians of all stripes and at all levels of government have conveyed upon themselves. Together these costly freebees contribute to an atmosphere of elitism and arrogance—an environment conducive to the idea that holders of political power can do no wrong. Take, for example, the nearly endless perquisites that members of Congress have graciously voted themselves at the expense of the nation's taxpayers (mostly middle-class families). According to Gross (1996, 190–193):

- Congress's 535 members employ a supporting staff of over 25,000 at a cost of well over $1 billion. The House chaplain's salary is $115,300. Congressional pay costs taxpayers $55 million per year, plus $30 million to maintain up to three offices in their districts, and $78 million in free mailing privileges (see below).
- There is an extra $3,000 income tax deduction given to Congress members simply because they are Congress members.
- Free personal income tax preparation gladly provided by the IRS (all other Americans pay—and pay dearly—when they hire tax experts to do their taxes).
- Members of Congress pay no Washington, DC, sales taxes on items purchased inside the Capitol Building—even if they live in the nation's capital. Congress members are likewise exempt from all Washington, DC, income taxes (comparable to state income taxes). This is somewhat significant because the nation's capital (currently headed by a convicted felon and recovering drug addict) is millions in debt.

- The National Gallery of Art lends original paintings, some of which are worth millions, to members of Congress for use in decorating their offices.
- A special gift office wraps packages free of charge to representatives, senators, and their senior staff. There are special stationary stores inside the Capitol that heavily discount all items sold. This congressional subsidy costs America's taxpayers $1 million annually.
- There are free photos with constituents taken, cropped, and sent out at no cost. The same service also frames posters and snapshots for free. Airport parking at both Dulles and Reagan airports—a few steps away from the terminal—is free. All other patrons must pay royally and at places sometimes far from these airports for airport parking.
- If airline tickets are paid for by the government (a not-infrequent occurrence), Congress members and their staffs are allowed credit for airline frequent-flyer miles. When using their privately owned vehicles, above-average mileage reimbursement is allowed.
- After leaving Congress, members may use their office desks and chairs free—at home! Some 79 senators with seniority are given second (hidden) offices inside the Capitol—in addition to spacious regular offices. Ordinary citizens must pay hundreds of dollars per square foot for offices outside their homes. Members of Congress and their staffs are also provided with free, unlimited long-distance phone service—even when calling from their own homes. Common folk are forced to pay dearly for every call made from their residences.
- The Library of Congress charges no fines on overdue books and other items for Congress members and their staffs. Each year, thousands of books go unreturned. Members of both houses hire children of friends and constituents to fill various patronage jobs—such as congressional page—at taxpayer expense. Likewise, the White House has numerous such posts. At this writing President Clinton is accused of having a sexual relationship with one such intern. Several members of Congress have been accused, prosecuted, and convicted of having sexual relations with these usually under-aged employees over the years. Likewise, a number of congresspersons have been caught by capital police engaging in oral sex in their vehicles with various pages (Kessler, 1996).
- Leaders of the House and Senate, of course, must be transported from one place to another, and they are provided (at taxpayer largesse) free limousines and chauffeurs. There are radio and television studios inside the nation's capital, used for free by elected officials there for making tapes that are subsequently sent out to media outlets in their districts. Challengers in elections must, of course, pay to have such messages made.
- People in Congress have free medical, life, and other insurance, as well as an unparalleled pension plan. Some 40 million U.S. citizens, most members of the "working poor," are without medical insurance during part of any given year largely because Congress refuses to pass national health care legislation.
- In 1996, the average retired Congress member received $100,000 from the government.
- Each member of Congress receives a postal budget of some $108,000—known as the franking privilege—paid for by the taxpayers. Most of the mail (printed for free) sent goes for reelection purposes. The cost of this self-serving subsidy is over $65 million a year in the House of Representatives alone. This great campaign aid is, of course, denied to those challenging Congress members in elections.
- Finally, there are congressional "junkets." These are merely free air and other forms of travel on government owned and operated airplanes. One recent junket involved four

congresspersons, their senior staffs, and twenty-five of their spouses going on a "fact-finding" tour of China and Japan at a cost of $550,000. Part of the tour included an entire day spent at a reserve for Chinese panda bears. Lest you think this ridiculous example unusual, other trips have included:

- Congress members, staffs, spouses, and guests—over 100 people in all—went to a Paris air show at a cost of over $200,000.
- Some 19 members of the House toured Saudi Arabia and Israel and billed America's taxpayers $322,402 for the privilege.
- House committee members "investigated" Eastern Europe with their mates for $99,000.
- A foreign policy investigation of Singapore by one senator, six of his friends, and their spouses cost $359,000.

The point is not simply that these game show-like prizes are unfair on their face. The key issue here is that such nonsensical expenditures create an atmosphere in which illegal and unethical behaviors are certain to flourish.

This claim is borne out by a similar examination of the White House environment. If the congressional atmosphere can be described as one of special privileges, the White House environment can only be termed one of royalty.

- A White House operator dials phone numbers for important personnel. The minute the president takes off his suit, a servant carries it off to be cleaned. There are helicopters available to transport the president and guests to a fleet of state-of-the-art jetliners awaiting at Andrews Air Force Base. The White House also has a fleet of 29 limousines and drivers, as well as Secret Service agents to transport the president. There are five calligraphers at an annual cost of $260,000.
- No one really knows how much all the White House perks cost. The White House has 132 rooms that are run and maintained like a world-class luxury hotel. Priceless paintings decorate the walls. The land it sits on is assessed at $314, 974, 600, and the building itself at over $25 million. There are also numerous executive office buildings for use by the executive branch. The president receives a $200,000 annual salary, which is nothing, considering it costs $9.7 million to run the White House executive residence, $24.9 million for the Office of Administration, $38.9 million for the White House Office, and an additional $93.8 million for remaining costs. In total, the executive office of the president is budgeted at over $300 million per year. In addition, the president's airplane costs $391 million because it is specially equipped. Another $356 million is spent by the Secret Service to protect the president and vice president. In 1992, the Office of Personnel Management tried to estimate all remaining costs and came up with a figure of $978.5 million annually, but this does not include the other support costs that are part of the budget of other agencies besides the Secret Service (Gross, 1993, 14; Kessler, 1996, 7–8).

Ronald Kessler (1996, 8–9) has assessed the consequences of all this largesse:

The dizzying combination of power and perquisites is corrupting. The percentage of White House aides who have had to consult psychiatrists is far out of proportion to the general population. The White House is an environment that magnifies character flaws, a catalyst that has led to such scandals as Watergate and the Iran-Contra affair.

Another attribute of the federal government that encourages corruption is its myriad of functions and their costs. In Chapter 1, we noted that government at all levels in the United States now constitutes 40 percent of the nation's gross domestic product, some $2.7 trillion. Two-thirds of this money is spent by the federal government, and it is spent for a bewildering assortment of purposes, both arbitrary and necessary. The government encourages the arts and humanities, preserves historic structures, and insures the rights of the handicapped. It spends hundreds of billions on national defense, oversees the design of automobile engines, the building of interstate highways and mass-transit systems, and even operates two zoos and a host of museums. In short, "nearly all national issues are ultimately resolved in Washington. [Moreover,] about half of all American families now receive some form of payment from the Treasury" (Caplow, 1991, 108).

The federal budget has increased from $92 billion in 1960 to well over $1.631 trillion in 1997. There are 700,000 federal employees, one third of all federal civilian workers, who control, manage, audit, or check up on other employees at a cost of $35 billion a year (Gore, 1993, 14, 121).

Likewise, as described in Chapter 1, numerous corporations make campaign donations and lobby Congress and the White House for favorable tax treatment. The result? Forty percent of American corporations with assets of $250 million or more paid either no corporate income tax or less than $100,000 in 1997 (Danaher, 1996, 40). Former Clinton staff member Betsey Wright now works for Washington's largest professional lobby firm, the Wexler Group. Former Reagan staff members Michael Deaver and Lyn Nofzinger (who was convicted of perjury) now have their own lobbying firms. According to White House rules, executive-branch employees must wait one year to lobby for clients with their former departments. However, they are allowed to lobby other governmental departments as soon as they leave government service. Moreover, members of the families of federal politicians may lobby at will. Likewise, former members of Congress who become lobbyists are allowed in congressional cloak and meeting rooms, a privilege not accorded ordinary lobbyists.

Another cozy relationship exists between former members of the U.S. Trade Representative's office and official Washington. Between 1974 and 1990, nearly half of all former senior trade officials registered with the Department of Justice as foreign agents. These lobbyists work for foreign corporations and governments, usually for Asian corporate entities like Nissan, the Japan Whaling Association, Toshiba, Airbus, Daewoo Electronics, Panasonic, Matsushita, or the European jewelry giant Cartier International, and governments like Taiwan.

Some of these agents lobby while still in federal jobs. Eight registered foreign agents were members of Clinton's White House staff in 1996, one of which worked for the People's Republic of China. Likewise, a large number of registered foreign agents are on the staffs of the Democratic and Republican National Committees.

Lobbyists and Consultants: An Incestuous Lot

Finally, there is an army of professional political consultants, advisors, so-called "spin doctors," and pollsters. Members of this profession specialize in candidate image creation, campaign strategies, running interference with the media when politicians experience crisis, and measuring the pulse of voters on a host of issues. The consultant industry is paid $1.5 billion a year to enhance the public images of candidates, engage in damage control, and otherwise mold the opinions of an increasingly alienated (hence apathetic) public. In 1996, one Democratic pollster alone, Stanley Greenberg, was paid $365,000 by the Democratic National Committee in just three months.

What has emerged in Washington is a shadow government made up of public relations firms, think tanks, and polling organizations, all funded by corporate interests. The results are staggering:

- Fifty-one U.S. senators and 146 members of the House of Representatives are either founders or officers of tax-exempt organizations that produce either research statistics or corporate propaganda for lobbying purposes (Greider, 1992, 51). In 1960 fewer than 400 lobbyists were registered with the U.S. Congress. By 1992, 40,000 were so registered (Perot and Choate, 1993, 120). Those 40,000 people represent mostly U.S. and foreign corporations. Much of this growth came in the 1970s and 1980s, when the capitalist class decided it was underrepresented in the nation's capital. Eighty percent of the *Fortune 500* corporations established "public affairs offices" (lobbies) in Washington.
- In the 1970s new think tanks were established and richly endowed by corporate money. The right-wing Heritage Foundation was started with a $250,000 donation from the Colorado beer tycoon Joseph Coors (Gilbert & Kahl, 1993, 224–225). The patrons of the American Enterprise Institute include AT&T ($125,000), Chase Manhattan Bank ($125,000), Exxon ($130,000), General Electric ($65,000), General Motors ($100,000), and Procter & Gamble ($165,000). The "institute" quickly became a "primary source of Washington opinion," shaping the policy positions of Washington politicians and the mass media (Greider, 1992, 48).

The system works in a manner that can only be described as incestuous. For example, Representative Bud Shuster (R-PA) chairs the House Transportation Committee, which dispenses hundreds of billions of dollars for government contracts and so-called "pork barrel" construction projects for his and his friends' congressional districts. Representative Shuster is frequently lobbied by Ms. Ann Eppard, a former member of his own staff. Her clients include corporate giants like FedEx, Conrail, Union Pacific, Amtrak, and Sealand, who pay her to secure government contracts and keep regulations favorable to the transportation industry. While working for these private firms, Ms. Eppard is also paid $36,000 as a political consultant to Rep. Shuster. (Eppard helped Shuster raise $650,000 in 1995 for his reelection campaign.) Eppard earns $600,000 a year in her two jobs.

The Shuster–Eppard connection is symbolic of a much more widespread condition. Professional lobbyists represent corporate and other interest groups that donate hundreds of million of dollars to the campaigns of federal politicians. A large number of these lobbyists are current and former members of Congress and their staff members, as well as former White House employees. The result of these arrangements is widespread corruption.

Corruption: An Institutional Regularity

Author Mark Twain once said that "there is no distinctly native American criminal class except for Congress" (Twain, 1899). The late Will Rogers, famous satirist of the 1920s and 1930s, once remarked that America has the best politicians that money can buy. In Chicago there is a standing joke that goes: "How can you recognize an honest politician in this town? Simple, it is the one who stays fixed (does what's been agreed on) after accepting a bribe." More recently, former Clinton administration Secretary of Labor Robert Reich stated, "a good friend in Washington is one that will stab you in the front." These jokes are an important symbol of a scandalous problem.

Looking at unethical and illegal political behavior today, such sayings seem prophetic indeed. According to a 1993 estimate, nearly 3,000 public officials are indicted, convicted, or awaiting trial in the United States each year. In 1974, there were only 523 corruption cases in the entire country. By 1989 the estimate was around 1,500 (Simon, 1997, 3), so the number of corruption cases has increased by 600 percent within two decades. Gross (1996, 67–69) argues that the actual number of corrupt public officials at all governmental levels may be as high as 10,000.

Of the 3,000 or so annual cases, nearly half (1,357 in 1993) are federal. The charges levied against various public officials vary widely, from padding expense accounts, to bribery, conflicts of interest, and illicit sex acts (usually with underaged employees). The list of recent cases is long and instructive.

- Richard Nixon's vice president, Sprio Agnew, confessed to accepting kickbacks on government contracts from a Maryland engineer, and resigned from office as part of a plea bargain in 1974. Agnew's greed fueled a constitutional crisis as it left the nation without a vice president at the time the president was about to face impeachment. The country came dangerously close to a situation in which the next person in line for the presidency was 87-year-old House Speaker John McCormick, a man on the verge of retirement, if not death.
- In 1980, an FBI sting operation called ABSCAM (short for Arab Scam) involved FBI agents dressing up as Arab sheiks to offer bribes to members of Congress. Representatives Ray Lederer (D-PA), Frank Thompson (D-NJ), and John Murphy (D-NY) were videotaped taking bribes.
- In 1992, another FBI sting operation, "Boptrot", discovered Kentucky lobbyist John Spurrier III offering a $50,000 bribe to a politician. In return for leniency, Spurrier agreed to cooperate, which meant playing the role of set-up man for the FBI. The lobbyist's hotel suite was quickly loaded with electronic surveillance gear, and Spurrier was given cash with which to bribe Kentucky state legislators. The results were shock-

ing. Sixteen legislators, including the speaker of the Kentucky House, John Blandford, were convicted or plead guilty to crimes (Gross, 1996, 59).

- In 1992, the House Ethics Committee issued a report summarizing all known ethic violations since the House's founding in 1789. The report cited 71 cases, the vast majority of which had taken place since 1967. The report was prompted by the case of Rep. Adam Clayton Powell, who paid his own wife a federal salary and used government funds for personal travel. (Powell liked to vacation in the Caribbean where he would relax with his favorite drink, scotch whisky mixed in milk.)
- U.S. House Speaker Newt Gingrich was fined $300,000 in 1997 by the House Ethics Committee because he misused funds from a nonprofit organization to promote his own goals and gave the House Ethics Committee "untrue information when it investigated that charge" (Wright, (ed.), 1997, 16).
- In 1994, Congresswoman Enid Waldholz (R-UT) received a mysterious campaign donation of some $1.8 million. The money was reported as being her own by her husband. Subsequently, her husband, who told his wife that there was no problem with the contribution, went on the lam from federal authorities due to a number of illegal acts, including misappropriation of his wife's campaign funds. Eventually, Mr. Waldholz plead guilty to 27 counts of fraud.
- In 1986, Senator James Weaver (D-OR) "lost" over $113,000 of his campaign money by speculating in the commodities market. No action was taken because Weaver had followed federal rules by reporting the speculation to the Federal Election Commission.
- Senator Alphonse D'Amato (R-NY), who chaired a Senate investigation into the Clinton Whitewater scandal in 1997, was charged by the Senate Ethics Committee with allowing his brother to write a letter to the Department of Defense on official senate stationery on behalf of Unisys, a major defense contractor. D'Amato was also cited for improperly lobbying the Department of Housing and Urban Development on behalf of real estate developers in return for campaign contributions.
- Senator David Durenberger (D-MN) was required to reimburse the government over $29,000 and donate over $93,000 to charity because he (1) was given $100,000 by his own book publishers for lecturing (in violation of senate honoraria rules) and (2) charged the government $65 for staying in his own Minneapolis condo.
- Representative William Clay (D-MO) was sued by the Department of Justice in 1976 for violations of the False Claims Act for submitting false travel vouchers to the House. The case was dropped after Clay agreed to pay $1,754.
- Representative Lewis Stokes (D-OH), two-term chair of the House Ethics Committee, was fined $250 in 1983 after being arrested for drunk driving. Senator Bob Kasten (R-WI) was arrested for drunk driving in 1985 and entered an alcohol-abuse course.
- 1984 Democratic vice presidential nominee Geraldine Ferraro was investigated for failure to disclose her husband's interests. She was cited for commission of ten violations of House Disclosure rules. A check for $53,000 was sent to the Internal Revenue Service for a 6-year-old underpayment error.
- Senator Mark Hatfield (R-OR) was cited by the Senate Ethics Committee for receiving over $42,000 in unreported gifts (which is illegal under senate rules). One of the largest freebees came from a university whose federal funding was controlled by a congressional committee of which Senator Hatfield was a member (Gross, 1996, 221).

- In 1989, Representative Tony Coelho (D-CA) resigned when it was revealed that he had invested in junk bonds with the help of an owner of a savings and loan and the Drexel, Burnham, Lambert investment firm.

Case Study: "Zippergate": Sexual Scandals and Political Corruption

In early 1998, the Clinton White House was reeling from news of a sleazy 3-year sexual relationship involving a former 24-year-old White House intern, Monica Lewinsky, and the 50-year-old president. Charges of Clinton's infidelities surfaced in the 1992 campaign when a former Arkansas state employee, Jennifer Flowers, sold her story of her affair with then Governor Clinton.

Mr. Clinton lied about the affair in a 1992 *60 Minutes* interview. Ms. Flowers had tapes, authenticated by audio experts, of her 12-year affair with Clinton. Flowers sold the tapes to a supermarket tabloid, *The Star,* for $175,000 after they had been reviewed by audio experts. It was probably the fact that a tabloid broke the news that led the still non-tabloid mainstream press not to take the story seriously. Clinton was soon thereafter elected president, and Ms. Flowers posed naked in the December, 1992 issue of *Penthouse.* Betsey Wright, Clinton's chief of staff when he was governor of Arkansas, expressed relief that yet another "bimbo eruption" (sexual affair with a tattletale) has been survived (Kessler, 1996:164).

Since being elected president, Clinton has been sued for sexual harassment by another Arkansas woman, Paula Jones. Shortly after giving a deposition in the Jones suit, the first by a sitting president, news of his alleged relationship with Monica exploded in the press on Jan. 21, 1998.

Charges of late-night phone sex, a gift of a dress containing a spot of the president's semen, and late-night trysts in the White House Theatre were countered with charges of a plot to get the president by right-wing Republicans and GOP independent prosecutor Kenneth Starr.

At first Mr. Clinton was slow to respond to the allegations, merely denying that any "improper" relationship had taken place. However, mysterious tape recordings of conversations between Monica Lewinsky and Linda R. Tripp, a Pentagon employee whose telephone call to Independent Prosecutor Star on Jan. 12 began the investigation, seem to indicate otherwise. There was also evidence of a late December, 1997 meeting between Clinton and Ms. Lewinsky after she had been subpoenaed in the Paula Jones sexual harassment case against the president, and of intensive efforts by presidential confidant Vernon E. Jordan, Jr., to help find the lowly White House intern a job at the time she prepared her affidavit (Balz, 1998, A–1).

Allegedly, Ms. Lewinsky had been instructed by the president to lie under oath concerning their affair, which, if true, amounts to a felony, suborning perjury, a possible impeachable offense. Likewise, allegations of the president lying under oath while being deposed in the Paula Jones case amount to, if valid, the crime of perjury (another possibly impeachable offense). Thus Mr. Clinton might be forced to resign, not because of his adulterous sexual affairs, or carrying on with a lowly underling, but because of lying about them and instructing others to lie about them, under oath.

The allegations stunned press and public alike, for this was the post-Watergate generation, familiar with scandals involving abuses of power, not sexual deviance in high places. Had more news media members or their public remembered the history of scandals on the federal level, the news may not have been so traumatic. Since Americans live in a culture with a long history of sexual repression and other sexual contradictions, scandals about their president's peculiar sexuality still evoke strong emotions.

Due in large measure to the American culture's numerous contradictions about matters sexual, the nation has a very long history of sexual scandal in places high and low. So far as we know, it all began in 1702 (before the nation's independence) when Lord Cornbury, the colonial governor of New York, addressed the state assembly wearing a dress, elaborate headgear, and waving a fan, supposedly to better represent his queen. From there, sexual scandals became a somewhat institutionalized feature of the trappings of political power in America.

- In 1730, Benjamin Franklin brought home an illegitimate child (by his mistress) for his common-law wife to raise. Franklin had numerous affairs throughout his life, most of which he wrote about in depth.
- George Washington, while single, wrote a love letter to his neighbor's wife, and Thomas Jefferson, while single, had children by one of his slaves, Sally Hemings. Jefferson also had affairs with Betsey Walker, wife of his next-door neighbor, and Maria Conway, spouse of an English miniaturist.
- Married Treasury Secretary Alexander Hamilton published accounts of his sexual liaison with Maria Reynolds, for which he paid her husband. Eventually Reynolds blackmailed Hamilton over the affair (Ross, 1988, 3–43).
- In 1880, President Garfield became the first known married president to have an extramarital affair, and in 1884, Grover Cleveland openly confessed to fathering an illegitimate child.
- During the 1920 presidential campaign, the Republican National Committee sent Senator Warren Harding's mistress, Mrs. Carrie Philips, on an all-expense paid trip to China. She was one of two of Harding's mistresses. The other, Nan Britton, had an illegitimate child with Harding.

In short, sexual scandal is a common phenomenon in American life, perhaps even more the norm than bribery incidents. It is also the case that sex, mixed with other morally questionable behaviors, has been the source of many recent federal scandals:

- As president, Franklin Roosevelt carried on an affair with Lucy Mercer Rutherford when his wife, Eleanor, was out of town. Mrs. Roosevelt carried on a lesbian relationship with Loreana Hickok, who actually lived in the White House in a room directly across from the First Lady's (Kessler, 1996, 2).
- Ms. Kay Summersby wrote a book about her extramarital affair with President Eisenhower when he was supreme commander of the Allied Forces during World War II.
- From 1961 until his assassination in 1963, John F. Kennedy seduced a wide variety of women in the White House, including a girlfriend of Chicago Mafia don Sam Giancana, Judith Exner. Kennedy was introduced to Exner by his close friend, entertainer Frank Sinatra, whose Mafia ties were already decades old. JFK broke off the affair after FBI

Director J. Edgar Hoover wrote a secret memo to Attorney General Robert Kennedy expressing alarm over the president's involvement with a woman with Mafia ties. Another women with whom JFK was involved was thought to be an East German spy. Kennedy may have swam nude with his brothers and various women in the White House swimming pool, while the Secret Service guarded the pool entrance (Hersh, 1997).

- JFK was involved with literally hundreds of women. Two blond secretaries, nicknamed Fiddle and Faddle, regularly brushed Kennedy's hair for him, as well as cavorted nude with the president in the White House pool. JFK and artist Mary Pinchot Meyer made love and smoked pot together in the White House. Actresses Jayne Mansfield, Angie Dickinson, and stripper Blaze Starr were some of his lovers, as was Marilyn Monroe, who had affairs with both President John and Attorney General Robert Kennedy. The Kennedys' sexual and other scandals were kept out of the public realm by an admiring press and their father's active discouragement of press leaks until 1969. Then Senator Ted Kennedy drove his 1967 Oldsmobile off a Chappaquiddick bridge, killing his companion, Mary Jo Kopechne, and dashing the senator's hopes as a presidential candidate. Supermarket tabloids and numerous additional press organs have detailed the personal lives of the senator and all Kennedy offspring ever since.

- Likewise, Lyndon Johnson made a habit of seducing members of his secretarial staff while president. Johnson once crawled into bed in the middle of the night with an aide (who was visiting his ranch) while uttering "Move over, this is your president" (Ross, 1988, 209). Johnson also had a special bell system installed in the White House so the Secret Service could warn him of his approaching wife as he was seducing various secretaries (Kessler, 1996, 1).

- Johnson's chief of staff resigned after being arrested for homosexual encounters at a Washington YMCA men's room.

- In 1974, House Ways and Means Committee chair, Wilbur Mills (D-AR) was arrested for drunk driving at Washington tidal basin. In the car with Mills was his mistress, striptease artist ("the Argentina Firecracker") Fanne Fox, who tried to flee by plunging herself into the water (Ross, 1988, 191–214).

- Richard Nixon, the only president to resign from office, had an off-again on-again relationship with Marianna Liu, attractive cocktail-lounge hostess at the Hong Kong Hilton's Den lounge. The affair lasted from 1958 to 1969 when Nixon's wife, Pat, insisted it cease. Nixon personally aided Ms. Liu in securing American citizenship.

- In 1976, Ohio Democratic representative Wayne Hayes resigned after revelations that his mistress, "secretary" Elizabeth Ray, was being paid $17,000 a year to use her sexual prowess to entice businessmen and politicians' associates to close deals with Hayes.

- In 1980, Maryland Republican representative Robert Bauman, who was fond of criticizing gay people, was caught soliciting sex from a 16-year-old nude, male stripper in a Washington gay bar. Bauman initially blamed his alcoholism for the incident, but later confessed that he was homosexual. He resigned from Congress, lost his family and conservative friends, and even contemplated suicide before writing a book about his contradictions.

- In a similar case, representative Jon Hinson of Mississippi called a 1980 news conference to admit his homosexuality (in part because he was about to be found out). Despite his announcement, Hinson was reelected by his constituents. His luck did not hold, however, and in 1981 he resigned his House seat after pleading no contest to a sodomy charge involving Hinson and another male in a public restroom.

- Another 1981 case involved several members of Congress and former lobbyist and attractive blond Paula Parkinson. Parkinson allegedly took three members of Congress, including vice president to be Dan Quayle, and six other males on a Florida golfing vacation. Rumors ran wild that Parkinson had videotapes of a number of her powerful guests in embarrassing positions. Parkinson was bewildered by all the press coverage, and claimed that she had had affairs with eight members of Congress, including a number of members of the ultraconservative Moral Majority. In the end, none of the politicians involved admitted much of anything about the incident, especially since it was being investigated by the FBI. Ms. Parkinson finally resigned her lobbying post, proudly proclaiming, "My morals might be low, but at least I have principles" (in Ross, 1988, 264). Following the scandal, Parkinson did the customary thing, posing nude for a men's magazine.
- Representative Gary Stokes (D-MA) was censured by the House in 1983 for having sex with a 17-year-old male congressional page.
- In 1988, Representative Jim Bates (D-CA) was accused of sexually harassing his female aides and using his congressional staff to do campaign work.
- In 1988, married Colorado Democratic Senator Gary Hart withdrew from the presidential race following the *Miami Herald*'s story that Hart had spent the night with a young model, Donna Rice, on board a yacht.
- In 1989, Representative Don Lukens (R-OH) was convicted of contributing to the delinquency of a minor by having sex with a 16-year-old girl. After spending 30 days in jail for the offense, Lukens was subsequently accused of fondling a Capitol building elevator operator and soliciting sex from her.
- In the early 1990s, Senator Robert Packwood (R-OR) resigned from office after it was revealed that he had sexually harassed numerous female staff members and campaign workers.

So what can be learned about corruption from this minihistorical review of the deviant sexual behavior of America's political officials? One way to draw useful conclusions is by using it to dispel a number of myths reported in conjunction with the 1998 Clinton sex scandal.

- *Myth:* The 1998 Clinton sex scandal is an aberration. Most American scandals are about abuses of power, not sex. When sex becomes an issue, usually the Democrats are involved. When money is an issue, it's usually a Republican doing.
- *Fact:* Both political parties have a long history of sexual scandals among their members. The key factor operating here is not sex or money, but the relationship between sexual scandals and all other abuses of power. Anyone in a position of authority who takes up with any underling is, almost by definition, abusing a basic form of power—the power to hire and fire. A review of the record reveals that most politicians accused of sexual misconduct also misbehave in other areas.

This brings us to a related notion, namely:

- *Myth:* What presidents (or other politicians) do in their private lives is unrelated to the performances of their jobs.
- *Fact:* In this post-Watergate, post-Chappaquiddick, era, tattling on celebrities, including politicians, has become a cultural obsession. As a result, politicians clearly put their careers at risk and endanger their chances for the party's future success by engaging in reckless sexual behavior or by committing perjury or obstruction of justice in order to cover it up. Sex with people affiliated with organized crime, or other unsavory interests (especially enemy spies), today would place any powerful politician in a vulnerable position, one that may result in blackmail, thus endangering the nation's security, and/or removal from office.
- *Myth:* Sexual scandals are only about sex.
- *Fact:* Sex, status, power, and money are increasingly interwoven in this most materialistic of cultures. Ms. Lewinsky was quickly offered $2 million by *Penthouse* for her photos and story. Many other women involved in political and sexual scandals with wealthy and powerful men have posed naked in men's magazines, written books, or starred in movies or nightclub acts due to the incidents that made them famous. This includes Elizabeth Ray, former congressional spouse Rita Jenrette, and prostitutes visited by televangelist Jimmy Swagart and actor Hugh Grant. The sex-scandal industry is a cottage industry in contemporary democratic societies. Women with a modicum of intelligence are well aware of the possibilities offered by sexual encounters with rich and famous men, and the Clinton sex scandal is no different.

  Given America's cultural contradictions concerning sexual goings on, its constant craving for knowledge of the "backstage" behavior of the powerful, rich, and famous, and the media's werewolf-like yearnings to make profitable commodities out of everything and anything, the sex scandal business can only continue to grow. Were the public to tire of such matters, were illicit sex to become unprofitable, and were those who related only the sleazy hearsay that initiates reportage of sexual scandal publicly condemned, the results might be quite different.

Trashy and tragic as it may sometimes become, sexual news is an economic mainstay of mass-media journalism, entertainment, and advertising. Given satellite TV news, tabloid journalism, and so many men and women on the make, the sexual scandalization of politics is probably in the infancy of a new era. As media critic John Carman (1998, A–1, A–11) relates, when it comes to sleazy and hearsay reporting of sexual deviance, the seemingly ashamed media behaves like the pet dog who has been scolded by its master for chasing cars.

> *Seemingly contrite and stricken, the dog trudges to a corner of the yard and plops down miserably to contemplate his bad behavior. The next car drives by and the dog bolts after it. It's difficult to change the nature of things.... Traditionally the greatest journalistic virtue was to get the story right. The next greatest virtue was to get it first. In the new climate... factualness and speed appear to have changed places.*

Given these realities, it would not be surprising if news broadcasts of videotape of politicians engaging in all manner of illicit sex became something of a custom in the near future.

Scandals of the National Security State

Another important trend causing scandal within the federal government has been the growth of the "national security state" (Moyers, 1988). In 1947, the National Security Act created a national intelligence apparatus composed of the National Security Council, the Central Intelligence Agency, and the various intelligence agencies of each of the armed services. Along with the national security apparatus came the growth of secrecy, and with secrecy has come regular episodes of scandal.

The writers of the Constitution intended for government to be both small in scope and very open in its business. Instead of being open to public scrutiny, secrecy, in the form of classifying information and conducting paramilitary operations hidden from public view, has become a way of life. The consequences include:

- Recurrent scandals within the executive branch of the federal government.
- Waste, fraud, and abuse regarding contracting for defense weapons systems.
- "Welfare" for rich individuals and corporations in the form of wasted monies and special tax privileges, all for the ultimate purpose in aiding corporations in amassing profits.
- Support for governments that violate basic human rights, while supporting the expansion of economic activity by First World multinational corporations (Parenti, 1995).

We begin with the scandals of the national security era.

Beginning in 1963 with the investigation into the assassination of President Kennedy, the U.S. federal government has experienced repeated scandals. When President Kennedy was assassinated in Dallas, Texas on 22 November, 1963, an alleged cover-up of the investigation into the crime may have been personally ordered by President Johnson, Assistant Attorney General Katzenbach, and FBI Director Hoover. These officials agreed that the public must be convinced that Lee Harvey Oswald acted alone in killing the president (Simon, 1999). This was President Johnson's motive in setting up the Warren Commission in December, 1963. The FBI, CIA, and other agencies of the National Security state all withheld valuable evidence from the Warren Commission. For example, the CIA never informed the commission that it had hired organized crime figures in an attempt to assassinate Premier Castro of Cuba. The FBI withheld information that it had received a handwritten note from Lee Harvey Oswald shortly before the assassination.

Moreover, the Warren Commission did find that Oswald had acted alone in killing the president, and that Dallas nightclub owner Jack Ruby had acted alone in killing Oswald (who at the time was surrounded by nearly 70 armed law-enforcement officers) in the Dallas police station.

Subsequent investigations into the crime by the House Special Committee on Assassinations (HSCA 1975–1978) found numerous inconsistencies in the case. The HSCA found that President Kennedy "was probably assassinated as a result of a conspiracy" (Summers, 1980, 14). Probable suspects included members of organized crime (Select Committee on Assassinations of the U.S. House of Representatives, Volume IX, 1979, 53). The HSCA concluded that Mafia bosses Marcello of New Orleans and Trafficante of Florida had the "means, motive, and opportunity" to assassinate the president, and/or that anti-Castro activists may have been involved.

The precise nature of the conspiracy—concerning the actual assassinators and those persons or organizations that employed them—was never determined, and, consequently, numerous theories have been advanced. Between 1966 and 1998, over 600 books and 2,000 articles were written about the Kennedy assassination. The dominant view in these writings is that government agencies killed their own president, theoretically because the president was gong to make peace with the Soviet Union and end the Cold War. There is also some evidence that Kennedy was going to withdraw U.S. troops (called "advisors") from Vietnam. The *investigation* of Kennedy's assassination marks not only the first major postwar scandal, but the beginning of a drastic decline in public confidence in government at all levels.

Following Kennedy's death, the United States escalated the Vietnam War. The war that began secretly with the CIA's training of the South Vietnamese police lasted from 1964–1975. Over 158,000 American men and women died, and the war's cost was nearly $160 billion. Moreover, numerous Vietnam-related miniscandals took place. For example, more than 40,000 Vietnamese civilians were murdered in the CIA-sponsored Phoenix program, mostly without trials.

Near the end of the Vietnam War, the Nixon administration collapsed in the Vietnam-related Watergate scandal. Watergate was actually an endless series of miniscandals, the causes of which remain unknown (Simon, 1992):

- Burglars, bankrolled by the Committee to Re-elect the President, burglarized and bugged the headquarters of the Democratic National Committee in the Watergate complex in Washington, DC, for reasons still unknown. Later, psychiatrist Daniel Ellesberg's office was burglarized. Ellesberg, who had leaked the Pentagon Papers to various newspapers, was standing trial at the time. The judge in the case was contacted about becoming FBI director while the trial was in progress. The judge proceeded to declare a mistrial.
- The burglars, all former CIA agents, some associated with the 1961 Bay of Pigs fiasco, were promised executive clemency and hush money by the White House.
- Mr. Nixon had secretly wiretapped his own offices and those of his top aides, planting microphones in White House offices to record conversations.
- The White House secret intelligence unit, called the plumbers (to stop leaks to the press), engaged in a host of dirty campaign tricks aimed at discrediting potential Democratic presidential candidates. Letters were written and distributed that allegedly came from Senator Muskie's campaign charging that Senator Jackson was a homosexual. Prostitutes were hired and planted at campaign rallies to embarrass opposition candidates.
- Nixon's administration generated an enemy's list of its critics inside and outside government and illegally misused the Internal Revenue Service by requesting tax audits of these critics. The FBI and CIA were manipulated into ceasing the investigation into Watergate, and the head of the FBI even destroyed vital evidence in the case by burning files along with Christmas present wrappings.
- Mr. Nixon lied repeatedly to Congress concerning both his involvement in the case and his possession of evidence that would reveal his involvement. Mr. Nixon offered his two aides, John Erlichman and H. R. Halderman, hush money in exchange for their silence. He had his personal attorney solicit illegal campaign contributions in exchange

for the promise of ambassadorships. Money from these contributions was illegally laundered to conceal donors' identities.
- Attorney General John Mitchell helped plan the bugging of the Democratic National Committee. Mitchell and numerous other Nixon administration officials were convicted of perjury and other crimes and sent to prison in record numbers.

Following the Watergate scandal in 1975, investigations into the postwar activities of the CIA and the FBI revealed that both agencies had engaged in systematic violations of the civil liberties of thousands of U.S. citizens. Such violations have continued to this day:

- Since 1947, the FBI has committed over 1,500 illegal break-ins of headquarters of U.S. organizations and foreign embassies. During the Reagan administration (1981–1988), the FBI spied on various citizens' groups and on citizens opposed to administration policy in Central America. Such groups included the United Auto Workers, Maryknoll Sisters, and the Southern Christian Leadership Conference (Shenon, 1988, A–1, A–8; Simon, 1999, 257).
- After his 1963 "I have a dream speech," the FBI illegally spied on the Rev. Martin Luther King, Jr., bugging his house and hotel rooms. The FBI even tried to induce King to commit suicide by threatening to reveal evidence that he had carried on adulterous affairs.

The CIA has been involved in a variety of illegal activities both inside and outside the United States. From 1947 to 1975 the CIA:

- Illegally experimented on a variety of U.S. citizens, scientists from the Army Chemical Corps, and some of its own agents (without their knowledge or consent) with knockout drops, incapacitating chemicals, and LSD (an hallucinogenic drug). The CIA even hired San Francisco prostitutes to give their customers drugs.
- Was involved in various assassination plots against foreign heads of state, including Castro (Cuba), Lamumba (Zaire), Trujillo (Dominican Republic), Diem (South Vietnam), and Allende (Chile) between 1950 and 1974. This practice continued into the 1980s when, in 1985, CIA Director Casey secretly arranged for the murder of Shiite Muslim leader Fadlallah in a deal with Saudi intelligence (Johnson, 1987; Corn, 1988; Simon, 1999, 270–272).

In 1987, news broke concerning what was to be the most damaging scandal of the Reagan administration, the so-called Iran-Contra affair. The root of the scandal involved the diversion of funds from profits on missiles sold to the Iranian government to the Nicaraguan Contras, a counterrevolutionary force virtually created by the CIA (Moyers, 1988). At first the entire episode was blamed on a Marine, Lt. Col. Oliver North, with virtually all high-ranking officials of the Reagan Administration claiming they were "out of the loop" concerning any knowledge of the events. Subsequent investigations and trial testimony, however, pointed to a massive cover-up by White House aides and others:

- North's 1989 trial revealed that at a 1984 National Security group meeting composed of Vice President Bush, the Joint Chiefs of Staff, several cabinet officers, and President

Reagan, a discussion on Contra aid based on solicitation of "third" parties (foreign governments) took place. This was adopted as a strategy of getting around the Boland Amendment, which forbid further military aid to the Contras (Draper, 1989).

- President Reagan personally solicited the largest contributions for Contra aid from foreign nations, and a number of Latin American governments were asked to falsify arms-sales transactions so knowledge that the weapons were for the Contras could be hidden. Those nations agreeing to falsify such documents were promised increased U.S. foreign aid. Both illegal arms sales and illegal solicitation of funds were orchestrated by a secret group, Operation Enterprise, set up apart from the CIA and other governmental agencies to assure secrecy. Operation Enterprise was composed of retired military and intelligence personnel, arms dealers, and drug smugglers. Thus, in 1994, North's Iran-Contra activities were linked to drug trafficking by former Drug Enforcement Administration agent Celerino Castillo III. Mr. Castillo was the DEA's principal agent in El Salvador between 1985 and 1991. He claims that North smuggled both guns and drugs through a Salvadoran military airport with the help of over two dozen cocaine traffickers. The drug traffickers were granted visas by the U.S. embassy, even though their criminal records were documented by the DEA.

Agent Castillo informed then Vice President George Bush of North's smuggling activities at a 1986 cocktail party. Bush simply shook his hand and walked away. When Mr. Castillo pushed for an investigation of North's activities within the DEA, he was suspended and then transferred to San Francisco in 1991. He also tried to give his documented information concerning North's activities to an FBI agent working with special prosecutor Walsh's investigation. Castillo never heard from the agent again, and none of North's drug and arm smuggling on behalf of the Contras was ever investigated by either congressional committees or the special prosecutor (Bernstein & Howard, 1994, 6).

According to *Webster's* Dictionary, the term *scandal* has various meanings. One notion of scandal relates to religious faith and involves the loss thereof, or violations of religious precepts (rules, sin). A second aspect of scandal refers to gossip, either true or false details damaging to an individual's personal reputation. Another notion of scandal concerns anger brought about by violations of morality. A final view of scandal relates to impertinent remarks or reproachful tactics used in a court of law (*Webster's International Dictionary,* 1986). While these definitions of scandal are suggestive, they have little resemblance to the scandals plaguing American life since 1963. All the scandals listed above share common characteristics:

1. They were all the result of secret actions of government agencies (e.g., the FBI, CIA, executive office of the president) that were either illegal or unethical and caused severe physical, financial, and/or moral harm to the nation.
2. All the episodes discussed were the subject of official government hearings or investigations. The Watergate and Iran-Contra hearings were nationally televised.
3. The original causes of most of these episodes remain unknown. Thus motives for President Kennedy's assassination, the reason(s) for the Watergate break-in, and the possible involvement of Vice President Bush, President Reagan, and CIA Director Casey in planning the Iranian arms sales and diversion of funds to the Contras remain matters of heated debate.

These scandals reveal that the combination of immense sums of money and great secrecy has created a situation characterized by great physical harm, corruption of democratic processes both at home and abroad, and increased governmental debt. These great harms are not limited to the major scandals of the postmodern era, however; they are also characteristic of U.S. defense policy in general.

Corporate Giveaways

The federal government has made a disturbing practice of using public money to bolster private profit. The modern practice of subsidizing corporations began in the 1950s, when the Eisenhower administration granted some $50 billion worth of off-shore oil reserves, rights to federally owned synthetic rubber factories, and various additional public facilities. A multi-billion-dollar interstate highway system was constructed, as was a national system of urban airports. These projects greatly benefited the automobile, trucking, and airline industries. Today there are $651 billion in federal subsidies, mortgage-interest deductions, loans, grants, and the like received annually by affluent individuals and corporations (Parenti, 1995, 77).

Because there is so much money to be had at the federal level, members of Congress and lobby groups usually cooperate with each other in various ways to obtain it. The results of this cooperation are some of the most bewildering, irrational, and debt-increasing programs imaginable. For example, during World War II, DuPont, Chase Manhattan Bank, Ford, General Motors, International Telephone and Telegraph, and Standard Oil all did business with Hitler's Nazi government. Some executives were even Nazi sympathizers. Standard Oil sold the fuel that powered the German submarines which took the lives of hundreds of U.S. merchant seamen. Many of these firms did business with the I. G. Farben Company, which was convicted of employing concentration-camp inmates as slave labor after the war. A number of the U.S. corporations had their German plants bombed by the Allies during the war and were actually awarded reparations (subsidies) by the U.S. Congress (Jensen, et al., 1997, 132–133; Simon, 1999, Chapter 2). Further,

- The government spent $500,000 for the construction of the home of President Lincoln's neighbor.
- The Farmer's Home Administration (FMHA) has lent the nation's farmers $56 billion, but it is continually unable to collect bad loans. In one instance, 43 large borrowers owing $79 million ($1.8 million each) had their loans reduced to $64 million when they could not pay. The FMHA has already written off some $10 billion in bad loans, and some borrowers are paying as little as 1 percent interest due to government subsidies on loans.
- The Department of Interior spends $100,000 a year to train beagles in Hawaii to sniff for brown tree snakes (Gore, 1993, 20).

The federal government subsidizes a variety of businesses and professions for little apparent reason. Government funds have been spent for all manner of nonsensical ends:

- $15 million to build a footbridge from New Jersey to Ellis Island.
- $1 million to restore a movie theatre in Cleveland.

- $2 million for a Toledo, Ohio, farmers' market.
- $6 million for something called the World University games.
- $161,000 to study Israeli reactions to being attacked by SCUD missiles. (To say the least, the Israelis did not enjoy the attacks.)
- $19 million for an International Fund for Ireland, part of which went to fund a golf course video center.
- $3 million for streetcars in Orlando, Florida.
- $120 million for a Phoenix, Arizona, courthouse.
- $96 million for a Portland, Oregon, courthouse.
- $57,000 to buy Vice President Quayle gold-embossed playing cards (Gross, 1993, 179–181; 1996, 133–134).
- $125,000 for a summer conference on photography and American identity.
- In 1990, Congress allocated $1 billion for the Department of Agriculture to aid in the advertising of U.S. agricultural products overseas. The money was allegedly supposed to help farmers and small, struggling firms, but some of it went to the nation's largest corporations, Gallo Wines, Sunkist, Blue Diamond Almonds, McDonald's, Ralston-Purina, Dole, Pillsbury (a British-owned firm), Wesson, Campbell Soup, Kraft, and even Newman's Own received from $100,000 to $6.2 million to promote the sale of their own products in what amounted to a grant in a strange "corporate welfare" program (Gross, 1993, 136).
- $105,000 to study the evolution of monogamy in two parent rodents (Gross, 1996, 134).
- The FDA inspects 1.5 million food products per year for labeling and safety standards. But the government, not food firms, pays for this service. Charging user fees could save an estimated $1.5 billion over a 5-year period (Gore, 1993, 105–106).

What all of this means is that much of what the federal government spends is wasted, and, aside from increasing debt, incidents such as those mentioned above cause considerable moral harm. Public confidence in government in early 1993 was at an all-time low.

- The average American believes government wastes 48 cents of every tax dollar.
- Five of every six Americans say they want fundamental change in Washington (Gore, 1993, 1).

There is good reason for such cynicism. The average citizen is done considerable financial harm by the government's financial favors to corporations. As taxpayers, we all pay for the costs of these subsidies, and we then pay again as consumers, because many subsidies keep the prices of the goods we buy, such as agricultural products, artificially high. Entire new technologies in such areas as biogenetics, computer systems, and aeronautics are developed at taxpayer expense and then handed over to private corporations for profit, all in the name of stimulating the economy. For example, in 1962 the entire satellite communications system was put under the control of AT&T after the government had spent $20 billion to develop it (Parenti, 1995, 78).

Another harmful practice supporting the accumulation of profits by multinational corporations involves supporting regimes that violate human rights.

Human Rights and Multinational Corporations

The United States is a signatory to two international agreements on human rights and renunciation of terrorism. The first of these was the International Bill of Rights passed by the United Nations in 1948. The agreement endorses the protection of a range of both economic and civil liberties and specifically pledges signatories not to subject anyone to "torture or to cruel, inhuman or degrading treatment, or punishment" or to "arbitrary arrest, detention, or exile" (Joyce, 1978, 239).

The United States is also a party to the Helsinki Agreement of 1975, which contains a detailed section on human rights, pledging signatories to "respect human rights and fundamental freedoms, including freedom of thought, conscience, religion, or belief, and without distinction to race, sex, language, or religion" (Buncher, 1977, 11–17).

The U.S. government has committed itself to the safeguarding of human rights on paper, but has violated human rights at home in some disturbing ways. In 1979, Project Censored reported widespread human-rights violations in U.S. prisons, including the exploitation of prison labor. In the 1990s, 30 states have contracted out prison labor to private firms. On average, prison laborers get to keep only 20 percent of the wages they earn, and in Colorado, one of the nation's largest corporations, AT&T, paid prisoners only $2.00 per hour as telephone solicitors (Jensen, et al., 1997, 80–81).

The United States also has a record of supporting governments that engage in violent repression of these rights. Since 1947 it has supported with military and foreign aid, as well as the training of police forces and death squads, some of the Third World's most repressive dictatorships. A number of these regimes, military dictatorships, have routinely engaged in the murder of innocent civilians, kidnapping, arbitrary torture, terrorism, and arrest, as well as wanton murder by roaming death squads.

- In 1975, the Indonesian military invaded East Timor and subsequently slaughtered between 50,000 and 100,000 people, 10 percent of the population. By 1996, 200,000 people had died. While the United States suspended military aid to Indonesia in 1992, aid was reinstated in 1996 and then suspended again in 1997. Indonesia, the site of large off-shore oil reserves, is closely watched by U.S. oil firms and their political allies. President Ford and Secretary of State Kissinger gave Indonesia their approval for the initial invasion. Mr. Kissinger is now a member of the board of directors of Freport-McRania, a U.S. company that operates the world's largest gold mine in Indonesia (Jensen, et al., 1997, 88).
- A link between the Nicaraguan Contras and cocaine smuggling had been alleged in the 1980s. Cocaine plantations in Columbia, airplane landing strips in Costa Rica, and phony seafood companies in Miami were all alleged to be part of the smuggling network. The Contras received funding from narcotics traffickers as well as illegal funds from the CIA and the Reagan-created Operation Enterprise. In 1997, the San Jose *Mercury News* alleged that the CIA sold crack cocaine to the Los Angeles-based criminal gangs who promptly sold crack throughout the United States (Jensen, et al., 1997, 203–05).
- In 1996, released manuals from the CIA-run School of the Americans (SOA) indicate the training advocated such tactics as murder, extortion, physical abuse, and paying bounty for enemy dead. Other tactics advocated included the use of blackmail, false

arrest, imprisonment of parents, and execution of all other members of the "enemy's" local cell. Such tactics are illegal for U.S. intelligence agents, in part because they violate the human-rights treaties to which the United States is a signatory. The SOA has trained members of so-called "death squads" throughout Latin America. The squads are responsible for the deaths of thousands of innocent civilians in Latin America.

Between 1954 and 1995, over 200,000 Guatemalan citizens were killed by their own government's death squads, many of the members of which were trained by the CIA. In El Salvador, 40,000 citizens were killed by right-wing death squads, many of whose members were trained at the CIA's school. The story is the same in several other Latin American nations from the 1950s to the early 1990s, where the CIA has either sponsored violent military coup d'etats (Chile in 1973) or trained and supported death squad leaders, and/or military aid was provided (Panama, Columbia, and Nicaragua) (Simon, 1999, Chapters 5 and 9).

- The terrorists responsible for the 1993 World Trade Center bombing were trained in Sudan and Afghanistan (Weiner, 1994, 53; Krulak, 1993, B–6)—the Sudan training operation is financed by a world terror network that is financed by seven nations, and an Afghan group has received extensive aid from the CIA.

- In 1991, the Haitian military, lead by the Haitian intelligence service, overthrew democratically elected President Aristide, and quickly imposed a reign of state terror involving death-squad assassinations and drug trafficking. In 1994, the Clinton administration sent troops to Haiti to restore a democratically elected government after buying off Haiti's dictators with promises of amnesty and an affluent exile (complete with relocation at United States expense). What is less known is that the CIA created the Haitian intelligence service in the 1980s as part of the United States' war on drugs. Ironically, a number of the Haitian officers were implicated in drug trafficking and money laundering.

- In 1991, the United States went to war with Sadaam Hussein's army in order to prevent a takeover of Kuwait. The Bush administration helped provide financing and arms to Sadaam Hussein in an effort to win him over and then covered up the policy after he invaded Kuwait. Banca Nazionale del Lavoro is an Italian bank whose Atlanta branch was used by Iraq to finance its arms building. Billions in loans to Hussein to finance his military were guaranteed by the U.S. Department of Agriculture in a labyrinth of deceit (Hagan & Simon, 1994).

Access to global markets, raw materials, and cheap labor, not the promotion of democracy or free enterprise, has been the stated goal of U.S. foreign policy since 1947.

- In 1996, Nigerian troops executed nine environmentalists, including a former Nobel prize winner. The activists were involved in protests against Shell Oil's parent company, which had destroyed large tracts of farmland in their quest for Nigerian oil. Shell refines and imports into the United States almost 50 percent of Nigeria's entire oil production. Evidence uncovered by *The Village Voice* in 1995 indicates that Shell Oil has been paying the Nigerian military to take action against environmental protesters, and that Shell has offered bribes to witnesses in trials of murdered protesters (Phillips, et al., 1997, 31–34).

- In Turkey, an automobile accident occurred in 1997 which killed Abdullah Catli, a convicted drug trafficker and murderer, and his girlfriend, Conca Us, a Mafia hitwoman and former beauty queen. Evidence found at the crash scene that Turkish officials had given special diplomatic credentials and various weapons permits. A subsequent investigation demonstrated that this same pattern of U.S. support for groups that are involved in the repression of democratic or revolutionary movements, accompanied by the most extreme types of physical and financial harm, has been repeated in numerous countries outside Latin America in the postmodern era (Simon, 1996, Chapter 5).

Discussion: The Undemocratic Government

This chapter has explored the harmful consequences of a society characterized by the principles of democratic government and the ethos of monopoly capitalism. A major consequence of attempting democracy in a society dominated by the profitmaking goals of business is a multifaceted corruption of government.

Since the investigation of the assassination of President Kennedy in 1963, the executive branch has experienced a parade of major scandals. These scandals have involved both personal enrichment on the part of some individuals and gross abuses of power on the part of governmental organizations, especially the CIA. The CIA was created by the National Security Act of 1947, and ever since deviant behavior (both criminal and noncriminal) has been institutionalized in a secret government (a National Security state) that has demonstrated itself beyond democratic controls.

Thus the CIA has attempted to assassinate foreign leaders, established narcotics routes in conjunction with organized crime, hired former Nazis, and illegally spent monies that were part of a black (secret) budget. The CIA has also played a major role in not fully cooperating or covering up investigations of the Kennedy assassination as well as the Watergate, Iran-Contra, and savings and loan scandals.

Another consequence of the National Security Act was the establishment of a permanent warfare state, with its high levels of military spending, especially on expensive weapons systems. Our examination of Pentagon contracting has revealed a long history of waste, fraud, abuse, and corruption within defense-contracting circles. There is also a long history of a revolving door wherein personnel are easily exchanged between Pentagon and weapons manufacturers.

In addition to the growth of the military-industrial complex, the federal government, since the 1930s, has experienced tremendous increase in various executive-branch departments and congressional staffs. The result is that the federal government now spends over $1 billion per year just for congressional staffs. The great influence of corporate money in politics and the quest for political power in Washington among politicians have resulted in a gravy-train mentality in which members of Congress secure subsidies and pork-barrel projects for their most influential constituents. These expenditures, along with the costs of the warfare state, have greatly increased the federal debt (which has nearly quintupled since 1980, and currently stands at over $4.5 trillion).

Finally, abroad, the influence of multinational corporations and the creation of the secret government have produced a foreign and defense policy whose central priority concerns the protection of the overseas holdings of multinational corporations and the arms sales of the military-industrial complex and its secret government. Support for terrorist governments by the United States was all too common during the Cold War and continues in other places today.

Critical Thinking Exercise 3-1: Subsidies without Reason

Senator William Proxmire used to present a "Golden Fleece" award for the most ridiculous expenditures by the federal government. One of his awards included things like funding research to discover why monkeys fall in love. As you can tell from the above discussion of subsidies, the federal government continues to spend money on wasteful projects. Do a search of databases like Infotrack, Proquest, or the Reader's Guide for the past 3 years. Make a list of what newspapers and magazines consider the most questionable expenditures. On what basis are most of these grants and subsidies questioned? Who are the recipients of most such programs?

Occupational White-Collar Deviance

Although Sutherland (1940) utilized the term "white collar crime," his research was concerned almost exclusively with corporate misconduct or corporate crime (1949). Most criminologists follow the lead of Clinard and Quinney (1986) in making the distinction between corporate (organizational) crime and occupational crime. While the former is committed in the course of a legitimate occupation on behalf of the organization, the latter also takes place within respectable employment activity but is done for one's own personal benefit.

Research on Occupational Crime/Deviance

Obtaining accurate empirical information on occupational crime or white-collar crime in general is difficult. Federal crime statistics such as the Uniform Crime Reports, the National Crime Victimization Survey, and self-report surveys virtually or totally ignore white-collar crime. Researchers tend to be forced to rely extensively on media reports, anecdotes, and secondary sources, as well as case studies. Higher professions tend to be self-regulating by professional organizations; and often codes of silence and protectionism—rather than disbarment, removal of license, or other sanctions—greet reports of wrongdoing. Rather than admit vulnerability to the public, many employers quietly ask for resignations from crooked employees. They may not even keep an official record of the wrongdoing. In fact, such records are not usually kept on any systematic basis by criminal justice agencies or professional associations (Hagan, 1998, 274).

Given the lack of official records, estimation of the cost of white-collar crime is difficult, although nearly all experts on the subject agree that it is far greater than that of standard street crime. While Uniform Crime Report estimates of the cost of all property crime in a given year are less than $20 billion, the cost of the savings and loan debacle of the 1980s alone was placed at $500 billion—one-third of which was believed to be due to fraud and criminal activity.

Figure 4.1 presents two of Edelhertz's categories of white-collar crime. The first category, "crimes by persons operating on an individual, ad hoc basis," illustrates the fact that white-collar crime/deviance may include nonoccupationally related offenses by respectable consumers and others. This might be viewed as "avocational crime." Such activities may include purchases on credit with no intention to pay or purchases by mail in the name of another. People cheat the government of more on income tax every year than is stolen by street criminals. Credit card and bankruptcy fraud are other examples. The federal and state governments are regularly cheated by individuals taking advantage of programs such as home improvement loans, social security, unemployment insurance, and welfare. Edelhertz includes violations of Federal Reserve regulations as well. Unorganized frauds on insurance companies and fraudulent "lonely hearts" appeals by mail are also mentioned.

Edelhertz's category, "crimes in the course of their occupations by those operating inside business, government, or other establishments, in violation of their duty of loyalty

---

Crimes by persons operating on an individual, ad hoc basis:

1. Purchases on credit with no intention to pay, or purchases by mail in the name of another
2. Individual income tax violations
3. Credit card frauds
4. Bankruptcy frauds
5. Title II home improvement loan frauds
6. Frauds with respect to social security, unemployment insurance, or welfare
7. Unorganized or occasional frauds on insurance companies (theft, casualty, health, etc.)
8. Violations of Federal Reserve regulations by pledging stock for further purchases, flouting margin requirements
9. Unorganized "lonely hearts" appeals by mail

Crimes in the course of their occupations by those operating inside business, government, or other establishments, in violation of their duty of loyalty and fidelity to employer or client:

1. Commercial bribery and kickbacks, i.e., by and to buyers, insurance adjusters, contracting officers, quality inspectors, government inspectors and auditors, etc.
2. Bank violations by bank officers, employees, and directors
3. Embezzlement or self-dealing by business or union officers and employees
4. Securities fraud by insiders trading to their advantage by the use of special knowledge, or causing their firms to take positions in the market to benefit themselves
5. Employee petty larceny and expense account frauds
6. Frauds by computer, causing unauthorized payouts
7. "Sweetheart contracts" entered into by union officers
8. Embezzlement or self-dealing by attorneys, trustees, and fiduciaries
9. Fraud against the government

    a. Padding of payrolls
    b. Conflicts of interest
    c. False travel, expense, or per diem claims

FIGURE 4.1   Edelhertz's Categories of Occupational Crime

Source: Herbert Edelhertz. 1970. *The Nature, Impact and Prosecution of White-Collar Crime.* Washington, DC: National Institute of Law Enforcement and Criminal Justice, Government Printing Office, 73–75.

and fidelity to employer or client," is what we have been calling occupational crime/deviance. Such activities may include bribery and kickbacks by buyers, insurance adjusters, contracting officers, quality and government inspectors, and auditors. Bank violations by bank officers, employees, and directors, or self-dealing or embezzlement by business or union officers and employees, are other examples in which employees benefit themselves at the expense of the employing organization. Other areas to be discussed in more detail later in the chapter include securities fraud by insider trading or brokers causing their firms to take positions in the market for their benefit. Employee petty larceny and expense account frauds, computer frauds, "sweetheart contracts," embezzlement or self-dealing by attorneys, trustees, and fiduciaries, and various frauds against government are other examples suggested by Edelhertz.

Occupational Crime in Historical and Comparative Perspective

Corruption, bribery, and kickbacks in both the public and private sectors arc hardly new developments and certainly are not restricted to—nor are they at their worst—in North America. Political corruption in the United States at the federal, state, and local levels has been rife since the beginning of the Republic. Shelley Ross (1988), in *Fall from Grace, Sex, Scandal and Corruption in American Politics from 1702 to the Present,* describes political scandals that have occurred in nearly every presidential administration.

Crimes of the Presidents

Nathan Miller (1976), in *The Foundling Finaglers,* describes corruption in various administrations that includes activities such as ordinary bribery, conflict of interest, till-tapping, and improper and illegal use of government authority for financial gain or political advantage. Such illicit activity goes back to the earliest colonies and to George Washington's administration in Alexander Hamilton's Treasury Office, where members of his staff benefited from inside knowledge (Miller, 1976, 100). In this review of past scandals, presidents themselves may not always be directly involved in wrongdoing; but, as James Madison suggested in the First Congress, a president is "responsible for the conduct of the person he has nominated and appointed" (Johnson, 1991, 184). Since merchants and thieves share the same god—Mercury—little surprise is engendered by noting that many early fortunes were made through swindles, often due to connections with crooked politicians (Myers, 1936).

The Reagan years have been described as a new "gilded age," the original term being derived from Mark Twain's novel by the same name, which was a satirical, political commentary on the corrupt post Civil War period in which the accumulation of material wealth was glorified.

The top five presidential eras for crime, corruption, and scandal were those of:

James Buchanan
Ulysses Grant
Warren Harding
Richard Nixon
Ronald Reagan

The seriousness of wrongdoing is not necessarily reflected by the ordering, however, which is chronological.

The Buchanan Era

James Buchanan is the only Democrat in the top five and may in fact represent an exception to the rule. Ross (1988, 235) points out, "If it's a sex scandal, you're more likely to find a Democrat involved; if it's a financial scandal, you're more likely to find a Republican." The Buchanan administration, which immediately preceded that of Lincoln, was marked from the very beginning with corruption. In addition to stealing votes by encouraging fraudulently naturalized aliens to vote for him, Buchanan gave fixed government contracts to campaign supporters. Moreover, enormous graft, kickbacks, and overpayments were common in the issuing of government printing contracts (this was before the creation of the Government Printing Office). Other supporters were privately sold a military reservation. His secretary of war was forced to resign in a financial scandal and finally on June 13, 1860, President Buchanan himself was formally censured by Congress (Ross, 1988, 84). And these activities were mild compared to the events of the Grant and Harding Administrations.

The Grant Era

The period after the Civil War was one of major corruption in both business and politics, and no previous presidential administration had been racked by the level of corruption as the two terms of Ulysses S. Grant. While Grant himself did not appear to be personally involved in corrupt practices, he expressed very poor judgment in choosing advisers and administrative officials. His vice president, personal secretary, and members of his cabinet were all involved in financial scandals. In 1869, business tycoons Jay Gould and James Fisk, in cooperation with the president's brother-in-law, attempted to corner the gold market, setting off a financial panic. The notorious "Whiskey Ring" skimmed millions of dollars in liquor taxes and involved Grant's personal secretary in their schemes (Ross, 1988, 100–103).

The real cause celebre of the Grant era was the Credit Mobilier affair of the 1870s, a scandal that would be the subject of four later presidential elections. Caught up in the corruption were a dozen congressmen, a Treasury secretary, two vice presidents, a speaker of the House, and a future president. The latter was James Garfield, then representative from Ohio, who admitted accepting stock from Credit Mobilier in return for legislative favors (Ross, 1988, xvii).

> *In the last century railroads were the S and Ls of their day, highly leveraged entities that spent lavishly to buy political clout in Washington. In 1862 the Central and Union Pacific railroads convinced Congress to subsidize the building of the first transcontinental railroad to the tune of $60 million (nearly $1 billion in today's money) and 20 million acres of land.*
>
> *The owners of both railroads soon realized that they could make far more money on construction contracts for the railroad than on shipping charges through the sparsely populated West. And so they set up dummy companies that paid them exorbitant building fees. The Union Pacific's front was Credit Mobilier of America, a finance company patterned after a French venture (Fund, 1991, A6).*

Those operating Credit Mobilier padded budgets and fees; and when Congress threatened investigations, they gave great deals on $33 million worth of stock to members of Congress. The individuals controlling Credit Mobilier contracted among themselves for construction contracts, manipulating the cost per track mile so that the final cost was not $44 million but $94 million—netting them $50 million in inflated profits (Kohn, 1989, 77). The waste, crime, and corruption of the Credit Mobilier Affair had its counterpart some 50 years later in the aftermath of World War I.

The Harding Era

The "Roaring Twenties" and a "return to normalcy" after World War I also represented a return to another period of corruption during the presidential administration of Warren Harding. Similar to Grant, Harding exercised poor judgment in his choice of appointees. Key cabinet members were involved in conspiracy, graft, fraud, bribery, and cover-ups. Three of these were forced to resign including Interior Secretary Albert Fall, the first cabinet officer in history to be imprisoned for crimes committed while in office. The head of the Veterans Bureau was caught bootlegging war surplus goods and drugs and accepting kickbacks. Many others took bribes (Ross, 1988, 157–159). But it was Albert Fall and a naval oil reserve in Wyoming named Teapot Dome that would gain the most lasting notoriety. The Teapot Dome petroleum reserve was so named because it sat beneath a rock formation that resembled a teapot. Fall convinced Harding to issue an executive order transferring naval oil reserves including Teapot Dome to the Interior Department under him. Fall secretly and without competitive bidding leased the oil rights in these reserves to friends in return for gifts (Kohn, 1989, 315). Mammoth Oil drilled at Teapot Dome in return for a $308,000 bribe and a herd of cattle. Fall kept the cattle at a ranch paid for with a $100,000 bribe received from Pan American Petroleum in return for rights to access Elk Hills, California, reserve (Ross, 1988, 158). In 1929, Albert Fall was convicted of bribery and served 10 months of a one-year sentence in the New Mexico State Penitentiary. It is ironic that prior to all of this President Harding was quoted as having said, "If Albert Fall isn't an honest man, I'm not fit to be president of the United States" (Kohn, 1989, 315).

The Nixon Era

On September 8, 1974, President Gerald Ford granted former President Richard Nixon an unconditional pardon for all federal crimes that he had "committed or may have committed or taken part in" while in the office of president. Due to the Watergate scandal and other misconduct associated with it, Nixon had become the first American president to resign in disgrace rather than face the certainty of impeachment.

Perhaps no one event evokes the visage of political corruption and deceit as does Watergate. This involved the discovery of the illegal break-in of the offices of the Democratic National Committee located in the Watergate complex in Washington, D.C., by agents in the employ of Richard Nixon. This scandal is discussed in detail shortly.

The Reagan Era

At the very least the Reagan era matched if not surpassed the foregoing political administrations with respect to graft and corruption. Between 1980–1988 over 200 Reaganites came under either ethical or criminal investigation, the greatest number of scandals in any administration in American history (Ross, 1988, 1). It is difficult to determine whether public or private corruption was greater during the "Roaring Eighties." The major public scandals of the Reagan era were corruption at the Environmental Protection Agency (EPA), the Wedtech scandal, the Pentagon procurement scandal, abuses at the Department of Housing and Urban Development (HUD), and the previously discussed Iran-Contra affair. In 1983, administrators of the EPA were charged with mismanagement, conflict of interest, and sweetheart deals with polluting companies. The administrator and her assistant either resigned or were fired amidst scandal, along with 20 other senior employees. Regulatory neglect of nuclear safety alone was estimated to cost $200 billion in deferred bills for cleanup after Reagan left office (Johnson, 1991). Wedtech was a former machine shop in the South Bronx that in five years (1980–1985) would be made into a major defense contractor through bribery and corruption. Eventually 25 persons would be convicted of influence peddling and kickbacks. Also accused, but not convicted, was former Attorney General Edwin Meese (Thompson, 1990).

In "Operation Ill Wind," the FBI conducted an investigation that uncovered major corruption in the awarding of defense procurement contracts by the Department of Defense. Forty-five contractors and Pentagon officials and five corporations were convicted, including former assistant Secretary of the Navy Melvin Paisley, who had accepted bribes. The HUD scandals were the biggest within the Reagan administration. By 1989, 28 of the 48 agency programs were affected by fraud, costing over $4 billion. The investigating congressional committee charged that HUD was "enveloped by influence-peddling, favoritism, abuse, greed, fraud, embezzlement and theft" (Pound, 1990, B8). HUD Secretary Samuel Pierce and his chief aides were forced to resign before being fired.

Other Corruption

At the local level, political machines such as New York City's Tammany Hall combined vice and corruption with political favoritism and voting fraud. A system of campaign finance that requires politicians to cater to special interests in order to fund their campaigns is a continuing national disgrace and often supports the old adage that we have "the best politicians money can buy."

As will be explored shortly, public crooks appear as amateurs compared to the private sector. The 1890s in the United States was the age of robber barons or captains of industry, of no income tax, no labor unions, and little regulation of industrial plundering in the name of "Social Darwinism" (the socially fit will survive). Vanderbilt, Rockefeller, Morgan, and others often swindled their partners and consumers, bribed legislatures, and made an oxymoron of the term "business ethics." When asked whether he was concerned with the legality of some of his operations, railroad magnate Cornelius Vanderbilt is cited as having said, "Law! What do I care about Law. Hain't I got the power?" (Browning and Gerassi, 1980, 201).

In the United States and Western society, developed professions convince legislatures to grant them the right of self-regulation; that is, only fellow professionals can protect the public from harmful occupational practice through self-governance. Theoretically, by enforcement of codes of ethics professions assure proper conduct and sanction the unqualified or deviant. More cynical observers view this as a snare, a smokescreen by which occupations gain power, monopoly, and high remuneration. None other than the capitalist version of Karl Marx, Adam Smith, in *The Wealth of Nations* (1953, 137), warned, "Seldom do members of a profession meet, even be it for trade or merriment, that it does not end up in some conspiracy against the public or some contrivance to raise prices."

Occupational deviance can be sanctioned in a variety of manners besides the criminal law itself. Professional associations such as the American Medical Association or American Bar Association may exercise removal of license or disbarment, whereby an individual is no longer permitted to practice. Civil law (private disputes) and administrative law (usually decided by regulatory agencies) enable occupational offenders to escape the stigma of being a criminal. Professional boards enforcing professional ethics may utilize censure, suspensions, or temporary or permanent removal of license and membership privileges. While civil action by government or private suits may include the awarding of monetary damages and license suspension, administrative penalties typically feature fines and seizure of illegal goods.

Surprisingly, in its early history the Federal Bureau of Investigation was heavily concerned with investigating white-collar crime such as antitrust violations, bankruptcy fraud, security sales violations, and the like. This was superseded by a public relations blitz and gangbuster image of the 1930s (Lowenthal, 1950). In the 1970s, the House Judiciary Subcommittee was accusing the FBI of being soft on white-collar crime and that its image of white-collar crime was that of small-time con artists (professional crime) (Simon and Swart, 1984). Interestingly, when the Bureau adopted more aggressive, proactive policies such as sting operations to root out upper-level white-collar crime, many members of Congress were not amused when its own members became the subject of investigation in Abscam (to be discussed shortly).

Crime by Employees

In 1997, the Ethics Officer Association and the American Society of Chartered Life Underwriters and Chartered Financial Consultants issued the results of their survey of 1,324 randomly selected workers, managers, and executives in multiple industries (Jones, 1997). Some of the findings of their study included:

- Nearly half, 48%, of U.S. workers admitted to ethical or illegal activities in the previous year.
- The list of such deviant actions included cheating on expense accounts, discriminating against co-workers, paying or accepting kickbacks, secretly forging signatures, trading sex for sales, and ignoring the violation of environmental laws.
- Workers were asked only to account for violations that they attributed to "pressure" on the job such as long hours, sales quotas, job insecurity, role conflicts between work and family, and personal debt. Not asked were deviations due to greed, revenge, or blind ambition.
- Fifty-seven percent indicated that they felt more pressure to be unethical than five years ago, and 40 percent believed that it had gotten worse over the last year. Some examples included,

  - Three Archer-Daniels-Midland executives were charged with conspiring to fix worldwide prices for livestock feed. While the executives faced trial in 1998, the company had already agreed to pay $100 million in fines, the largest criminal anti-trust fine in history (Jones, 1997, 1).

- Facing indictments for obstruction of justice, the company had already agreed to pay [as of April 1997] $176 million to settle a racial discrimination suit.
- Columbia/HCA, the largest hospital company in the United States, is being charged with cheating and overbilling on Medicare and Medicaid payments.
- Eastman Kodak is suing a former manager for selling company film secrets.
- Centennial Technology's stock rose 450 percent the year before stockholders were informed that earnings were inflated; and the company's CEO, Emanuel Pines, was arrested for alleged insider trading.
- In a 1997 civil suit, Dow Chemical sued General Electric, alleging that GE recruited more than a dozen Dow employees in order to acquire trade secrets (Jones, 1997).

In an earlier National Institute of Justice–sponsored study ("Satisfied Workers Don't Steal," 1983), one-third of the workers surveyed from 47 corporations indicated that they had stolen company property. Nearly two-thirds admitted counterproductive work prac-tices such as abusing sick leave, substance abuse while at work, and longer-than-permitted lunch and break periods. Unhappy workers were found to be involved in more counterpro-ductive activity and theft. Guardsmark, an employee-screening company, estimates that employee theft costs U.S. companies about $120 billion a year (Jones, 1997). While those working in manufacturing and health care reported the most pressure to behave illegally or unethically, the incidence of such behavior among high-tech employees was the highest. They were twice as likely as the average workers to "put inappropriate pressure on others, withhold important information, discriminate against coworkers, engage in copyright/soft-ware infringement, forge someone's name, and misuse or steal company property" (Jones, 1997, 3).

Public Corruption

As previously noted, current examples of public wrongdoing reflect a long legacy of such behavior; and in fact there probably is a higher standard of expected conduct by public ser-vants today than in the past. Crime and deviant behavior by public officeholders and civil servants include influence peddling (performing services in return for gifts or bribes), fur-nishing favors to private businesses such as illegal commissions on public contracts, fraud-ulent licenses, favorable zoning, tax exemptions, and even lower taxes. In their *Crimes of the Criminal Justice System,* Joel Henderson and David Simon (1994) note widespread cor-ruption throughout the various segments of the criminal justice system.

In the early 1990s, the Mollen Commission in New York City documented extensive corruption and wrongdoing within that city's police department. Similar widespread cor-ruption had been revealed two decades previously by the Knapp Commission. Inside infor-mants revealed police extortion, theft and resale of drugs, robbing dead people, rolling drunks, and brutality in poor sections of the city ("NYC's Mollen Commission," 1993). Such occupational deviance by police is certainly not restricted to the nation's largest city, but has been noted throughout the country. O. J. Simpson's acquittal in the murder of his wife, Nicole, and Ron Goodman in 1995 was in part due to racist statements made on tape by one of the investigating officers, Los Angeles Police Detective Mark Fuhrman, as well as in reaction to the beating of Rodney King by Los Angeles police officers. Scandals have racked New Orleans, Philadelphia, Jersey City, Atlanta, Miami, Cleveland, and Detroit police departments, among others (Hagan, 1998, 281). While media attention to wrongdoing seems to focus on the police, the police symbolize the law in the public mind while at the same time the occupation provides greater opportunity for deviant activity than most other occupations.

Police corruption is mirrored in other segments of the criminal justice system as well as other agencies of government. A Pennsylvania police raid of Graterford Prison (near Philadelphia) arrested 13 guards for, among other things, the drug overdose deaths of 11 inmates ("Drug Raid," 1995); and a similar raid in Philadelphia (Jacoby, 1988) netted 30 guards involved in smuggling drugs and weapons and even aiding escapes. Judgscam, or "Operation Greylord"—a 1983 FBI sting operation of the Cook County, Illinois, judiciary—resulted in the convictions of at least 61 persons including police officers, lawyers, judges, and other court officials.

Scandals of presidential administrations in the post–World War II era, such as we have discussed, have spawned a growth industry of political humor. Did you hear that "President Kennedy was on vacation in the Virgin Islands? After he returned, it was called 'the former Virgin Islands.' An imitator of Richard Nixon, as part of his act, said, "There is a bright side to everything. My administration has taken crime out of the streets and put it in the White House where I can keep an eye on it." During Watergate, "The Reverend Billy Graham's Bible readings at the White House now extend from Revelations through Exodus"; and "Carter does the work of two men—Laurel and Hardy." The Iran-Contra investigations were said to be "causing President Reagan a lot of sleepless afternoons." Or the campaign button at the Republican National Convention that read, "Nixon in '96. Death is No Excuse" (Shafer, 1997).

Alleged political scandals of President Bill Clinton's administration included the Paula Jones affair, Whitewater, the White House travel office case, questions regarding Hillary Clinton's billing records with the Rose law firm, FBI files kept by the White House on political opponents, foreign fund-raising sources, and other events. While Clinton's handling of these affairs has been viewed by some as less than candid, the events pale in comparison to the all-time political scandal—Watergate.

Watergate would begin on June 17, 1972, with the burglary of Democratic National Committee headquarters in the Watergate complex by five well-dressed men wearing surgical gloves and carrying sequentially numbered, new $100 bills.

I had no prior knowledge of the Watergate break-in . . . I neither took part in nor knew about any of the subsequent cover-up activities. I neither authorized nor encouraged subordinates to engage in illegal or improper campaign tactics. That was and is the simple truth.

. . . Not. Richard Nixon had lied on national television to the American public and on August 9, 1974, would resign in disgrace rather than face certain impeachment, the first president ever to do so. He was later pardoned of all criminal wrongdoing by his successor,

President Gerald Ford. The details of Watergate were presented in Chapter 3. As previously indicated, major public scandals of the Reagan administration far exceeded those of any presidential administration, including the Grant administration, with its Credit Mobilier affair, and the Harding administration, with its Teapot Dome scandal. But the biggest scandal, perhaps second only to Watergate as a threat to the Constitution, was the Iran-Contra affair (Hagan, 1997), also detailed in Chapter 3.

In the Iran-Contra affair, Ronald Reagan and members of his administration, as we had discussed, conducted secret foreign policy operations that had been specifically prohibited by the United States. Televised Congressional hearings and a subsequent trial found members of the administration lying and perjuring themselves—most notably Lt. Col. Oliver North, who finally admitted under testimony that "Ronald Reagan knew everything" despite Reagan's own testimony claiming, "I don't recall," 187 times under sworn testimony. Despite a five-year investigation by independent counsel Lawrence Walsh and convictions, the final chapter of Iran-Contra was written by President George Bush, Ronald Reagan's successor who, shortly before leaving office, issued full pardons to most of those charged or convicted of wrongdoing in the affair, including Ronald Reagan (Draper, 1991; and Bandow, 1991).

Abscam

Not all corruption and scandal at the federal level have attached themselves to the executive branch. The congressional branch has had more than its share of wrongdoing. So much so, in fact, that it led satirist Mark Twain (1899, 98) to remark, "There is no distinctly American criminal class except Congress." Abscam (Arab or Abdul scam) was an FBI sting operation in 1978–1979 in which agents and cooperating con artists posed as rich oil sheiks interested in bribing members of Congress. Eight members of Congress were convicted, even though they charged entrapment on the part of the government. Entrapment involves causing a crime to happen that would not have if the stimulus had not been put there, in this case, by the government.

Such occupational crime of a political nature has not been restricted to the United States. Bakseesh (Middle East), bustarelle (Italy), pot de vin (France), mordida (Latin America)—the bribe is widespread and international. Countries such as Italy, Japan, and Mexico have been shocked by high-level corruption in the nineties. Former President Raul Salinas of Mexico was imprisoned for selling influence to corporations to the tune of $120 million. In March 1995, U.S. drug enforcement authorities estimated that at least half of Mexico's federal police chiefs and attorney generals receive illegal payoffs from drug dealers (Lloyd, 1995). In February 1997, this charge was in part substantiated. Mexico's drug czar, General Jesus Gutierrez Rebollo, was fired after it was revealed that he had accepted bribes from the head of the Juarez drug cartel (Anderson, 1997). Elsewhere, former Venezuelan President Carlos Perez was found guilty of misusing a $417 million secret fund, a dozen Argentinian officials were convicted of a multimillion dollar fraud involving IBM, and Ecuador's vice president fled to Costa Rica to escape embezzlement charges.

This high level of political corruption has led one investigative journalist, James Mills, in *The Underground Empire, Where Crime and Governments Embrace* (1986), to charge that the largest narcotics conspirator in the world is the U.S. government, whose intelligence agencies ignore the complicity of or conspire with high officials in at least 33 countries (1160). As part of his four-year field investigation in Latin America, he concludes that the State Department and Central Intelligence Agency often sabotaged the efforts of the Drug Enforcement Agency in the name of foreign policy (Hagan, 1987). He described the "underground empire" as a "fourth world" of nations of institutionalized, state-supported crime. Mills (1986, 1140–1141) states:

> *The international narcotics industry could not exist without the cooperation of corrupt governments. Our own government leans over backward to conceal this from the public. To recognize it would cripple foreign relations.... The highly connected tuxedo-clad criminal is left in place to provide intelligence to the U.S.— and drugs to its citizens.... To assuage the public, politicians will continue to wage a civil war, one above-ground sector of the government attacking the drug traffic on the front page and the seven o'clock news, another underground sector secretly permitting the traffic, at times, promoting it.*

The arrest and conviction of former President of Panama Manuel Noriega, who was a paid CIA informant, lends some credibility to Mills' charges.

Gottingen University constructed an "Internet Corruption Perception Index," which ranks 54 countries in 1996 with respect to corruption. Employees of multinational firms and institutions were surveyed with respect to their perception of the degree of misuse of public power for private benefits. The scale ranged from 10—totally uncorrupt—to 0—perceived to be totally corrupt—and used ten sources including ratings by executives in top and middle management, senior banking executives, American, European and Australian managers, embassies and chambers of commerce, a global risk service, and a political risk service. A selection of country ratings included the highest (least corrupt)—New Zealand (9.4)— followed by Denmark (9.3), Sweden (9.1), and Finland (9.1). Others included Ireland (8.5), Germany (8.3), U.S.A. (7.7), Japan (7.1), Portugal (6.5), Poland (5.5), South Korea (5.0), Spain (4.3), Italy (3.4), Mexico (3.3), Russia (2.6), China (2.4), Pakistan (1.0), and the lowest (most corrupt)—Nigeria (.7) (Internet Corruption Rating, 1997).

While public corruption raises the animus of the public, the far more extensive and costly private illegalities are sometimes not subject to the same ire. The tie-ins between public and private corruption can be illustrated by the influence of campaign donations in protecting the interest of private groups at the expense of consumers. For example:

> *The federal government last week finalized one of the largest interest-group giveaways in recent history. The Federal Communications Commission began implementing a law passed by Congress last year that gives to each television station—for free—a second frequency that will handle tomorrow's extra-sharp digital pictures. If these channels had been sold, as a broad range of political leaders wanted, they would have generated a staggering $30 billion in revenues to the treasury in a single year (Glastris, et al., 1997).*

Furthermore, the issue of free television time also could have been forced on broadcasters as part of the telecommunications bill. The station owners got free television licenses without being required to give free television time to political candidates. Campaign donations sabotaged the best opportunity to reduce the power of political money (Glastris, 1997, 7). Similar donations blocked other legislation that would have benefited consumers. Congress extends the patents on brand-name drugs, preventing generic-drug companies from offering the same product for less than half the price. Lobbyists for banks and credit card companies gave more than $3.6 million PAC (political action committee) and soft money to prevent a bill that would have reformed late fee charges on credit cards. Heavy lobbying prevented passage of legislation that would have forbidden health insurance companies from selling redundant cancer and other insurance to individuals who already have such coverage under Medicare or Medicaid.

Private Corruption

Private corruption, fraud, and deceptive business practices far outweigh those of the public sector. Such activities can take many forms, from accepting kickbacks to commercial bribery to embezzlement. Contracting officers, inspectors, insurance adjusters, or buyers may all accept bribes in the form of gifts or cash in return for awarding contracts, approving products, assessing damages, or ordering merchandise.

Crime by Employees against Employees

One area of occupational crime consists of crime and deviance by employees against other employees. There are at least three types of activities that fit this category—sweetheart contracts, workplace violence, and sexual harassment.

A "sweetheart contract" involves collusion between management and labor leaders to make secret deals to the disadvantage of workers whom the labor officials represent. The officials might take a bribe and then cheat the workers out of what would have been a higher raise.

"Workplace violence" has become a growing concern in post-industrial society. While murder is the most publicized form of such violence, it may also include assaults, rapes, suicides, shootings, as well as psychological and mental health episodes. Drug and alcohol abuse and absenteeism may also impede a healthy, productive workplace. The increasing stresses and demands of the modern workplace combined with a breakdown in primary group ties such as family, neighborhood, and community and poor management have been fingered as playing a role in the increase in such violence.

A number of incidents have brought the issue of "sexual harassment" to the forefront of public attention, including the Anita Hill incident, the Tailhook convention, and cases in the military particularly related to coed training environments. Anita Hill's charge of sexual harassment against then Supreme Court nominee Clarence Thomas was unsuccessful before an all-male Senate confirmation committee, but it was successful in bringing public notice to the issue. The Navy Tailhook convention of 1992 found 26 women in attendance (many fellow officers) being sexually assaulted by both retired and fellow active duty aviators. Incidents related to military training instructors taking advantage of female charges have also made the news. "Sexual harassment" involves unwelcomed, uninvited, coercive, or threatening sexual attention, usually in a nonreciprocal relationship. This could include unwanted comments or sexual suggestions, coercive sexual behavior, threats in an attempt to secure compliance with sexual requests, threats of punishment if the victim is uncooperative in sexual requests, a demand for sexual favors in order to secure jobs or grades, and the like. A hostile, intimidating, and offensive sexual work environment may foster sexual harassment, sexual assault, and untold psychological and other damage.

Employee Crime against Organizations

Embezzlement is perhaps the preeminent example of occupational crime/deviance in that the employee steals from his or her employer for his or her personal benefit. It involves theft from an employer by an individual who is in a position of financial trust. Donald Cressey's *Other People's Money* (1953) is the groundbreaking study on this subject. On the basis of his interviews with 133 incarcerated embezzlers, Cressey describes the process of embezzlement as involving the development of a "nonshareable financial problem" by an individual trusted by the firm. Often gambling, addiction, sexual affairs, and the like are factors. The trust violator "temporarily borrows" the money without permission from the employer in order to resolve this problem. Finally, the embezzler comes to the realization that he or she will be unable to repay the money, and his or her "rationalization" of temporarily borrowing breaks down.

A contrary view of embezzlers was presented by Gwynn Nettler (1974), whose own study of "trust violators" found no "nonshareable problem," but simple greed and opportunity as the primary motivations. He felt that Cressey's description may be applicable only to caught embezzlers. Many caught embezzlers, those for whom statistics are kept, tend to be more lower-level employees (tellers) rather than higher-level executives (bank presidents). The latter are often handled more informally, but not always. In 1995, Michael Modus, former president of Phar-Mor, Inc., received a nearly 20-year sentence for embezzling more than half of the company's net worth (roughly $350 million in losses).

Erwin Smigel and H. Laurence Ross in *Crimes against Bureaucracy* (1970) indicate that the very wealth, impersonality, and size of large employing organizations enable employees to rationalize stealing from them. In fact, the larger the organization the less guilt the deviant employee feels in ripping off his employer. In her classic work on retail theft, *The Booster and the Snitch,* Mary Owen Cameron (1964) estimates that the majority of "inventory shrinkage" (retail loss) is due not to boosters (professional shoplifters) or snitches (amateur shoplifters), but to employees—who security personnel estimate may account for 75 percent of all retail theft. There are an endless number of ways employees can cheat their employers including cheating on expense accounts, company vehicle usage, till tapping (simply stealing from the cash register), not ringing up purchases and pocketing the money, and not charging friends for items, as well as receiving clerks who steal merchandise and truck drivers who fake gasoline purchases and repairs.

Computer Crime

The most burgeoning area of crime is crime by computer. Speaking before an international computer crime conference in March 1997, FBI Director Louis Freeh cited three recent cases that illustrate the range of the challenge of computer crime. The first involved someone with a laptop computer in St. Petersburg, Russia, who tried to gain access to millions of dollars in a U.S. bank; in the second, a terrorist used a laptop to create plots to blow up U.S. airliners; in the third, Swedish hackers broke into computers in Florida to shut down a 911 emergency system for an hour. New FBI recruits now leave their academy training furnished with laptops (Milton, 1997). In 1997, the Computer Security Institute reported that three-quarters of the 563 U.S. corporations, government agencies, financial institutions, and universities that responded to their survey indicated financial losses in the previous year due to compromises in their computer security. Losses suffered by the 249 organizations that gave estimates totaled $100 million in 1996. These broke down into $24.9 million in financial fraud losses, $22.7 million due to telecommunications fraud, $21 million in proprietary information theft, $4.3 million due to sabotage of data or networks, $12.5 million from computer viruses, and $6.1 million from theft of laptops ("Security Group Sounds Alarm . . . ," 1997).

While some crimes are specifically computer related, others are computer facilitated. The latter are traditional crimes such as robbery, burglary, and embezzlement, which can now be committed via computer. The variety of computer crimes can be illustrated by the following types: insider crime, malicious hacking, activities in support of criminal enterprise, telecommunications fraud, on-line pedophiles, and high-tech espionage (Spernow, 1995; and Hagan, 1998, 288). There is a major problem of the "dark figure of computer crime"; that is, for every one reported there are many others that go unreported. Many companies, particularly banks, do not report some computer crimes for fear of adverse publicity and the potential subsequent loss of customers.

It is estimated that about 80 percent of computer crime is committed by insiders, mostly employees. Malicious hackers (sometimes called "crackers") often exhibit the "hacker ethic," which assumes that it is their right to explore cyberspace and there should be no restrictions on their right to surf the net and break into other systems. Computers may be used to plan, keep records, and support criminal operations. They can also be used for money laundering, child pornography, gambling, production of counterfeit documents, and any number of other illicit activities. Kevin Mitnick, alias "Condor," had stolen about 20,000 credit card numbers from computer systems. After nearly destroying a computer service in 1995, he was arrested. Telecommunications fraud involves activities such as stealing telephone access codes as well as stealing cellular phone numbers and then using these stolen codes to make millions of dollars in illegal calls.

Pedophiles use the web to entice young victims. Cybersleuthing by high-tech spies is also a burgeoning business for industrial espionage. A computer analysis and recovery team was established by the FBI in order to attempt to keep up with this growing area (Icove, Seger, and VonStorch, 1995). While the term "hacker" refers to those skilled in computer usage, the term "cracker" has emerged to refer to those who break into computer systems.

Some of the jargon of computer crime is becoming increasingly familiar. "Viruses" are rogue programs that copy themselves onto other programs or disks, destroying or altering data. Ready-made viruses are even available through a computer bulletin board service in France. These can be downloaded and then introduced into a targeted computer (Carter and Katz, 1996, 5). "Salami techniques" are a form of embezzlement in which small amounts (slices) from the assets of many sources are transferred to the thief's account. A fraction of a percent of many accounts could be retained for the thief's account. "Time bombs" (logic bombs) are hidden computer programs set to go off and perform a destructive function, such as destroying data, at a future date. "Trojan horses" are hidden subprograms that contain a virus, bomb, or some other destructive feature. "Sniffer" programs secretly copy vital information such as passwords from legitimate users when they log onto the system. In August 1995, managers at the Naval Command, Control and Ocean Surveillance Center in San Diego discovered unauthorized files labelled "sni 256" and "test," which turned out to be sniffer files that were eventually traced to intruder Julio Ardita using Telecom Argentina ("Hacker Traced," 1996). "Spoofing" involves gaining external access to another computer by forging the Internet address of a friendly machine. Once "root" status is gained, a cracker can install damaging programs. The variety and extent of computer-related crime is only in its infancy and will represent an enormous challenge to law enforcement in the twenty-first century, as our final example illustrates.

This example both illustrates the danger of computer crackers as well as underlines many of the points that have been made regarding this type of crime. "Phantomd" (26-year-old Matt Singer) had participated in underground Internet chat channels regarding targets and techniques of electronic burglary. On these he acquired the electronic equivalent of burglars' power tools such as Trojan horses, replicas of legitimate programs, which made it possible to enter networks covertly without detection. A program called "Crack" guessed passwords by systematically trying every word in the dictionary, common names, geek slang words, and the like (Freedman & Mann, 1997). Believed to have broken into several thousand systems including classified military sites, nuclear weapons labs, banks, and *Fortune 100* companies, Phantomd often collaborated with someone called "Jsz," who had written a "sniffer" program to read all data passing in or out of a computer searching for signals—words such as merger or proxy, for example. At places such as the Naval Research Laboratory, Phantomd rifled files, established phony accounts, and planted Trojan horses. In 1995, a new tool, "Rootkit" (a cracker version of a software suite), was distributed via the World Wide Web. This program grabs control of a computer, installs Trojan horses, and sets up a descendant of Jsz's original sniffer. An inexperienced cracker simply types "make all install" (Freedman & Mann, 64). Although both were eventually caught and prosecuted, the relative ease of their escapades is a mild harbinger of future cracker activities.

Crime/Deviance in the Professions

The concept of "profession" in sociology has three dimensions. It refers to occupations that possess esoteric, useful knowledge and that provide service to the public. On the basis of having these traits, occupations may then convince the public and the state to grant them autonomy, as well as its concomitants high prestige and remuneration. Not all developed professions live up to the trust of the public.

Medicine

The medical industry is the nation's largest with almost $1 trillion in annual revenue. An estimated $100 billion of this is lost to insurance fraud on the part of crooks ranging from hospital executives to average citizens (Davis, 1995). In 1997, federal auditors estimated that the Medicare program had lost $23 billion from improper payments in 1996. While not all of this was fraud, such a figure exceeds the cost of all property crime as annually measured in the FBI Uniform Crime Reports. Medical misconduct was addressed by President Bill Clinton, who announced in March 1997 efforts to reduce the amount of fraud in the government's Medicare program. Noting that efforts to bilk the system force seniors to pay billions of dollars a year in higher premiums, he indicated that the best way to prevent fraud is to keep dishonest doctors and other scam artists out of the Medicare system in the first place. Until recently, weak monitoring of medical claims to Medicare—referred to facetiously as a welfare program for doctors—has invited cheating. These ripoffs include nursing home purchases of boats and trips to Hawaii, laboratory kickbacks for new accounts, charges for fake services, and unnecessary treatments and tests.

Unnecessary operations and medical malpractice may kill more people every year in the United States than crimes of violence. A House subcommittee estimates 2.4 million unnecessary surgical procedures per year costing $4 billion and causing nearly 12,000 deaths (Coleman, 1994, 37).

Unnecessary operations are of particular concern. Some 420,000 Caesarean baby deliveries were performed unnecessarily in 1994, according to the Public Citizen's Health Group. While accounting for about 6 percent of births in 1970, C-sections, by 1988, were nearly 25 percent (Neergaard, 1994). Such procedures pay more money than standard deliveries.

Other violations may include sexual misconduct involving health professionals. The number of such cases has been increasing, according to state agencies that discipline doctors and other caregivers (Barlas, 1997). Other violations by physicians include such practices as "fee splitting," in which doctors refer patients to others in return for splitting the fee. Another involves "gang visits" or billing for unnecessary multiple services. Quinney's (1963) classic study of "Prescription Violations by Retail Pharmacists" found a higher number of violations by those who identified with business than with the profession. Such offenders view their clientele as customers rather than as clients. Violations include filling prescriptions with unauthorized generic drugs while billing for brand-name products and charging Medicare or insurance companies multiple times for the same prescription as well as for unfilled prescriptions.

Law

Violations by lawyers include the practice of ambulance chasing—encouraging unnecessary or fraudulent lawsuits in order to collect commissions. Blumberg (1967), in his classic article "The Practice of Law as a Con Game," describes cases in which lawyers collect fees for defending clients while routinely "plea bargaining" cases in order to expedite them, with little concern for the client's well-being. Home closings yield set fees for very little work.

The collection of contingency fees on civil liability cases (in which lawyers receive a percentage—say, one-third—of anything won) has flooded television with advertisements for personal injury firms with punch lines such as "and there is no charge for our services unless we win money for you." Often class action suits intended to benefit the public serve instead to enrich law firms specializing in such cases, as the following case illustrates:

When Keith Long set up his new computer, something struck him as not quite right. The monitor he bought was advertised as having a 14-inch screen. Long's tape measure told him his was 11.6 inches. Feeling cheated, Long complained.

> *Three years, more than 100 lawyers, more than 40 law firms, and mountains of legal documents later, tens of millions of Americans are now receiving in the mail a dense legal notice informing them that if they buy a computer monitor in the next three years, they will be entitled to a cash rebate of $13.*
>
> *For their work, the lawyers who negotiated this settlement on behalf of the nation's computer owners will receive $5.8 million, plus up to $250,000 in expenses (Fisher, 1997, 29).*

In 1994, a settlement of the airline price-fixing case netted passengers discount coupons worth $25 million, while the lawyers won $16 million. Ironically in many cases the lawyers collect huge fees from companies that usually settle the cases out of court, and the consumers are rewarded by the privilege of being able to buy more of the product of the company that ripped them off in the first place (Fisher, 1997).

Concern has been expressed that the United States, with probably the largest per capita lawyer population in the world, has become an overlitigious society, one that has far too many lawsuits. The United States is the only country in the world that encourages such litigation with the custom that lawyers are paid a portion of lawsuits won. This was illegal under early English law with offenses such as "barratry"—instigating and maintaining suits and quarrels in court—and "champertry"—lawyers receiving benefits of the successful action (Crovitaz, 1991, A17).

While legal training has always preached the right of defendants to a vigorous advocacy and defense, it does not encourage participation in criminal activity. The nature of legitimate legal representation does not extend to relaying death threats from Colombian drug cartel chiefs, drafting false affidavits to clear clients, or disguising the drug origins of money for legal fees (Associated Press, 1997). In May 1997, the U.S. Justice Department filed criminal charges against the cartel's lawyers, including one accused of revealing to the cartel the identity of a government informant who was killed. While doctors and lawyers are the most visible of occupational offenders within the professions, white-collar deviance can be found in all manner of lines of work.

Inside Traders

Fraud and inside dealing on Wall Street among brokers and traders have cost clients and the public billions in personal losses as well as pension fund losses. James Stewart, in his book *Den of Thieves* (1991a), describes the four Wall Street operators—Ivan Boesky, Michael Milken, Martin Siegel, and Dennis Levine—who made millions in the eighties by fixing stock market trading. "Insider trading" involves agents or brokers making use of confidential market information for their trading advantage and often to the disadvantage of clients and other traders. In 1986, Dennis Levine, a broker with Drexel Burnham Lambert, made $12.6 million in illegal insider-trading profits. Along with another former investment banker, Martin Siegel, he agreed to cooperate with the government and gave information on Ivan Boesky, a major stock speculator and inside trader. He also received a reduced sentence of two years in prison, as well as $100 million in fines and restitution. Boesky informed on Michael Milken.

Milken, a broker at Drexel, used junk bonds to finance Boesky in leveraged buyouts (hostile takeovers) of companies. Facing charges including stock manipulation and insider trading, Milken plead guilty to six felonies and paid a fine of $650 million. Among the other charges were robbing clients by trading on confidential information for personal gain, manipulating securities prices to force deals and earn huge fees, cheating clients on junk-bond trades, and stealing their securities (Stewart, 1991b). None of the "Den of Thieves" served more than two years in prison. Ironically, Charles Keating, the king of the savings and loan thieves, was able to buy Lincoln Savings and Loan, using as collateral junk bonds borrowed from Michael Milken.

Other offenses by stockbrokers include practices such as "churning," collecting high commissions by making a large number of unnecessary buy-and-sell orders. In May 1985, an inexperienced client opened an investment account with broker Peter Ryan with the objective of "appreciation with safety." Without the customer's knowledge, Ryan made numerous trades for which he earned $47,000 in commissions, while the client's investment dwindled from $114,000 to $8,800 (Power, 1991, C17). In 1991, the New York Stock Exchange kicked Peter Ryan out of the securities business for having cheated numerous customers. Some other examples include,

- In the practice of "loss dumping," a stockbroker buys stock options without attaching the customer account numbers. Those trades that declined in value were dumped into family trust accounts, while the winners were credited to his account and the accounts of two other brokers (Hagedorn and Barrett, 1991).
- In 1989, shortly before declaring bankruptcy, Drexel Burnham Lambert paid out over $260 million in employee bonuses, twice the amount of the debt on which it had defaulted.
- In 1991, three securities firms and 21 brokers were accused of a price-rigging scam costing customers $10 million in losses. They had manipulated the prices of over-the-counter stocks by buying and selling over and over again among themselves ("21 Brokers," 1991).
- In 1995, in the largest settlement of its kind, the Securities and Exchange Commission reached an agreement with Merrill Lynch Company and Lazard Freres and Company to have each pay roughly $24 million in fines due to a secret fee-splitting scheme with municipal bond underwriters and officers and municipalities ("There's a New Sheriff," 1995, C1 and C7).

A United States Supreme Court decision in 1997 expanded the definition of "insider trading" in the James O'Hagan case. The court ruled that insider trading laws apply to people who have confidential information, even if they do not have a direct connection to the company whose shares are being traded. James O'Hagan, a lawyer, earned $4.3 million trading Pillsbury stock after he learned of a hostile takeover bid. The company's stock soared after the offer was disclosed. The new standard applies to anyone who obtains confidential information that should not be used for trading (Norris, 1997). However, incidental knowledge picked up in bars by unconnected people is not covered in this interpretation.

Other examples of crimes by professionals against consumers abound, from merchants short-weighting customers or overcharging for products to bait-and-switch advertising in which the product advertised is suddenly unavailable, while a more expensive version is pushed on the customer. Phony or unnecessary repair work is not the monopoly of professional scam artists, but part of the repertoire of legitimate repair services. Abuses in nursing homes involve owners placing profit ahead of the well-being of elderly patients. And even the dead and their survivors are not immune from victimization. In *The American Way of Death,* Jessica Mitford (1963) describes abuses in the funeral business such as the misuse of the coroner's office to obtain business, "steering" by bribed hospital workers, reuse of coffins, and duplicate billings in welfare cases.

Lest students reading this work feel sanctimonious in condemning the wrongdoing of professionals in all lines of work, consider the following "Coded-Pencil Caper," which was busted in 1996. Taking advantage of the U.S. time zone difference, those taking the Graduate Record Exam, the Test of English as a Foreign Language, and Graduate Management Admission Test on the East Coast would phone the questions and answers to collaborators, who prepared coded pencils, with the answers written on the side, to be taken into the examination on the West Coast. Federal officials reported that hundreds of prospective graduate students had paid $6,000 to American Test Center, which advertised a "unique method" of preparing for the examinations. They were flown to Los Angeles to take the tests (Richardson, 1996) and probably would have had "uniquely" high scores had the entire scam not been busted.

William Cook (1995) describes a corruption scandal in the New York City school system in 1988. Members of the school boards were involved in scandals related to patronage, extortion, bribery, theft, and fraud.

> *The* New York Times *reported the following allegations about school board members: (1) during a search for a new superintendent, a forged letter was used to ensure that the "preferred" candidate would be hired, while other, more qualified candidates were excluded; (2) relatives of some school board members were placed on the payroll with the agreement of five other members (this is permitted by Board of Education policy); (3) two or more board members were believed to have taken expensive equipment (e.g., computer equipment) that had been purchased for use by the schoolchildren; (4) board members used district funds to pay for trips to professional conferences in such places as Las Vegas and South Hampton (Cook, 1995, 275).*

Espionage

A secret June 14, 1997, meeting in a Philadelphia hotel was to seal Kai-Lo Hsu's scheme. A technical director of a Taiwan paper company seeking diversification into biotechnology, he had been dealing over a year with a technology information broker to obtain confidential data on Bristol-Myers Squibb Company's cancer drug, Taxol, which had sales of $813 million in 1996. The meeting was secretly videotaped and raided by the FBI as part of a sting operation, one of the first under the Economic Espionage Act of 1996—which made theft of trade secrets a federal crime. A survey by the American Society of Industrial Security (ASIS) had shown that such crimes had increased 323 percent from 1992 to 1995, costing U.S. companies $25 billion. In 1996, the FBI reported 800 pending probes of economic espionage by foreign companies or governments, double the 1994 figures (Crock and Moore, 1997).

In his book *War by Other Means, Economic Espionage in America* (1997), John Fialko describes what he calls "locators." These are groups or individuals who do not necessarily steal technology, but ferret it out, locate and identify it, and leave the next stage—stealing—to someone else. In 1997, growing concern was expressed with respect to JETRO, the Japan External Trade Organization, which is regarded as one of the most sophisticated commercial-intelligence gathering bodies operated by a foreign government in the United States (Holstein, 1997). Under the ostensible purpose of helping U.S. companies do business in Japan, JETRO has eight offices in the U.S.; but as an arm of Japan's powerful Ministry of International Trade and Industry, it appears to have more of an intelligence-gathering function than export mission. With 160 employees and a $30 million budget, it has established key relationships with governors and mayors, which have given it tremendous access to identifying American technologies that Japanese companies may wish to adopt, as well as funding advanced research. About 100 JETRO researchers and "on loan" trading company executives visit thousands of small U.S. companies every year. Few positive payoffs in exports have taken place (Holstein, 1997).

"Spying" (espionage), the secretive theft of information, has been a practice since the earliest of times. In the Bible, God instructs Moses to send spies to Canaan; and fifth-century sage Sun Tzu (1963) in *The Art of War* has an entire chapter on spies and secret agents. Despite images of James Bond, Mata Hari, cloaks and daggers, and sable-coated countesses traveling on the Orient Express, there has been a major shift in spying since the end of the Cold War. This is to be found in the burgeoning area of economic espionage, in which government agents as well as private individuals steal trade secrets for rivals.

Industrial and Political Espionage

Industrial espionage is performed by three different groups—intelligence agencies, competing firms, and disloyal employees. With the end of the Cold War many intelligence agencies that previously spied on other countries now conduct industrial espionage. French intelligence, the Direction Generale de la Securite Exterieure, has been the most active, going so far as bugging the seats of business people on flights and burglarizing their hotel rooms for documents (Waller, 1992). As early as 3000 B.C., commercial secrets related to porcelain and silkworms were stolen from China. Patent laws were passed during the Middle Ages to attempt to control widespread economic spying. Such industrial piracy may in fact have been responsible for the rapid spread of the Industrial Revolution.

Similar to political spies, industrial spies may have a variety of motivations. Frank Hagan (1997) has developed a typology of spies, which classifies them in terms of their motivation. The types of spies include mercenary, ideological, alienated/egocentric, buccaneer, professional, compromised, deceived, quasi-agent, and escapee. These types were developed to describe primarily political spies operating for or against intelligence agencies. The most common type of spy, either political or economic, is the mercenary spy, who trades secrets for personal monetary reward. Motivated by strong ideological beliefs, ideological spies are political criminals heralded as heroes or condemned as traitors, depending on the observer. While alienated spies may betray for personal reasons such as getting even with an employer, buccaneer spies seek adventure and the excitement of the world of a spy. Professional spies are careerists, employees of intelligence agencies, while compromised spies are reluctant traitors who betray for romantic reasons or as a result of blackmail or coercion. The former Soviet KGB used the term SMICE to identify various strategies for compromising subjects: *S*ex, *M*otivation, *I*deology, *C*ompromise, *E*go. The recruiter had to identify which button to push.

Deceived spies are "false flag recruits," those who are led to believe that they are working for one group when, in fact, they have been duped and are really working for another. Peter Maas's *Manhunt* (1986) provides the example of Edwin Wilson, an ex-CIA employee, who recruited technicians and operatives, including high-level CIA types, as moonlighters for Libya. They believed it was a "company" operation, which it was not (Epstein, 1983; Goulden, 1984). In a further analysis, however, Block and Weaver (1997) claim that it was a CIA "false flag" against Libya, hoping that Wilson would be accepted and they would expose their terrorist operations to him. Industrial spies who believe they are spying for a rival company may, in fact, be doing the bidding of a rival power. Quasi-agents are whistle-blowers, those who reveal secrets not to rivals, but to the general public; while escapee spies defect in order to avoid personal problems. These are intended as "ideal types," overgeneralizations for discussion purposes; in fact, most spies show mixed motivations.

Jacques Bergier, in *Secret Armies* (1975), provides some interesting examples of industrial espionage. A Detroit company found television transmitters hidden in the air vents of its drafting room, probably providing their latest designs free of charge to the competition. Over 60,000 phone lines were discovered tapped in Manhattan, presumably to pick up secret information. Many companies no longer offer plant tours, since they provided far-too-useful photographs of their operations to competitors. IBM charges that it has lost $1 billion in profits due to French and Japanese espionage. A survey of directors of security of the American Society of Industrial Security found that 48 percent of their industries had experienced the theft of proprietary information (trade secrets) the year prior to the survey (1987), and over 90 percent had been victims within the past ten years (Mock and Rosenbaum, 1988, 18). The targets were research and development, new technology, customer lists, and programming plans, while the major tools were misuse of position, physical theft, computer compromising, subversion of employees, and false documents or authorization (Mock & Rosenbaum, 1988).

In political espionage, "white intelligence" (technological spying using space satellites, listening devices, and the like) has long superseded "black intelligence" (covert cloak-and-dagger human intelligence operations). Similarly in industrial espionage, in free societies about 95 percent of the information is publicly available. Such sources include published material and documents, disclosures from a competitor's employees without subterfuge, market surveys, consultant reports, financial reports, trade fairs, and the like. "The Wade System of Sources of Information on American Industry" also lists covert and/or illegal sources such as false negotiations with a competitor for a license, use of spies, hiring a competitor's employee to get information, break-ins, bribing a competitor's employees or suppliers, planting one's agent on competition's payroll, eavesdropping, outright theft, blackmail, and extortion (Hamilton, 1967, 222–223).

Discussion: Occupational Deviant Identity

Occupational criminals and deviants differ from professional criminals and deviants primarily in the degree to which crime is a basic part of their occupation. For occupational criminals, crime is an avocation (a hobby), not the central focus of their work life; whereas for professional criminals, crime is a livelihood, the main purpose of their occupational activity. Occupational and organizational offenders usually do not view themselves or their activities as criminal, and they identify with conventional society. They often find support for their deviant activities in occupational organizational environments or subcultures (Frank & Lombness, 1988).

Since they tend not to perceive of themselves as criminals, many occupational and white-collar deviants use rationalizations to explain away responsibility for their conduct (Clinard & Yeager, 1980, 69–72). Many feel that legal regulations of business are examples of government "red tape" and interference with free enterprise, and that such regulations are unnecessary and serve only to reduce profits. Such laws are viewed as too complex and as creating too much paperwork; they are not needed and govern unnecessary matters. There is little criminal intent (mens rea) in such violations and, after all, "everybody is doing it" and "I have to keep up with the competition." Since the cost and damage is spread out among a large number of consumers, little individual loss is suffered. If profits do not increase as a result of the action, there is no wrong; and, finally, such violations are necessary in order to protect consumers.

While speaking of corporate crime, Clinard and Yeager (1978, 255–272) and Geis and Meyer (1977, 3–4) discuss reasons for the lack of research on corporate crime (as well as occupational crime):

> Many social scientists lack experience in studying such crime. Such investigations may require expertise in areas of law, finance, and economics.
>
> Such violations are often handled under civil law, an area with which social scientists are less familiar.
>
> Enforcement of laws counteract that white-collar crime is usually the province of state and federal regulatory agencies and professional associations and not state and local police.
>
> Funding for such studies has been meager.
>
> Such crimes tend to be complex.
>
> Research data are not readily available.
>
> White-collar crime raises special problems of analysis and research objectivity.

For these reasons, much of the material presented on white-collar deviance remains anecdotal and reliant on media reports. This is likely to remain the case.

Critical Thinking Exercise 4-1: Scandal, The Hidden Dimensions

This chapter and Chapter 3 contain a discussion of some of the characteristics of modern scandal on the federal level. One of the most interesting aspects of contemporary scandal concerns lingering questions that remain the subject of controversy and debate. For example, after nearly 25 years, we still do not know why the Nixon administration decided to bug Democratic National Committee headquarters in the Watergate complex. Such unanswered questions are the subject of this exercise.

Select one of the following scandals:

- Watergate
- Iran/Contra
- Inslaw
- The savings and loan scandal
- Iraqgate

Look up articles about any one of these; then write a paper answering the following questions:

- What remains unknown concerning the causes of the scandal?
- What other scandalous events are speculated about by writers as occurring during the scandal? For example, some people have speculated that the Nixon administration hired Arthur Bremmer to assassinate George Wallace during the 1972 election campaign.
- What reforms are proposed to prevent such scandals from taking place in the future?

Chapter 5

Professional White-Collar Deviance

In 1996, a full-scale rebellion and civil disorder of massive proportions broke out in the formerly Communist country of Albania. Insurgents blew up bridges, seized police stations, and looted military arsenals. Freshly armed with automatic weapons, grenades, and reportedly even tanks and patrol boats, the rebels prevented government troops from entering their areas of control. What was unique about this revolt was its cause—the anger of thousands of Albanians who had been swindled in a huge Ponzi scheme that many believed involved the complicity of high government officials. Reportedly almost every Albanian lost money in the scheme (Nelan, 1997). Ponzi schemes as well as other swindles will be discussed in this chapter.

On the evening of October 29, 1964, at the American Museum of Natural History in Manhattan, Jack "Murph the Surf" Murphy and his accomplices scaled an eight-foot fence, climbed a ladder from a courtyard to the fourth-floor ledge, opened a window, and lowered themselves into the Museum's Morgan Hall of Minerals and Gems, where they proceeded to steal 24 precious stones. These included the celebrated Star of India, a 530-carat gem, the largest in the world, with an estimated value of over $1 million in 1986 (Preston, 1986, 210–211).

Prior to the burglary and before settling on their target, the thieves had cased the Guggenheim Museum and Metropolitan Museum of Art. Ten days of reconnaissance at the museum included an actual dry-run, nighttime burglary. Despite elaborate plans and a successful heist, the trio were shortly arrested and convicted. The subject of a made-for-television movie starring Robert Conrad in 1975, "Murph the Surf" and his accomplices represent the more glamorized, romanticized public view of crime. Another celebrated professional criminal, bank robber Willy Sutton, when asked why he robbed banks, quipped, "Because that's where the money is." While "Murph the Surfs" or Willy Suttons stand in the public eye as epitomizing the crime scene, former California Savings and Loan Commissioner William Crawford advises, "The best way to rob a bank is to own one" (cited in Pizzo, Fricker, & Muolo, 1989, 318). Charles Keating must have taken this advice.

Charles H. Keating, Jr., 68 years of age in 1991, controlled American Continental Corporation as well as Lincoln savings and loan and has come to personify the savings and loan scandal of the 1980s. Keating's name has been assigned to the famous "Keating Five" (Senators Cranston, DeConcini, McCain, Glenn, and Riegle) who, in return for campaign donations from Keating, pressured regulators to delay closing the bankrupt Lincoln S&L. One federal regulator (William Black) characterized Lincoln as "probably the worst (S&L) institution in America" and charged that Charles Keating operated it like a "Ponzi scheme" (Abramson, 1990, A18). The eventual failure of Lincoln is estimated to have cost American taxpayers about $2.6 billion, the costliest thrift collapse in history. That is about 2,600 "Star of India" burglaries, but do not expect a movie about "Keat the Cheat" (Hagan & Benekos, 1992).

By Spring 1991, seven federal and state government agencies were investigating or had charged Keating in connection with violations of securities laws or fraud (Salwen and Conner, 1991, B8). Instructing his salespeople to remember that "the weak, the meek, and the ignorant are always good targets," Keating's agents hustled American Continental (a subsidiary) bonds to gullible elderly, who lost their life savings when it turned out the bonds were not federally insured, as the investors had been led to believe ("Charles Keating," *Frontline,* PBS broadcast). Keating plundered Lincoln's deposits to finance highly speculative real estate and other investments. He concocted phony land sales, made insider loans, and was charged by the government with engaging in a dozen types of "illegal, fraudulent, and imprudent actions" (McCombs, 1990, 6). Besides being generous to politicians with S&L money, Keating and members of his family took $34 million in salaries from 1985–1988. Keating had the active assistance of skilled lawyers, accountants, appraisers, politicians, and, in some cases, regulators. After long, televised hearings, the Senate Ethics Committee delivered the judgment that the meeting of regulators with five senators ("The Keating Five") on Keating's behalf "gave the appearance of being improper" (Abramson, 1990, A14). In charging only one senator, the committee viewed such activity as "constituent service."

Both Jack "Murph the Surf" Murphy and Charles "Keat the Cheat" Keating serve as metaphorical comparisons to illustrate the theme that a metamorphosis, a hybridization or cross-breeding, may be taking place within traditional white-collar crime categories of occupational, corporate, and professional crime/deviance.

As indicated in Chapter 1, within Sutherland's (1940) initial concept of "white-collar crime," most criminologists find useful distinctions between "professional crime," "occupational crime," and "corporate (organizational) crime" (Clinard & Quinney, 1986; Hagan, 1998). "Professional crime" is generally defined in terms of possessing varying degrees of certain characteristics such as a full-time, lifelong pursuit of crime; extensive skill; high status in the criminal world; successful avoidance of detection; extensive criminal subcultures; a high degree of planning; and "fixing" of cases.

"Occupational crime" refers to crime committed by those in a legitimate occupation for their own personal benefit, whereas "corporate (occupational) crime" indicates violations committed by those in a legitimate occupation for the benefit of their employers or organizations. Traditionally, professional criminals have been viewed as acknowledged criminals clearly "beyond the pale" of legitimate society; "occupational/corporate criminals" are seen as avocational offenders who are primarily involved in and identified with legitimate activities. *Professional crime,* then, is assumed to differ from occupational and corporate crime in that the former has as its sole purpose of business the performance of criminal activity, whereas in "occupational/corporate crime" criminal activity is incidental to legitimate business or professional service. David Friedrichs (1996, 10) prefers the term "contrepreneurial crime" to refer to "swindles, scams, and frauds that assume the guise of legitimate businesses." Avocational crimes are illegal—but nonconventional—criminal acts committed by "white-collar" workers outside a specifically organizational or occupational context, including income tax evasion, insurance fraud, loan/credit fraud, customs evasion, and the purchase of stolen goods. Friedrich credits Francis (1988) with the actual coining of the concept "contrepreneurial," the intersection of "con artist" with entrepreneur.

As a sociological rather than legal concept, professional crime is distinguished from other crime not in legal definition but in the manner in which it is performed. Clinard and Quinney (1986, 246) identify the following characteristics of professional crime:

> Crime as a sole livelihood
> Crime for economic gain
> Highly developed criminal careers
> Considerable skill
> High status in the criminal world
> Success at avoiding prosecution

The beginning point in American Criminology of research on professional criminals was the pioneering work of Edwin Sutherland (1937), *The Professional Thief.* Based on extensive interviews with an incarcerated professional thief, Chic Conwell (a pseudonym), Sutherland attributed to professional thieves such characteristics as crime as a full-time career, careful planning, technical, shared sense of belonging, rules and codes of conduct, and argot (specialized language).

The *professional crime model* assumes that the professionalism of criminal activity is a matter of degree rather than kind. The greater the degree to which criminal activity exhibits these characteristics, the more it is an example of professional crime. Professional crime might be viewed as a continuum: The more a criminal activity involves key factors, the more it is an example of professional crime. These elements of the professional crime model as identified by Sutherland and Clinard and Quinney include crime as sole livelihood, extensive career in crime, technical skill, high status among criminals, successful avoidance of detection, a criminal subculture, high degree of planning, and avoidance of prosecution.

Figure 5.1 presents another category of the Edelhertz typology of white-collar crime, other categories of which have been presented in previous chapters. This category, while described as "white-collar crime as a business, or as the central activity," is more commonly known as professional crime. As Edelhertz's description indicates, the sole purpose of the business in professional crime is to perform criminal activity; while in occupational or corporate (organizational) crime/deviance, the criminal activity is incidental to legitimate occupational activity. In the following section we will detail only some of Edelhertz's examples as well as add others. The reader is referred to Edelhertz's book (1970) for details on those not discussed here. Some of the activities listed are not solely illustrations of professional crime, but they become so the more they exhibit the characteristics of the professional crime model.

White-collar crime as a business, or as the central activity:

1. Medical or health frauds
2. Advance fee swindles
3. Phony contests
4. Bankruptcy fraud, including schemes devised as salvage operation after insolvency of otherwise legitimate business
5. Securities fraud and commodities fraud
6. Chain referral schemes
7. Home improvement schemes
8. Debt consolidation schemes
9. Mortgage milking
10. Merchandise swindles:

    a. Gun and coin swindles
    b. General merchandise
    c. Buying or pyramid clubs

11. Land frauds
12. Directory advertising schemes
13. Personal improvements schemes:

    a. Diploma mills
    b. Correspondence schools
    c. Modeling schools

15. Fraudulent application for, use, and/or sale of credit cards, airline tickets, etc.
16. Insurance frauds:

    a. Phony accident rings
    b. Looting of companies by purchase of overvalued assets, phony management contracts, self-dealing with agents, intercompany transfers, etc.
    c. Fraud by agents writing policies to obtain advance commissions
    d. Issuance of annuities or paid-up life insurance, with no consideration, so that they can be used as collateral for loans
    e. Sales by misrepresentation to military personnel or those otherwise uninsurable

17. Vanity and song publishing schemes
18. Ponzi schemes
19. False security frauds, i.e., Billy Sol Estes or De Angelis type schemes
20. Purchase of banks, or control thereof, with deliberate intention to loot them
21. Fraudulent establishment and operation of banks or savings and loan associations
22. Fraud against the government:

    a. Organized income tax refund swindles, sometimes operated by income tax "counselors"
    b. Frauds, where totally worthless goods are shipped
    c. FHA frauds

        (1) obtaining guarantees of mortgages on multiple family housing far in excess of value of property, with foreseeable inevitable foreclosure
        (2) home improvement frauds

23. Executive placement and employment agency frauds
24. Coupon redemption frauds
25. Money order swindles

FIGURE 5.1   Edelhertz's Category of Professional White-Collar Crime

Source: Herbert Edelhertz. 1970. *The Nature, Impact and Prosecution of White-Collar Crime.* Washington, DC: National Institute of Law Enforcement and Criminal Justice, Government Printing Office, 73–76.

Medical and health frauds are widespread. Here we are not speaking of legitimate medical professionals occasionally skirting the law, but of crooked operators whose entire reason for going into business is to cheat the government, insurance companies, or their clients. Billing for false or useless treatment, multiple billings, quackery (unqualified practice), and the like are routine business. An outrageous example of medical fraud is the case of Dr. Richard Kone, a legitimate doctor whose avocation (ripping off the system) became his vocation (he became a professional criminal). Kone would finally plead guilty of defrauding the government and health companies of $500,000 in Medicare payments. From November 1977 until the fall of 1980, he submitted over $1.5 million in false claims for services that he had never performed. He asked Medicare patients to fill out false claim forms, and he filed ridiculous requests for reimbursement that he claimed "begged discovery." He felt that the system invited being "ripped off." In a Social Security scheme, Kone had himself admitted to a hospital, claiming a massive heart attack, which was verified by fake blood tests that he supplied. Against his doctor's order he checked out of the hospital for his tennis lessons, after which he saw another doctor to evaluate a fake stress test that he misrepresented as his own. This enabled him to collect $1,000 per month in disability payments for 19 months. As part of his federal plea bargain, Kone agreed to resign from medicine in ten states and repay the government $500,000 ("Cheating Medicare," 1981).

Advance fee swindles involve charging individuals an advance fee for services, such as finding them a loan or other opportunity, and having no intention of providing such a service and skipping with the money. Phony contests have been a common scam. This could be everything from selling tickets for a raffle that is fixed or for which there are no winners, to charging entry fees to phony contests, to phone solicitations telling people that they have won in a fictitious contest they had never entered but must submit a shipping and handling fee in order to collect their prize. The latter turns out to be something that is virtually worthless. A recent variation took place at a home fair, when it was discovered that individuals filling out entry forms to win an automobile failed to read the small print. It read that those signing agreed to join a veteran's organization for $50 and that the charge would be included on their telephone bill. Bankruptcy fraud can be illustrated by the old, organized crime practice of the "bustout." Organized crime figure Vincent Teresa (1973, 108–109) describes an arson-related "bustout" scam. Through intermediaries with "clean" records, he opened a bank account using a corporate name, leased a building prior to Christmas, ordered goods, and paid half the bill in order to build a credit line. Of the large orders he placed prior to the Christmas season, he removed any unsold items from his building and sold them to a fence. Next, he burned down the building, collected the insurance, and declared bankruptcy. It is also convenient if criminals control the insurance company.

Securities and commodities fraud takes advantage of investors' naivete in esoteric investment markets. With descriptions of supervisors in Superman or gorilla outfits urging telephone solicitors on and bells and cheers applauding each sale, a bizarre picture is drawn of a boiler room (dishonest telemarketing operation) run by James Carr, president of Lloyd, Carr and Company, a Boston commodity firm with high ratings by both Dun and Bradstreet and the Better Business Bureau and operating 11 branch offices throughout the United States. In a huge scam grossing as much as $75 million in just 18 months, the company was run by a career criminal, Alan Abrams, who had escaped from a New Jersey prison in which he had been incarcerated for security scams. He sold commodity options futures, which he claimed were bought on the London Commodity Exchange. Investors were urged to buy futures of coffee, soybeans, and other products with the assumption that the price would go up by harvest time. Abrams did not even bother to buy any futures on the London market, pocketing all of the money ("An Option to Run," 1978, 24; "Options Scam in Boston," 1978, 49).

A number of other professional scams involve chain referral schemes and home improvement schemes. The latter can be illustrated by traveling groups of professional con artists such as the "Irish travelers" from Georgia who, for a very reasonable rate, offer to pave your driveway with materials left over from a job up the street or spray your roof with a clear silicone sealant (really water). After the roof treatment, the first rain finds the mixture of old crankcase oil and dirt floating down the sewer. Other swindles of note are land frauds, the proverbial selling of useless swampland in Florida, which is portrayed to the buyer as the next Key Biscayne; and directory advertising scams, which use lists of suckers who were willing to advertise in other directories. Often little or no money reaches the organization for which the solicitation takes place.

Charity and religious frauds literally steal in the name of the Lord or take advantage of the good will of people. Under the protection of "freedom of religion," many religious groups and cults have been able to capture the hearts, minds, and assets of their members. The difficulty in policing such activity can be illustrated by one televangelist, who told his television audience that God was going to strike him dead unless he raised $4.5 million by the next week. Not having met the target and still alive, he extended the deadline. The son of the late L. Ron Hubbard, author of *Dianetics* (1963) and founder of the pseudoreligious movement Scientology, claimed the organization was a front for enriching Hubbard and to buy drugs ("Scientology Fraud," 1983). Hubbard even had his own police organization, "the guardians," who broke into an Internal Revenue Service (IRS) office to steal tax records. An IRS audit in the 1970s found that Hubbard had skimmed millions of dollars from the church and laundered it in Panama and Switzerland. Other televangelists such as W. V. Grant, Larry Lea, and Robert Tilton were nailed for pocketing immense amounts of tax-free funds ("Men of God," 1991). Perhaps the best known of religious frauds were the activities of Jim and Tammy Bakker and their PTL (Praise the Lord) Ministry. In 1987, the IRS charged the Bakkers with skimming $9.3 million; they were charged by others (ABC, 1987) with being responsible for the biggest religious fraud in history, siphoning off an additional $100 million in church funds (Carey, 1988). Collections for phony charities include selling franchises for donation boxes for charities in which those organizations actually receive only a small percentage of the money collected.

Personal improvement schemes are very popular given the general public's interest in bettering themselves. Diploma mills are educational programs (often unwittingly buttressed by federal guaranteed educational loans) that overpromise employment on completion. Many such programs, particularly correspondence schools, accept all applicants, flunk no one, and have a terrible record of actual placement. Some such programs in California, which has poor licensing laws, simply sell diplomas through the mail. Modeling and talent scout frauds appeal to a person's vanity and promise great success, often to those of little talent, in return for advanced fees. This is related to vanity song and publishing schemes in which songs are recorded or books published for a fee. Legitimate publishers do not charge authors or artists such fees.

Insurance fraud, which is widespread, will be discussed later in the chapter as will Ponzi and pyramid schemes. False security frauds involve deceiving investors by pledging false or phony collateral for loans. The purchase of banks in order to control or loot them is illustrated throughout the chapter with the case of the savings and loan scandal of the 1980s.

The biggest victim of all of these frauds is the federal government. This includes organized income tax fraud as well as planned rip-offs of numerous public programs. Some final examples provided by Edelhertz include executive placement and employment agency fraud, coupon redemption fraud, and money order swindles. Pseudo employment agencies may collect advance fees, promising to find employment, and then skip town, leaving behind a bevy of disappointed job seekers. Coupon redemption fraud costs companies millions of dollars. In this scheme, coupons are redeemed without the customer every buying the product. Finally, fake money orders can leave the consumer or merchant high and dry when it comes time for redemption.

Sutherland, in *The Professional Thief* (1937), and other treatments of the subject of professional criminals describe boosters (professional shoplifters) (Cameron, 1964), cannons (professional pickpockets), professional burglars, box men (safecrackers), fences (dealers in stolen property), paper hangers (counterfeiters), professional robbers, professional arsonists, professional auto theft rings, and hit men (professional killers). While some investigators have forecast a demise of professional crime since its heyday during the Depression (Inciardi, 1974, 1975; Klein, 1974; Shover, 1973), others (Staats, 1977; Chambliss, 1984; Hagan, 1991) see it shifting into other areas of operation. The "professional street crime" characteristic of an industrial society has given way in post-industrial society to "white-collar professional crime." While professional burglars and pickpockets may have declined, there has been an increase in sophisticated con artists, particularly in the decade of the eighties.

In *Whiz Mob,* David Maurer describes the following steps in "the big con" (1964, 15–16):

Putting up the mark (investigating and locating likely victims)
Playing the con (gaining the confidence of the victim)
Roping the mark (steering the victim to meet the inside man or woman)
Telling the tale (showing the victim how he or she can make big money dishonestly)
Giving the convincer (permitting the victim to make a profit)
Having the victim invest further
Sending the victim after the money
Playing the victim against the store and fleecing him or her
Getting the victim out of the way
Cooling out the mark (having the victim realize that he or she cannot turn to the law)
Putting in the fix (bribing or influencing action by the law)

Maurer (1964, 55) cites the following use of criminal argot by a pickpocket (circa 1930s) when asked in court what he had done:

Well, Judge, your honor, I was out gandering around for a soft mark and made a tip that was going to cop a short. I eased myself into the tip and just topped a leather in Mr. Bates' left prat when I blowed I was getting a jacket from these two honest bulls. So I kick the okus back in his kick and I'm clean. Just then this flatfoot nails me, so here I am on a bum rap. All I crave is justice, I hope she ain't blind.

In the 1980s, financial thieves ("financiopaths") developed a whole new jargon—S&L-ese. It sounded something like the following: "Using RAP accounting and beards and straw borrowers, go-go thrifts busted out many S&L's as well as Fizzlic itself. With "cash-for-trash" and "dead horses for dead cows," land flips and paper parking, they managed to Ponzi the American public—"the weak, the meek and ignorant" as well as the feds. With daisy chains and inflated appraisals paper was kissed, loans scraped, and walking money was produced from brokered deposits and invested in junk bonds. If revolving doors or fees could not buy off the professionalism of accountants, lawyers, and members of Congress, white knights could be used to rescue zombie thrifts."

Not only did many in the S&L industry begin to "talk that talk" of "hip" professional criminals, they also began to "walk that walk." Before it was over, the S&L scandal of the eighties would cost the American taxpayer $500 billion dollars, the greatest financial public policy failure in American history.

Emerging Professional Crime Patterns

Boiler rooms, slammers, taps, mile busters, abusive tax shelters, and dirt pile swindles are all part of the jargon of the new professional crime. Some newer examples of professional crime that are likely to be seen more in the future include:

Abusive tax shelters	Oil and gas investment frauds
Art theft	Oil and gas lease lottery frauds
Boiler room frauds	Penny stock frauds
Business opportunity and franchise frauds	Phony accident claims
Commodity frauds	Precious metals bank financing programs
"Dirt pile" gold swindles	Pyramid scheme frauds
Gold and silver investment frauds	Renaissance of Ponzi schemes
The investigator scam	Vacation timesharing scams
Mile busting (odometer tampering)	

As previously indicated, while there appears to be a decline in the traditional street variety of professional crime—that is, pickpockets, burglars, and the like—much of the growth in professional crime has taken place in the area of financial frauds, particularly investments scams. Some examples of newer or updated forms of such professional criminal activities will be detailed next. Many, but not all, of these come extensively from investigations by the North American Securities Administrators Association (NASAA), the organization that represents all 50 state securities regulators, as well as materials from the Council of Better Business Bureaus (CBBB). Many of these scams, while well known to these organizations, are less familiar to a general criminological audience (Hagan and Benekos, 1992).

Phony Accident Claims

Phony accident claims (insurance frauds) persist. SEPTA (the Southeastern Pennsylvania Transportation Authority) paid $47 million in injury claims in fiscal 1990—which amounted to about 18 percent of fare collection. In one publicized bus crash, eleven "passengers" filed suit, even though the bus was unoccupied (Steig, 1990, 16A). Phony accident artists team up with "ambulance-chasing" lawyers and cooperating physicians to sue "deep pocket" companies and insurance organizations.

The Insurance Information Institute describes one auto accident ring that involved a total of 173 people, including five doctors and two lawyers. The law firm that ran the operation was seized by federal authorities. In 1989, the estimated loss to insurance companies due to fraudulent claims was $17 billion ("Super Sleuths," 1991, 3–4). "Crashers" or "cappers" fake car accidents in California to the tune of roughly $500 million per year in fake insurance claims. "Hammers" (crash cars) are used in a carefully orchestrated script using stunt drivers, crooked doctors, and "ambulance-chasing" lawyers who split the settlement.

Mile Busting

Mile busting, the practice of rolling back odometers, is estimated to cost American consumers $4 billion annually. One former used car dealer estimates that 25 to 40 percent of used cars sold in the Houston area have been "whipped" or "mile busted" (CBS, 1990). One buster claims to earn $50,000 per month tax free.

Such systematic fraud is not restricted to crooked used car lots. In 1990, the Chrysler Corporation was accused of selling previously wrecked autos as new and disconnecting the odometers on about 60,000 vehicles. Chrysler pleaded no contest and was fined $7.6 million ("Chrysler Fined," 1990). In 1992, Sears was accused of overcharging and making unnecessary repairs at its auto service centers in California and New Jersey. Undercover investigators in California discovered overcharges in 90 percent of the cases (Yin, 1992).

Art Theft

Art theft is now estimated by Interpol as being the second largest international trafficking crime after drugs, and only 10 percent of such cases are ever solved (Plagens, Starr, & Robins, 1990, 50). The International Foundation for Art Research began keeping track of art theft in 1976. By 1979 there were 1,300 recorded thefts, and by 1989 this had risen to over 30,000 cases on file. Various groups, many of them professional criminals, are involved. French police speculate that the Japanese Yakuza, as well as networks organized by French and Italian antique dealers, were involved in recent French and American thefts. They also claim that the international art, narcotics, and arms underworlds overlap (Dickey, 1989, 65–66). Periodic explosions in art prices contribute to the increase in thefts, as has the quick willingness of insurance companies to negotiate with thieves.

Boiler Room Frauds

"Boiler room" operations (dishonest telemarketers) involve rented offices with banks of telephones operated by high-pressure salespersons who solicit funds or tout products with outrageous promises. Slick-talking telephone solicitors (called "slammers" in the trade) are masters at telemarketing fraud, which is becoming more widespread because the perpetrators know the laws and how to avoid the mail by using other means of delivery. Phone calls without back-up letters leave little or no proof of wrongdoing (Cary, 1987).

In 1990, the Pennsylvania Attorney General's Office filed suit against Florida-based professional fund-raisers for collecting large amounts of money and giving less than 4 percent of what was collected to charity. Events International and Community Benefit Services (both of Sarasota, Florida) act as solicitors for various legitimate organizations (e.g., the Jaycees or police organizations). The "boiler rooms" conduct solicitations for various events such as a "Kids Against Drugs Program."

> *Consumers received calls asking them to buy $12, $18, or $24 worth of tickets for the Kids campaign and make their checks payable to "Kids Tickets." The callers claimed they would see to it that the kids would get the tickets to visit the museum (a traveling exhibit organized by the boiler room).... A telephone solicitation for funds apparently was conducted for two different museum visits. The first was scheduled for March 20, and according to authorities the museum failed to show.... Preate's [the Pa. Attorney General] suit alleges... that the defendant's unsponsored campaigns have raised a minimum of $50,000, none of which has been used for any charitable purpose (Fry, 1990).*

These phone solicitors often used "sound-alike charities," or names for their organizations that sound very similar to known legitimate organizations. They use lists of suckers or "taps," as they are called in the fund-raising game, since they can be tapped again and again. Slammers boast about their ability to "reload" customers, a term borrowed from target practice to describe a tactic of barraging previous victims with multiple sales pitches. Scam artists buy sucker lists of previous victims for "recovery room schemes" in which fraud promoters promise to help consumers recover their losses for a fee.

In 1991, the Federal Trade Commission persuaded Salomon Brothers to drop rare U.S. coins from its annual investment survey. Fraudulent telemarketers had been generating over $100 million a year by persuading the elderly to diversify their investments by citing the Salomon investment survey, even though the 20 coins cited in the index were truly rare collectibles and a misleading indicator for investment in lesser quality coins (Tanouye, 1991, C3).

Telephone sales of bogus products and services via 900 phone numbers is a major scam that began in the late eighties. The primary aim is to keep the victim on the line for expensive charges for each minute of service. Phone sweepstakes—in which "winners" are encouraged to call a 900 number for details—and employment scams are favorites. In the latter, customers are finally given information they could have obtained for free in the local newspaper.

"Cross border scams" are one of the newest. Imagine that you have received a pager message to call 809-555-5555. Or, you find an urgent message on your telephone answering machine indicating that a relative has had an accident, and to call 809-111-1111. Or you receive an e-mail message about an unpaid bill, and are urged to call 809-555-2222 to clear up the matter. What do you do?

Unless you actually have relatives in the Caribbean, which is where the 809 area code is located, *don't return the telephone or pager messages to this area code.* The call is directed to a pay-per-call line, similar to a 900 number, and you risk getting billed outrageous amounts for the call ("FTC Telemarketing Fraud," 1997).

The Investigator Scam

In a variation of the old "bank examiners' scam" (in which "marks" [victims] are asked to put up their money in order to help investigators catch dishonest tellers), con artists now use the telephone in an attempt to get credit card holders' numbers. Such operators may pose as investigators for the credit card company or telephone long distance service and claim to need the person's card number and expiration date in order to check whether it has been used fraudulently. They may even give the victim a toll-free 800 number to call the following day to verify the call. When called, the number is, of course, no longer in service.

Names in the eighties, such as Ivan Boesky, Michael Milken, or Charles Keating, personified the deregulated, free-wheeling financial investment environment of that period. Even though their tactics were similar to those of professional criminals, these individuals were occupational or corporate criminals in that their predominant enterprise had a legitimate product. Their tactics of inside trading and fraud share common qualities with those of professional criminals. Donald Anspach (1990) describes how legitimate companies such as First Investors pushed contractual investment plans with high prepaid commissions, which were not suitable for most investors but were highly lucrative to the sales representatives. Similarly much of the savings and loan scandal of the eighties involved questionable practices that compete with the activities of professional criminals (Hagan & Benekos, 1990) and, in some cases, involved professional criminals.

This same financial environment of the eighties and particularly the "Black Monday" stock market crash of October 19, 1987, developed a number of high-risk, ill-understood investment strategies that caused some investors losses not seen since 1929. Much of the following information is drawn from the Pennsylvania Securities Commission's *Investor Alert* series, which was reproduced from original releases by the North American Securities Administrators Association and the Council of Better Business Bureaus.

Abusive Tax Shelters

While there are many legitimate ways individuals can save on their taxes using tax shelters, the Internal Revenue Service describes "abusive tax shelters" as those:

> *that involve transactions with no economic foundation, inflated appraisals and where claimed tax benefits are disproportionate to any economic ones. Abusive tax shelters are entered into with no expectation of a positive financial outcome, but*

rather with the sole expectation of evading taxes. Such tax shelters often involve movies, master recording tapes, real estate ventures, lithographs, books, gold and precious metal mining ventures (Pennsylvania Securities Commission, 1983c, 1).

When the IRS challenges abusive tax shelter schemes, it is the investors who lose deductions, pay penalties or interest, and also may be stuck with large loan repayments.

Oil and Gas Lease Lottery Frauds

In the early eighties, "boiler rooms" contacted consumers offering quick profits by buying entry into oil and gas lease lotteries run by the U.S. government and the state of Wyoming. Many of the firms charged exorbitant fees, used high-pressure sales techniques, and misrepresented their services and the government leasing system. Individuals were not made aware that they could enter these leasing systems directly by themselves without contacting a leasing service. Although they were offered the hope of a "sleeper lease" (a valuable lease with few filing on it), some parcels had 10,000 filings with only one to be granted. Although "cease and desist orders" had been filed by security administrations in various states, over 250 companies charged as much as $300 a filing, with some investors putting up as much as $20,000 (Pennsylvania Securities Commission, 1983b). Related to these frauds were oil and gas investment frauds.

Oil and Gas Investment Frauds

The rise in oil prices in 1990–1991 gave rise to increased investment scams related to oil and gas exploration.

In November 1985, a federal grand jury indicted an Illinois couple on 722 counts of securities, mail and wire fraud conspiracy and selling unregistered securities. Three hundred investors in 20 states and several foreign countries had allegedly been bilked out of nearly $6.5 million through the sale of investments in Southern Illinois oil wells. The indictments charged that the couple exaggerated the value and productivity of about 72 wells, retained the best wells for themselves and diverted investor funds to buy themselves Rolls Royces, a jet plane, a helicopter and other luxury items (Pennsylvania Securities Commission, 1986a, 1).

In similar frauds, wells were never drilled, and fake wells were claimed to exist in inaccessible areas in order to discourage investor inspections.

Gold and Silver Investment Frauds

Recessionary economic climates often raise interest in such investments as precious metals and coins. Many of the firms offering such investments, however, are relatively unregulated and also use misrepresentation and high-pressure sales tactics. A recent operation involved a deferred delivery agreement scam. Some practices of unscrupulous firms include not actually buying the ordered materials, hoping that the market will go down. A real "red flag" is the dealer's refusal to deliver purchased gold after it is requested. Many coin and bullion dealers are not subject to regulatory oversight.

Business Opportunity and Franchise Frauds

The freedom of being a self-employed entrepreneur has been part of the American dream for many. Business opportunity swindles cater to this desire and are estimated to cost $500 million per year. Such scams include "raise them in your guest room" worm farms, distributorships for worthless gas-saving devices for cars, a few hundred dollars for a "start-up" inventory of industrial-strength cleanser, to a $12,000 "equity investment" in a money-losing car wash in a nonexistent franchise chain. Many phony franchise dealers are recidivists with extensive careers involving fraud, embezzlement, and deceptive practices (Pennsylvania Securities Commission, 1984a).

> *The classic business opportunity swindle unfolds this way. The con man places ads filled with glowing promises. (They may also rent booths at business opportunity shows.) Potential investors are invited to call a toll-free number for more information and application forms. Once the unwary investor expresses interest, the swindler arranges a meeting at a nearby motel or restaurant, where he promises prompt delivery, high-quality merchandise, low costs, untapped markets, and minimal risk of loss. After turning his cash over to the promoter, the investor is left with a slick catalog book and an order form. The swindler leaves town and, if he is ever heard from again, supplies the investor with a small amount of overpriced, shoddy merchandise and none of the promised "100 percent, sure fire, can't miss" aid and assistance (Pennsylvania Securities Commission, 1984a, 2).*

A variety of scams are directed at business owners. In the "Nigerian letter scam," no Nigerian has ever gone to jail for mail fraud owing to believed connections with high Nigerian government officials:

> *The scam is usually introduced by a letter stating that the writer has access to huge sums of government money ranging from $25 million to $80 million. All he needs to transfer the money out of Nigeria he says is a foreign bank account. Letter recipients are promised 25 percent to 35 percent of the sum for the use of their account, but takers invariably end up losing thousands of dollars in advance payments to con men (Ojo, 1997).*

"Phony invoice schemes" involve con artists mailing thousands of phony invoices and solicitations disguised as invoices, netting an annual loss of billions to businesses. This may involve initial phone contacts, actual mailed invoices, phony past-due notices, phony advertising solicitations, fake Yellow Pages bills, and fraudulent fax directory schemes (Better Business Bureau, 1997).

Commodity Frauds

Commodity future contracts are fast paced, volatile investments in the future prices of everything from soybeans and pork bellies to precious metals and treasury bonds. Unscrupulous dealers rely heavily upon unsolicited, high-pressure phone calls; claims of inside information; "you must act at once!" pitches; and claims of no-risk, large, "get rich quick" profits. The National Futures Association (the commodity industry's self-regulatory organization) warns that many firms are unlicensed and unregulated. They often use impressive "sound-alike" names such as "Dunn and Bradford" or "Forbes and Lloyds," as well as impressive addresses such as "Wall Street" or "One Corporate Plaza," and usually prey upon individuals who can least afford to lose in the risky area of commodity investing (Pennsylvania Securities Commission, 1984b).

Penny Stock Frauds

"Penny stocks" are traded at very low prices to promote new, untested products. They are highly speculative, but also sometimes a fixed, inside game. State security regulators have taken a variety of actions against crooked promotions.

Forty-five percent of 78 new penny stock issues surveyed by *Venture* magazine had participants who were convicted felons, securities violators, targets of securities investigations, reputed crime figures, or principals who faced serious charges of insider financial misdealing (Pennsylvania Securities Commission, 1984c, 1).

Promoters of classic penny stock fraud assign themselves millions of shares of stock at a fraction of a cent per share at no cost to themselves. A prospectus is prepared and stock offered at five or ten cents per share, and the market is inflated through high-pressure sales. After the prices reach several dollars per share, the "smart money" bails out and the stock nosedives. After the stock collapses and product development dies, the company goes bankrupt; but not before the promoters line their pockets. Most investors lose most of their money.

Vacation Timesharing Scams

Timesharing programs offer weeks (intervals) at vacation resorts for a fee that can be financed through installment payments. Additional fees are charged for maintenance and other costs. Some timeshares involve a "right-to-use (lease) agreement" only, in which case, if the project fails, the entire investment is lost. Timeshares are often sold through "free vacation" promotions or other incentives and are accompanied by high-pressure sales tactics. Many timesharing programs are unregulated and do not produce as promised (Pennsylvania Securities Commission, 1984d).

One state closed a timeshare company that did not own some of the property it was selling, and another for overselling property it did own. Some timeshares are offered before adequate financing or construction has begun. When companies go bankrupt, the investors are often left out in the cold.

Renaissance of Ponzi Schemes

"Ponzi schemes" involve paying high rates of interest to initial investors from funds obtained from later investors (Hagan, 1990, 313). In 1985, the North American Securities Administrators Association, Inc., and the Council of Better of Business Bureaus found over 30 major Ponzi schemes involving investments of over $750 million during a three-year period. The explosion of financial services, deregulation, and bewildering number of new investments available to the public all contribute to recent growth in Ponzi schemes.

Many of the new Ponzi schemes rely upon the "herd instinct" to line up new investors. Initial stages may zero in on members of a specific pro football team, law office, or military base and rely upon initial victims to enthusiastically recruit new customers (Pennsylvania Securities Commission, 1985).

Many Ponzi-schemers pose as financial planners, a largely unregulated, unscrutinized industry. Six red flags or warning signs that characterize a con artist Ponzi who is operating as a financial planner are:

1. Promises of unrealistically high return (e.g., 20–40 percent annually)
2. Guarantees of investment against loss
3. Statements that the investment strategy is too complex to explain and you must trust the promoter
4. Unclear or unstated investment purpose such as a blind pool for investing at the planner's discretion
5. Exotic elements in sales pitch, e.g., off-shore banks, top-secret technology, inside information, and the like
6. Promoters flying solo and operating tiny offices that are little more than mail drops (Pennsylvania Securities Commission, 1988b, 4–5).

In 1977, John Bennett, Jr., pleaded no contest to federal charges in the collapse of his New Era Foundation, a philanthropy that promised to double investors' money in six months. More than 500 religious, charitable, cultural, and educational groups, including the Philadelphia Orchestra and the Franklin Institute, invested over $354 million beginning in 1989. When the foundation declared bankruptcy in 1995, hundreds of investors lost about $135 million in a giant Ponzi scheme in which early investors were repaid with money from newer ones (Slobodzian, 1997).

Pyramid Scheme Frauds

Recent renewed interest in entrepreneurship has also generated customers for pyramid scheme operators. Pyramid schemes resemble chain letters combined with high-pressure techniques to recruit new investors. A recent pyramid scheme had investors buy "lactic activator" kits, which produced a mold-type culture that an affiliated company supposedly would repurchase for use in the cosmetics industry. Investors lost $6 million when the bankrupt company was found to have no use for the substance in cosmetics.

In 1991, the Securities and Exchange Commission charged Melvin Ford and his International Loan Network, based in Washington, D.C., with operating a pyramid scheme defrauding more than 40,000 investors. Promising investors returns of 500 to 1,999 percent in as little as 180 days, the organizers charged clients $125 to $1,000 for initiation fees, but promised them bonuses for anyone they recruited—thereby setting up a pyramid chain. Later members could join additional income-opportunity programs. International Loan Network had not been paying promised returns, and its only source of income was the continued recruitment of new investors (Salwen, 1991, B8).

More recent wrinkles involve "self-motivation programs," self-improvement and nutritional programs, and a credit card sales scheme that claimed individuals would somehow never have to pay the balance due. Pyramid schemes mainly involve transferring money from new investors to those who got in on the ground floor. The later investors have a slim chance of getting the riches promised, and pyramid schemes always collapse.

Precious Metals Bank Financing Programs

In the late eighties, notice was made of the large growth in off-exchange commodity futures. Particularly of concern was the increase in sales of gold, silver, and platinum in conjunction with bank financing. In these transactions the typical soliciting dealer is unlicensed and unregulated.

> *To make a precious metal purchase pursuant to a bank financing program, the customer places an order with the soliciting dealer to purchase bullion. The customer must put 20% to 30% of the purchase price down and pay an additional "buy charge." The difference between the down payment and the total purchase price is financed from the proceeds of a loan obtained from a bank which the dealer will suggest to the customer. . . As part of the sales pitch, the investor is told that the firm can sell his metal for him at any time and will deduct the unpaid loan balance and fees from the proceeds of the sale.* In many instances, the sales load and other costs, such as loan origination fees, are extremely high and are not fully disclosed at the time of sale *(Pennsylvania Securities Commission, 1987a, 2).*

A major problem with these purchasing programs is whether the metal supposedly sold to each investor is in fact being held for the investor by a reliable institution. Many of the operators are boiler room scam artists. Legitimate precious metal investing is highly volatile and risky, a high-stakes game that is compounded if the investments involve leverage; margin; high commissions; hidden costs; and unregistered—possibly crooked—sellers. The hazards of a leverage purchase (buying on margin) can be illustrated in the area of coin purchasing. Some coin brokers advertise purchase of coins at a fraction of the sale price through a deferred payment or leveraged contract program. The balance of the price is financed by a bank loan. This increases the potential for profits as well as losses. If coins lose value, it is possible to lose substantially more money than the initial investment (Pennsylvania Securities Commission, 1987b, 5).

The "Black Monday" stock market crash of October 1987 drove many investors into what they thought were safer, more stable investments such as precious metals. Many, however, fled directly into the arms of con artists and boiler room scam operators.

"Dirt Pile" Gold Swindles

The fools' gold rush of 1988 found tens of thousands of Americans losing roughly $250 million to at least 52 known phony gold mine operations promoted by boiler rooms.

> *At the heart of the "dirt pile" swindle is the promise of gold at bargain basement prices; the catch is that the gold, if there is any at all, is still in the ground. A*

typical "dirt pile" investment involves a payment of $5,000 for unprocessed dirt guaranteed by the promoters to contain 20 ounces of gold, which works out to a price of $250 an ounce, well under the prevailing world spot market price. Delivery of gold is deferred for 15 months to three years (Pennsylvania Securities Commission, 1988a, 1).

How are people convinced by strangers to invest thousands of dollars, often their life's savings, on unprocessed, worthless dirt? The classic dirt pile scam could be illustrated by the following:

* A $5,000 investment is attracted by a boiler room slammer for 100 tons or more of dirt, which supposedly will yield at least 20 ounces of gold.
* Deferred delivery (1–3 years) is required supposedly due to start-up costs.
* Unqualified guarantees for the yield of each ton of dirt are made. Investors are reassured that the promoter will pay the difference if the mine fails.

Promoters even suggest they have a new alchemy for extracting gold. They send "lull letters" (progress reports), which are intended to reassure and head off questions. In the end, promoters simply vanish with the cash. Often no mining or extraction has taken place (Pennsylvania Securities Commission, 4).

A California entrepreneur named Murray Brooks sold investors dirt for $16,000 a ton from the Comstock Mines in Nevada. Brooks said his purported bonanza relied on new technology that could extract gold left behind by miners in the 1870s. "Our inspector took a backhoe, dug the dirt himself, did an analysis and showed there wasn't a speck of gold to be found...." That wasn't surprising. The Comstock Lode was a famous silver strike (Neff, 1991, 11A).

Many victims, hoping against hope, keep the faith with their promoters. The latter take advantage of this when facing legal action. In what sounds like a familiar litany used by savings and loan thief Charles Keating, promoters indicate they would be producing the promised gold were it not for all the legal and governmental red tape and harassment. Shifting blame is a typical tactic in almost every swindle that unravels (Neff, 1991). Many professional swindlers simply change the name of their firm and open up shop in a different state. In 1997, investors lost close to $500 million in investments in Bre-X Minerals Ltd., a Canadian company that had made bogus claims of a huge gold strike in the jungles of Indonesia (Wyatt, 1997).

Professional White-Collar Deviance and the S&L Crisis

Having examined some selected activities of recent professional crime, a few themes or related trends with respect to some likely directions of professional crime in the twenty-first century include:

* Professional crime is not dying, but it is changing in nature.

- There probably has been an overall decline in "street professional deviance" (professional robbery, burglary, and the like) and an increase in many types of "white-collar professional deviance" (particularly consumer and financial swindles of the type described in this book).
- The deregulated economy since the eighties attracted professional criminals to big business, as well as found many occupational and corporate criminals adopting their tactics, rationalizations, and even jargon.
- Concentration and focus of attention on the activities of professional criminals by federal agencies and law enforcement groups—while warranted—is still "the minor leagues" compared to the continuing relative inattention to, and lenience with respect to, the far more costly occupational/corporate crime such as in the "great savings and loan scandal."
- Increasingly, the activities of legitimate companies and professionals will overlap with and resemble activities that have traditionally been described as professional crime.

Savings and Loan Scams

Most criminologists are familiar with some of the jargon utilized by professional criminals revealed to Edwin Sutherland in his classic, *The Professional Thief* (1937), by informant Chic Conwell. Terms such as "booster" and "cannon" have their counterpart in the relatively flamboyant jargon of financial scams:

Alligators	Inflated appraisals	Revolving doors
Beards	Kissing the paper	Scraping
Bust-outs	Land flips	Straw borrowers
Cash-for-trash	Lender participation	Walking money
Daisy chains	Participation loans	White knights
Dead horses for dead cows	RAP accounting	Zombie thrifts

The savings and loans that were most active or on the fast track in risky ventures were called "go go thrifts." With deregulation, many formerly conservative thrifts fell into the wrong hands. It is common practice for S&Ls to pay private auditors to check their books, and many of these auditing firms were very cooperative in issuing positive results when, in fact, many institutions were very shaky financially. Some of these accounting firms (which included six of the former "Big Eight") and their auditors were offered kickbacks, gifts, and in some cases higher-paying jobs with the S&L in return for "cookin' the books" (General Accounting Office, 1989a,b,c). If auditors refused to cooperate with the S&L, the institution would change auditing firms (Pizzo, Fricker, & Muolo, 1989, 48). In addition to such pressure on auditors, some thrift owners allegedly practiced the classic "revolving door" technique with Federal Savings and Loan Insurance Corporation (FSLIC) inspectors. Federal employees (inspectors, contract officers) were offered future positions (usually upon retirement) if they were cooperative in overlooking their regulatory duties. Such a practice constitutes a "deferred bribe"; that is, cooperate now and we will pay you later with a cushy retirement job (Waldman, 1989).

As previously discussed, Vincent Teresa in *My Life in the Mafia* (1973) describes an organized crime–sponsored "bust out" scam as one in which intermediaries who lack criminal records open a bank account under a corporate name and lease a building. They order goods with half the bill paid to build a credit line; place large orders prior to Christmas; remove unsold items from the building and sell them to a fence; then burn the place down, collect the insurance, and declare bankruptcy (Hagan, 1990, 497). After deregulation of thrifts, organized crime groups began busting out thrifts. Pizzo, Fricker, and Muolo (1989), in their investigation of the collapse of Centennial S&L, found that often the same people showed up at various insolvent S&Ls in a coordinated system of fraud. A network of professional swindlers such as Rapp, Bazarian, and Renda heard about each other and cooperated mutually in looting S&Ls. One of these, Michael Rapp, was really Michael Hellerman, who had previously written an autobiography, *Wall Street Swindler* (Hellerman, 1977). Pizzo, Fricker, and Muolo (1989, 59) claim they uncovered a cast of "bank fraud artists" who were working every single S&L they examined. Similar conclusions were drawn by the General Accounting Office (1989a,b,c).

Land Flips and Daisy Chains

Many rogue S&Ls made heavy use of inflated appraisals of property as well as "land flips" and "daisy chains." Land flips involve selling property or a project back and forth and artificially increasing its value. For example, one condo project in Lake Tahoe was acquired for less than $4 million and sold back and forth until it cost $40 million. Often the transactions took place in the same room, with deeds and bills of sale passed around a table in signing parties. Land flips are really an example of daisy chains (linked financing). The latter had been common practice a decade earlier during the "Great Oil Scam" of the seventies, in which the major oil companies conspired to raise oil prices.

> *... phony paper transactions enabled the companies to claim that old oil (that which was produced from old wells and which was lower priced due to regulation) was new oil (which was unregulated and more than double the price). The companies simply created a chain of middlemen, to buy and resell the oil to each other, increasing the price each time (Hagan, 1990, 386).*

No actual cash changed hands in these "flips"; only new deeds were recorded each time, reflecting higher prices. "Once the desired value was reached, the borrower would get a loan for that amount and later default on it, leaving the lender stuck with a grossly over-encumbered property" (Hagan, 1990, 373). Kane (1989) describes such S&L legerdemain as financial black magic, the product of "smoke and mirror accounting" producing "zombie" thrifts. The latter were hopelessly insolvent thrifts that survived only through the black magic of federal guarantees (Kane, 1989, 4).

Paper Parking

Thrift operators collaborated to thwart regulators in discovering violations. They made loans to each others' officers in order to circumvent the $100,000 regulatory limit on loans to one of the banks' own officers. They shuffled loans and properties among themselves like cards in a monopoly game in order to hide liabilities from regulators (Pizzo, Fricker, and Muolo, 1989, 371). Drexel and Columbia Savings and Loan practiced illegal "stock parking" (paper parking), a sham sale of a security that is intended to hide the true owner for tax or disclosure purposes (Schmitt, 1990, A5).

Kissing the Paper

Deregulated S&Ls became very convenient places to launder money whether it was drug money, organized crime proceeds, Iran-Contra money, or even CIA money (Pizzo, Fricker, & Muolo, 1989, 138). In an eight-month investigation, which was not picked up by the national media, *Houston Post* reporter Pete Brewton alleged that the CIA had intervened in S&L investigations and was in part responsible that some suspected fraud had gone unprosecuted. Shaky institutions used laundered drug money to make long-term investments in real estate. The underworld used S&Ls to buy casinos through "beards" or "straw borrowers," individuals with clean records who could front for mobsters. Since thrifts were limited by law from lending too much to any one borrower, straw borrowers were a way around this. Related to this was the practice of "kissing the paper," in which a weak borrower joined with a person of good credit history to receive a loan. Once the loan was received, the good partner was bought out. In effect, the partner received a fee for the use of his name or for having "kissed the paper." Imagine financing casino purchases with federally guaranteed deposits. Mob lawyer and Dunes owner Morris Shenker made a massive assault on the thrift industry and had 105 corporations among which he moved money (Pizzo, Fricker, & Muolo, 1989, 175). Many S&Ls, particularly in Texas, began to resemble a massive Ponzi scheme. A Ponzi scheme, as described previously, is a con game named for swindler Charles "Get Rich Quick" Ponzi, who in 1919 devised a pyramid scheme in which early customers were paid off with money obtained from later investors. Such schemes often involve a nonexistent product (Hagan, 1998). The paying of high interest on "brokered deposits" (often involving junk bonds) and the loaning of this money on high-risk ventures or overappraised real estate (which showed paper profits) made money for everyone but the taxpaper, who would eventually be stuck with "alligators" once FSLIC took over. Alligators (which take bites out of the taxpayers) were properties that either produced no income or were losses because of large carrying costs that FSLIC was stuck with (Pizzo, Fricker, & Muolo, 1989, 370).

Cash for Trash

Many thrift owners and appraisers received "kickbacks" or payments in return for fraudulent or shaky loans, favors, or inflated appraisals. As some thrifts became zombies, they had to resort to even more "creative" schemes:

> *With supply vastly exceeding demand in 1985, many Texas thrifts kept from going under only by turning more deals and inflating their financial statement with more fees and upfront interest. Their portfolios became little more than huge pyramid schemes, Ponzis that required constant trades, refinancing, swaps, participations, and loans on yet more new projects. They had to take in more brokered deposits to fund more loans so it would appear that they were making more profit, even though the loans were risky.... (Pizzo, Fricker, & Muolo, 1989, 184).*

Some common practices of troubled thrifts were the use of "participation loans" and "cash for trash deals." A "participation" is the selling of a loan to other thrifts. Rogue thrifts could sell off loans that were likely to go into default. At Vernon S&L, when examiners were about to call, thrift executives would farm out their bad loans to other shaky thrifts until the examiners left (Pizzo, Fricker, & Muolo, 1989, 248). This, of course, made the thrift look more solvent than it really was. In "cash for trash" deals, borrowers were required to borrow more money than they wanted and use the extra cash to purchase one of the thrift's repossessed properties (trash). At Neil Bush's Silverado (called Desperado by other Denver banks), borrowers were sometimes required to buy stock in the S&L. Occasionally Silverado loaned money to developers to buy distressed properties. This replaced bad loans with new ones, which on the books looked as if they might be repaid (Purdy, 1990, A2).

Dead Horses for Dead Cows

"Dead horses for dead cows" was a practice of collusion among shaky thrifts in which bad assets (dead horses) would be swapped with other S&Ls to keep thrift examiners in the dark. "If you buy my dead horse, I'll buy your dead cow." A purchased delinquent loan could be "rolled over" or refinanced, thereby postponing the due date. "Lender participation" involves a practice in which loans are issued on the condition that the thrift gets a piece of the action or receives a portion of the project or profits. Through "beards" or "straw borrowers" many thrifts also violated regulations that set limits on loans to people affiliated with the institution or to a single borrower. Many zombie thrifts unwisely violated conservative loan-to-value ratios, which limited loans to no more than 80 percent of property value. They lent the entire 100 percent routinely and often made loans in excess of the value of lands. Money in excess of that needed for the project was called "walking money." Related to this was the practice of "scraping," so named in that swindlers "scraped off some of the loan" or stole some of the proceeds such as through double invoicing or keeping two sets of books or bills—the real price versus the phony price (Pizzo, Fricker, & Muolo, 1989, 375).

White Knights

Many of these questionable and risky practices were encouraged by an accounting system specifically designed for thrifts called RAP accounting (Regulatory Accounting Principles). This permitted the booking of such items as "goodwill" as assets and enabled the hiding of worsening economic conditions, which could have been apparent under the more traditional GAAP system (Generally Accepted Accounting Principles). When foreclosures threatened, often a "white knight" appeared to stave off "the feds."

> *White Knights were employed by thrift crooks and high fliers to forestall unpleasant actions like foreclosure or seizure of their thrift by federal regulators. The White Knight would suddenly appear, offering to pay top dollar for a troubled asset. Sometimes the deal would never close, but negotiations bought the owners additional time. When a deal did close on a White Knight purchase, it would usually be discovered that the White Knight got his money for the purchase from another friendly thrift and that loan would later go into default (Pizzo, Fricker, & Muolo, 1989, 375).*

The layperson or taxpayer, uninitiated to the world of finance, need not understand all of the intricacies of these financial swindles in order to realize that financial crime of unprecedented proportions has been perpetrated and Congress and regulatory agencies have not performed their jobs properly.

High Living

Some additional illegal and/or unethical activities are related to self-dealing or inside trading, that is, the use of insider information for personal advantage. Such insider abuse included making loans to insiders above that permitted by the law; S&L owners paying themselves and employees huge salaries and benefits even while the thrift was failing; abuse of institutional funds for high living, including parties, vacations, and automobiles; and blatant nepotism, all courtesy of the American taxpayer (GAO, 1989c). In the case of Charles Keating and his American Continental and Lincoln Savings and Loan, he and his many family members on the payroll together earned in excess of $34 million over five years. As an illustration of such extravagance, Pilzer and Deitz (1989, 100–101) described the operations of Don Dixon of Vernon Savings, who cultivated public figures such as then House Majority Leader Jim Wright, who later resigned in 1989 due to charges of unethical behavior. According to lawsuits filed by federal regulators, Dixon placed his Potomac River yacht and fleet of six aircraft at the disposal of members of Congress.

> *Not only did he live rent free for eighteen months at a $2 million mansion purchased by Vernon Savings in Del Mar California, according to the FSLIC, he also billed Vernon for more than $500,000 in personal living expenses, including $36,780 for flowers, $37,339 for telephone calls, $13,446 for catering services, and $44,095 for "out of pocket" incidentals. When Dixon and his wife, Dana, filed for personal bankruptcy in California in April, 1989, an action that prevented the FSLIC from seizing their personal assets, the Dixon's possessions included an art collection valued at almost $1 million; twenty-four cases of wine valued at $1300 each; six Fabbri shotguns and other expensive firearms valued at almost $170,000; a Victorian-era Steinway piano worth at least $15,000; hundreds of thousands of dollars' worth of jewelry; and several luxury cars, including a Rolls-Royce and a Ferrari. The list of possessions filed with the bankruptcy court was as long as it was opulent. Between 1983 and 1986, Dixon allegedly withdrew more than $8 million from Vernon in salary bonuses and dividends, not counting the bills paid by Vernon for living and entertainment expenses. In all, according to the FSLIC lawsuit, Dixon and six other former executives looted Vernon of $40 million in inflated compensation and dividends while they squandered some $350 million of the institution's assets (Pilzer & Deitz, 1989).*

Discussion

"All the King's horses and all the King's men couldn't put Humpty together again."

While changing economic forces had created the initial thrift crisis, Congressional and regulatory response exacerbated the problem, causing it to metastasize. Consistent with conservative "conventional wisdom" of the early eighties, deregulation and encouragement of venture capitalism was viewed as an appropriate means of improving the thrift industry. Unfortunately, deregulation created a climate of criminal opportunity—perverse incentives, according to Kane (1989)—and an invitation to financial looting. Deregulation removed many of the controls over S&Ls but failed to remove a fiduciary responsibility and the backing of a "junk bond speculative environment" with federal deposit insurance. Potential profits were private, while losses were socialized and guaranteed by the government.

In his classic examination of "white collar crime," Sutherland (1940) noted the relative leniency with which such crimes were treated by the criminal justice system. Four decades later, Clinard and Yeager (1980, 96) wondered "why such small budgets and professional staffs are established to deal with business and corporate crime when billions of dollars are willingly spent on ordinary crime control including 500,000 policemen, along with tens of thousands of government prosecutors and officials." Pizzo, Fricker, and Muolo (1989, 284) note:

> *For some reason our system has seen nothing unjust in slapping an 18-year-old-inner-city kid with a 20-year prison sentence for robbing a bank of a couple of thousand dollars while putting a white-collar criminal away for just two years in a "prison camp" for stealing $200 million through fraud.*
>
> *The average sentence for an executive who defrauds an S&L and gets sentenced to prison is three years, compared to 13 years for someone who sticks up the same institution. Of 960 people convicted in federal court of fraud against lending institutions in one year, only 494 were sentenced to prison terms. But of 996 people convicted of robbing banks and S&Ls, 932 went to prison.*

While the banking and thrift industry became increasingly sophisticated and a game for "high rollers," the regulatory mentality remained trapped in the thirties (Pilzer & Deitz, 1989, 47). The Federal Home Loan Bank Board, Justice Department, and FBI were unprepared to deal with the new thrift environment and S&L scandal. When the FSLIC filed civil suits and spent millions to get a civil judgment, the settlement was often a farce. It is perhaps ironic that, as America's homeless population grew in the late eighties, greedy, wealthy criminals robbed HUD and the S&Ls, the very institutions that had been designed to provide for decent housing.

The previous review of professional crimes as well as occupational/corporate crimes (S&L scams) sets the stage for a metaphorical comparison of "Murph the Surf" (con artists and professional criminals) and Charles Keating (savings and loan violators and criminals). Many of the operations of S&L crooks bear a startling similarity to the professional con games that have been described. The analogy of a federally sponsored Ponzi game in which zombie thrifts were kept alive only through the wizardry of creative RAP accounting is particularly appropriate.

Dwight Smith (1980), in "Paragons, Pariahs, and Pirates, A Spectrum-Based Theory of Enterprise," develops a theory specifically to analyze organized crime. It also provides a useful model for examining professional and occupational/corporate deviance. Much criminal activity is an extension of legitimate enterprise. Professional deviance derives from the same fundamental assumptions governing entrepreneurship in the legitimate marketplace, profit. Smith sees the pharmacist and narcotics dealer performing similar functions in providing drugs, the one legitimately and the other illegitimately, the one as paragon and the other as pariah or pirate. Deposit insurance became the "crack cocaine of American finance" (Mayer, 1990, 20), and the paragons (legitimate thrift operators) adopted the principles of con artists.

In the classic model of the professional criminal, the cons rely upon professionals, lawyers, and politicians to "put in the fix" and "cool out the mark." Fixers prevent adverse legal proceedings, while mark cooling involves convincing marks (victims) that they have little recourse. The S&L crooks were aided and abetted by the "best and brightest" professional talent America had to offer. More than eighty law firms represented Charles Keating to the tune of about $70 million in legal fees. Six of the then "Big Eight" accounting firms were charged by federal authorities with illegal conduct. Wall Street brokerage firms also unethically took advantage of unsophisticated thrift managers. In *The Greatest-Ever Bank Robbery, The Collapse of the Savings and Loan Industry,* Martin Mayer (1990, 298) indicates:

> *What makes the S&L outrage so important a piece of American history is not the hundreds of billions of dollars, but the demonstration of how low our standards for professional performance have fallen in law, accounting, appraising, banking and politics—all of them.*

Paper hanging (passing bad checks and other documents) has been a favored business of professional criminals. Phony credit cards, records, tapes, spare parts and products are a burgeoning business of professional hustlers. Jerome Jackson (1994) studied "fraud masters," professional thieves who obtain credit cards via fake applications or electronic theft and then market these internationally. None of the individuals in his five-year case study was caught. Such fraud is not restricted to professional criminals. In 1985, E. F. Hutton plea bargained to 2,000 counts of defrauding hundreds of U.S. banks through a check-kiting scheme. The company agreed to a then record $2 million fine and other settlements (Taylor, 1985).

In 1997, the brokerage firm of A. R. Baron and 13 employees were charged in a $75 million fraud against thousands of clients ("A. R. Baron," 1997). The defendants were said to have lied to investors, forged documents, made unauthorized trades, manipulated stocks and markets, ignored customer complaints, and disobeyed customers' requests to sell securities. Manhattan district attorney Robert Morgenthau claimed that the firm was set up with the sole intention of defrauding their clients.

One of the largest areas of fraud has been in the medical and insurance business. For example, in 1997 Blue Shield of California paid $12 million to settle charges that it submitted false Medicare claims, the biggest case of health fraud in Northern California (Howe, 1997). The insurance business appears to have attracted the biggest cases of systematic fraud that would put professional con artists to shame. In 1993, Metropolitan Life was fined $20 million for cheating its customers; and in 1996, Mutual of New York paid $12.5 million to Alabama consumers for deceptive sales practices. But the biggest case is that of Prudential, which had for 13 years "churned" accounts by duping roughly 10 million customers into using the cash value of their old insurance policies to pay premiums on new, more expensive policies without advising that this would eat up their equity and leave them with premiums they could not afford and often with no coverage. Prudential was fined $35 million in 1995 and agreed to pay more than $1 billion in restitution to fleeced policyholders (Sherrill, 1997).

The "Everybody Does It" Defense

In his closing presentation of January 16, 1996, to the Senate Ethics Committee, which had been deliberating the Keating Five Case, outside counsel Robert Bennett states,

> *Let's talk about the most important defense that's been raised throughout this case. It comes back time and time again. It's the "everybody does it" defense. A couple of senators, to avoid personal accountability, have raised the "everybody does it" defense. They threaten you with the opening of the floodgates. . . . I don't see any floodgates ("Everybody Does Not," 1991, A14).*

Many of the participants in the S&L scandal used such techniques of neutralization or rationalizations comparable to the now-classic statement of a G.E. executive in the Great Electrical Conspiracy trial who, when asked if he knew the price-fixing meetings were criminal, responded, "Illegal, yes; but not criminal." While the Senate Ethics Committee concluded that what Senator DeConcini did had "the appearance of being improper," Neil Bush indicated, "I know it looks fishy," in describing insider loans and conflict of interest at the failed Silverado Savings and Loan, where he sat on the board of directors.

Deregulation created a climate of criminal opportunity for likely offenders such as Charles Keating, Herman Beebe, Mario Renda, Charles Bazarian, and other "Godfathers of Financial Scams" (Pizzo, Fricker, & Muolo, 1989, 44). While criminal elements were involved, the lack of enforcement encouraged many of the financial scams examined in this section. While some analysts view the S&L failures as primarily due to economic flaws in the system, others such as Pizzo, Fricker, and Muolo (1989, 289) view much of the losses as due to financial thieves:

> *A financial mafia of swindlers, mobsters, greedy Savings and Loan executives, and con men capitalized on regulatory weaknesses created by deregulation and thoroughly fleeced the thrift industry. While it was certainly true that economic factors (like plummeting oil prices in Texas and surrounding states) contributed to the crises, Savings and Loans would not be in the mess they are today, but for rampant fraud.*

In signing the 1982 Garn-St. Germain Act, then President Ronald Reagan stated, "I think we've hit the jackpot." Perhaps unknowingly he had opened a financial gambling casino with taxpayers' depositor funds. The fraudulent potential of such a deregulated climate can be illustrated by an analogy to the fabled "Cat Rat Scam," a legendary, fictitious swindle by short confidence artists seeking a foolproof investment to sell to clients. Buyers were asked to invest in a self-sustaining cat pelt farm. Cats were fed rats. Later the cats were slaughtered and their fur sold for coats. The cat remains were fed to the rats. As long as both populations propagated, there were no expenses. Junk bonds from Drexel Burnham Lambert were used to finance savings and loans; and then the savings and loans bought junk bonds from Drexel (Knight, 1990, 19). Keating bought Lincoln with $50 million in junk bonds purchased from Michael Milken and then used the S&L's money almost exclusively to buy junk bonds from Milken. Such operators could also afford to buy off members of Congress, accountants, and lawyers with the equivalent of scraps. So many politicians were involved that there were few left to point the finger. Millions in campaign donations and a mistaken overemphasis upon constituent service led members of Congress to ignore their oversight function, and left the savings and loan industry as a playground for professional scams with the taxpayer as the hapless victim.

Critical Thinking Exercise 5-1: The Scamming of America

This chapter described a wide variety of fraud schemes to which Americans fall prey each year. The categories of schemes indicate that fraud schemes change over time. Some older schemes are discontinued while new ones are created. What are the most common fraud schemes of the 1990s?

In order to answer this question, go to the Info Track or other database and do a search under the heading of "fraud," or "white-collar crime." You may classify schemes from 1990 to the present date. Classify article topics based on the following categories:

Phony accident claims	Business opportunity and franchise frauds
Mile busting (odometer tampering)	Commodity frauds
Art theft	Penny stock frauds
Boiler room frauds	Vacation timesharing scams
The investigator scam	Renaissance of Ponzi schemes
Abusive tax shelters	Pyramid scheme frauds
Oil and gas lease lottery frauds	Precious metals bank financing programs
Oil and gas investment frauds	"Dirt pile" gold swindles
Gold and silver investment frauds	Other: (Name)

With your instructor's help, make a table that clearly presents your results. What patterns of fraud do you see being reported in the press?

C h a p t e r **6**

Organized White-Collar Deviance

Edwin Sutherland (1956, 93–95) saw many parallels between the deviant behavior of occupational and corporate offenders and that of professional and organized criminals,

- They are recidivists, committing their crimes on a continual and frequent basis.
- Violations are widespread, and only a relatively few are ever prosecuted.
- Offenders do not lose status among their peers or associates as a result of their illegal behavior.
- Like professional thieves, business people reveal contempt for government regulators, officials, and laws that they view as unnecessarily interfering with their behavior.

Organized white-collar crime has traditionally referred to the infiltration of organized crime groups such as the Mafia into legitimate business, but it may also refer to behavior on the part of legitimate businesses that resemble organized crime operations or alliances between organized crime and legitimate businesses. Organized crime has been the subject of a variety of definitions by the media, legislatures, law enforcement agencies, criminologists, and members of organized crime groups themselves. A content analysis of such definitions in selected criminologists' works by Frank Hagan (1983) found many did not even provide a definition. Federal agencies such as the Federal Bureau of Investigation and the U.S. Department of Justice use the Federal Task Force on Organized Crime's operational definition, which is quite broad in its sweep,

Organized crime includes any group of individuals whose primary activity involves violating criminal laws to seek illegal profits and power by engaging in racketeering activities and, when appropriate, engaging in intricate financial manipulations....

> *Accordingly, the perpetrators of organized crime may include corrupt busi-*
> *ness executives, members of the professions, public officials, or any occupational*
> *group, in addition to the conventional, racketeer element (National Advisory Com-*
> *mittee, 1976, 213–215).*

Features of the Organized Crime Control Act of 1970, specifically the RICO provision (Racketeer Influence in Corrupt Organizations), broaden the classification of organized lawbreaking to include political corruption and white-collar crime. This will be discussed in greater detail below.

In a clever title, Jay Albanese (1982) in "What Lockheed and La Cosa Nostra Have in Common" also pointed to many parallels between organizational criminals and organized criminals. At the McClellan Commission Hearings in the 1960s, informant Joseph Valachi described the secretive, inner workings of the Cosa Nostra; while in Senate hearings in the 1970s, the president of Lockheed Corporation exposed the system of secret corporate pay-offs and bribes to foreign governments. Howard Abadinsky, (1997), provides interesting parallels between Cosa Nostra control of the New York City Garment District and the classic case of the Great Electrical Conspiracy, which came to a head in 1961. The garment industry in New York has been the subject of racketeer control since the 1930s and the days of Louis "Lepke" Buchalter. The nature of the industry requires quick transit of cloth to a number of jobbers in order to meet the year's fashion fads. Until 1993, Tommy Gambino, the eldest son of Carlo Gambino, and his brother owned the major garment center cartage firm and, along with another mob-controlled firm, divided manufacturers among a limited number of truckers. This cartel controlled everything that moved in the garment district. After a successful 1992 FBI sting operation, the Gambino brothers pleaded guilty to restraint of trade, paid a fine of $12 million, and agreed to quit the business in return for avoiding prison (Abalinsky, 1997, 424–425).

Even though it had been going on since the thirties, the "Great Electrical Industry Conspiracy" came to light in May 1959, when a young reporter with the *Knoxville News Sentinel,* Julian Granger, did a double take when reading a press release from the Tennessee Valley Authority that stated:

> *On this bidding for a transformers contract which was awarded to Westinghouse*
> *in the amount of $96,760 Allis Chalmers, General Electric, and Pennsylvania*
> *Transformer quoted identical prices of $112,712 (Fuller, 1962, 9).*

The release also indicated that two other firms quoted the same prices on a $273,000 contract, and seven companies gave the same bid on another, down to the penny, $198,438.24 (Fuller, 1962, 10). Granger was flabbergasted. How, under a system of independent, sealed, competitive bids, was it possible to have such identical prices quoted? In publishing his story, he had begun a process that would become, at the time, the largest antitrust case in U.S. history. Price-fixing and collusion had become a common practice in the electrical industry. Firms took turns submitting the lowest bid, costing the American public billions in higher prices. When asked whether he was aware that meeting to fix prices with fellow salespeople from rival firms was illegal, one G.E. executive rationalized, as previously observed, "Illegal, yes; but not criminal" (Punch, 1996, 95–101).

By February 1961, a strong warning was sent to such price fixers when seven executives from firms such as General Electric and Westinghouse were given jail terms of thirty days, an unprecedented benchmark. G.E. was also fined $437,500 and Westinghouse $372,500; and, in all, 29 companies and 45 executives were convicted of fixing prices on roughly $2 billion worth of electrical equipment. The executives met secretly under fictitious names in hotel rooms, calling their meetings "choir practice" and the participants "the Christmas card list" (Herling, 1962).

These two illustrations, the Gambino garment industry cartage cartel and the electrical industry conspiracy, serve as examples of the overlap between organized and white-collar deviance. The former shows an organized crime group moving into and monopolizing legitimate business operations, while the latter involves legitimate companies operating like a gang to monopolize and control markets. Both involve stealing from consumers in the form of higher prices. What is the difference? If the perpetrators are ethnic, speak gangster English, and do bad imitations of *The Godfather* or *Guys and Dolls,* we call it organized crime; while if they have fancy educations and are well groomed and well connected, we call them white-collar violators. In short, there is little difference. A blurring has obviously occurred. Before we explore organized white-collar crime further, let us first discuss the nature of organized crime and its infiltration of legitimate business.

Shover indicates:

> *The category of organizational crime excludes crime committed in the context and in pursuit of goals of avowedly illicit organizations. The crime of La Cosa Nostra and drug smugglers is organized, but is not organizational. In practice, this conceptual distinction can become blurred, as when a legitimate business is converted gradually into one that is criminal, or when it serves as the organizational context for one that is exclusively criminal (Passas and Nelken, 1993).... Legitimate organizations also may establish and maintain mutually beneficial relationships with criminal organizations (Ruggiero, 1996; Shover, 1998, 8).*

The view of organized crime as an outside entity infiltrating the purity of business is an oversimplification. This infiltration is often aided and abetted by legitimate organizations themselves whose operations may resemble those of organized crime groups. Bribery and corruption of national or international public leaders, violence through the purposive sale of unsafe products or directly in secret assassination attempts of foreign leaders, even the pushing of legitimate drugs in excess of public need by pharmaceutical companies may serve as illustrations.

The problem with attempting to define organized crime is that there are really two different types of organized crime being defined—a generic definition and a more specific criminological definition (Hagan, 1998, 369–371). The generic definition plays very heavily on the term "organized" and really reduces to group crime. Joseph Albini (1971, 37) offers a generic definition of organized crime, one quite compatible with operational policy definitions employed by federal agencies. Organized crime consists of:

> *any criminal activity involving two or more individuals, specialized or nonspecialized, encompassing some form of social structure, with some form of leadership, utilizing certain modes of operation, in which the ultimate purpose of the organization is found in the enterprise of the particular group.*

As previously indicated, one of the authors (Hagan, 1983), in a content analysis of authors of professional articles and books on organized crime, found the following variables identified in their definitions: an organized (continuing) hierarchy, rational profit through crime, use of force or threat of force, and corruption to obtain immunity. This supports a core, *specific definition of organized crime,* which consists of "criminal organizations that use violence or threats of violence, that provide illicit goods in public demand, and have immunity of operation through corruption and intimidation."

Organized crime might be best viewed as a continuum in which the greater degree to which criminal groups have these three core characteristics as well as others such as hierarchy, restricted membership, and codes of secrecy, the more it is an example of organized crime. Dwight Smith (1980, 371) proposes in his "spectrum-based theory of enterprise" that illicit enterprise is at the core of organized crime; that enterprises take place along a spectrum (or continuum) of possible behavior ranging from the legal to illegal, the saintly to the sinful; and that the separation of legitimate business from crime, where on the range one begins and the other ends, may be arbitrary.

Organized Crime

Ralph Salerno and John Tompkins in *The Crime Confederation* (1969) provide a description of "the classic pattern of organized crime," the evolution of criminal gangs to large, powerful, organized crime syndicates. In their model, organized crime groups can exhibit a gradual evolution from strategic and tactical crimes to illegal businesses and activities to legitimate businesses to big business. Strategic and tactical crimes involve activities such as assault, blackmail, extortion, and murder. While others commit these crimes as well, organized criminal groups are more persistent and better at it. Success at these crimes enables them to dominate and be successful at illegal businesses such as loan sharking, gambling, drugs, and protection rackets; and success at these requires money laundering and investment in legitimate businesses.

Annelise Anderson (1977) provides six reasons for organized crime to want to infiltrate legitimate business, profit, diversification, transfer, services, front, and taxes. Legitimate businesses can serve as profitable enterprises that provide diversification from total reliance on illegal activities. Such legitimate companies can be transferred to dependents and provide the service of offering legitimate employment, even if it happens to be "no show" employment for parole purposes. Very importantly, a legitimate operation can act as a front and meeting place for illegal activities and provide a tax cover to avoid income tax evasion charges. It can also assist in money laundering operations. Legal businesses can also be used to perpetrate other crimes; for example, a mob-owned insurance company may ask few questions in investigating a mob-inspired arson bankruptcy. Yet another, not to be overlooked, reason for the mob to infiltrate legitimate businesses is their realization that the criminal justice system is far softer on white-collar criminals than on gangsters.

Not just legitimate business but also labor unions have been a favorite target for organized crime involvement. "Labor racketeering" entails mob infiltration of unions for their own personal profit. Bribery, kickbacks, violence, and extortion are used to gain access to union pension funds, to offer "no strike" insurance (a guaranteed no strike contract), and "sweetheart contracts" (secret deals between union officials and management to the disadvantage of workers) and other criminal operations. Such infiltration of unions contains the same advantages as mob infiltration of legitimate business. Four unions that historically have been plagued by organized crime influence have been the International Longshoreman's Association, the Hotel and Restaurant Employees Union, the Laborer's International Union, and the International Brotherhood of Teamsters. Jonathan Kwitny in *Vicious Circles, The Mafia in the Marketplace* (1979) documents organized crime's infiltration and control of the meat industry, bakeries, cheese processing, the garment district, banks, stockbrokerages, as well as unions. An interesting testament to the corruptive power of organized crime takes place in Pennsylvania in the early 1990s. In the 1960s the Pennsylvania Crime Commission was established as an independent, state-funded commission to investigate organized crime; and it became a model of its kind. It made the mistake, however, of interpreting the concept of organized crime broadly and began investigating illegal campaign donations to then Pennsylvania Attorney General Ernie Preate. Even though Preate would eventually be sent to jail, the Pennsylvania Crime Commission as an independent agency was abolished by the state legislature, mainly through the efforts of Preate.

Earlier, we discussed how the seeds of many great American fortunes were made a hundred years ago by "robber barons" who, a generation later, were regarded as pillars of society. Similarly, Francis Ianni in *A Family Business* (1972) sees some American fortunes beginning with "dirty business" and progressing after time into "respectable business," a natural "ethnic succession" or evolution. He is concerned that such a progression not be entirely blunted. This all depends, of course, on whether the organized criminals do or do not abandon criminal activity once they move into legitimate business. This notion of ethnic succession has also been elaborated on by Daniel Bell (1953), who feels that organized crime has often represented "a queer ladder of mobility," an illegitimate opportunity for upward, vertical mobility for various groups. Groups that were the most recently arrived, lowest on the totem pole, or denied legitimate opportunity found opportunity in organized crime. Often, within a generation, these groups became successful enough to move into legitimate opportunities and were replaced by the next group in the pecking order.

The Mob Is Bullish on America

The mob has always been a fan of the profits to be made in the free enterprise system; they simply have been a bit fuzzy on the approved or legitimate means of doing so. In February 1997, perhaps prematurely, the *New York Times* reported, "Officials Say Mob Is Shifting to New Industries" (Raab, 1997). With successful law enforcement crackdowns on traditional organized crime activities such as extortion and bid-rigging rackets, Mafia crime families in New York were reported as shifting their focus to frauds in health insurance, prepaid telephone cards, and small Wall Street brokerage houses.

> The authorities in New Jersey said they uncovered what might be the prototype of the mob's medical care strategy in August, when they arrested 12 men accused of being members of a Genovese crew, or unit. The crew's leaders were charged with siphoning payments from Tri-Con Associates, a New Jersey company that arranged medical, dental, and optical care for more than one million patients in group plans throughout the country. Investigators said that the mobsters set up Tri-Con, invest-

ing their own money and using employees as managers, and intimidated some health plan administrators into approving excessive payments to the company. New Jersey authorities said Tri-Con in effect became a broker, linking networks of health-care providers, including physicians, hospitals and dentists with group plans for companies and unions (Raab, 1997).

Prepaid phone cards are a relatively new business, grossing about $1 billion in 1996 and offering a new target for organized crime. The Gambino crime family set up a company that stole over $50 million from companies and phone callers. According to one account, the Gambinos sold $20 cards that became worthless after only $2 or $3 in calls because they had not been programmed for the correct amount. The telephone carriers also lost money due to credit they extended to the phony company, which never paid them for the calls. John "Junior" Gotti was involved in the telephone card business but, as of this writing, appeared to be operating it as a legitimate business (Bastone, 1997).

At least three New York City crime families were involved in frauds with initial public offerings in over-the-counter stocks handled by small brokerage firms. In these swindles the mob lends money to brokers who are in debt or wish to expand their business. They then force the brokers to sell them most of the low-priced shares in a company before its stock is available as initial public offerings. The mob and brokers quickly inflate the value of the shares by fake transactions or trading among themselves. The brokers are forced to inflate prices further by pushing them on unsuspecting investors. The mobsters then sell, making huge profits before the overvalued stock plunges (Bastone, 1997).

Mob infiltration of big business can threaten the heartline of our nation's economy. Organized crime becomes such a central part of core institutions that it can compromise the government itself. In "Operation Mongoose," the Central Intelligence Agency used members of the Mafia to attempt to assassinate Fidel Castro. When one of these figures, John Roselli, was scheduled to appear before the House Assassinations Committee investigating the assassination of the late President John Kennedy, he was mysteriously killed (Anderson & Whitten, 1977). Correctly or incorrectly, the conclusion of the U.S. House of Representatives Select Committee on Assassinations (1979) was that there was a conspiracy in the assassination of JFK; and more specifically, as the title of the chief counsel to the committee's book claims, *The Plot to Kill the President, Organized Crime Assassinated JFK* (Blakey & Billing, 1981). It is alleged, *not proven,* that the Mafia felt betrayed by John Kennedy because they claimed major responsibility for getting him elected by stuffing ballot boxes, particularly in Illinois. Once elected, John Kennedy appointed to the post of Attorney General his brother, Robert Kennedy, who waged war against organized crime. RFK had crusaded against the mob and labor racketeering since his days as counsel to the McClellan Commission, which was investigating mob rackets. He continued his attacks on figures such as Teamster leader Jimmy Hoffa. This did not sit well with a particular "subordinate," J. Edgar Hoover, Director of the Federal Bureau of Investigation. It has been charged, *not proven,* that Hoover had avoided any efforts against organized crime because he had been compromised, receiving favors from gamblers and perhaps blackmailed due to an alleged secret sexual life. Columnist Jack Anderson and others (Anderson & Whitten, 1977) allege that John Kennedy was killed for two reasons: one, in retaliation for the attempt on Castro (one of the would-be assassins, Santo Trafficante, may have turned); and two, a mob plot to eliminate RFK's campaign against the mob by taking out the head (his brother). Much of this is speculation and perhaps we will never know; but the day after the president of the United States was assassinated, Hoover, the nation's top law enforcement officer, spent the day at the racetrack.

Organized Crime Myths Exposed

As mentioned, the distinction between organized crime and various forms of white-collar deviance is often a very fine line. Related to this reality is another that is often overlooked in discussions of organized criminal syndicates. That is, it is usually assumed that organized crime members are part of some alien conspiracy who bully their way into various neighborhoods and businesses, guns ablazing, with no cooperation or invitation from people or organizations. This is one of the great myths about crime syndicates (Kappeler et al., 1996, 110ff).

The reality, more often than not, is just the opposite (Quinney, 1975, 145). As Lyman and Potter state,

> ... *organized criminals, legitimate business people, and government officials are all equal players in the market place of corruption. Each comes to the market place with goods or services wanted by others, and a rather routine and institutionalized series of exchanges takes place.... Who initiates such a deal depends on the circumstances, and the initiator is as likely to be the legitimate actor as the criminal (1997, 359).*

Thus organized crime syndicates have long been useful to so-called legitimate corporations and certain government agencies and politicians, who have need of illegal goods and services that only crime syndicates can provide. One of us (Simon, 1999, 82ff) has described in depth the uses political organizations and government agencies (including the CIA) have found for the goods and services of organized crime syndicates. The U.S. Mafia has been used to:

- Attempt to assassinate Cuban premier Castro
- Raise secret funds for aid to the Nicaraguan Contras and other causes from the profits of narcotics sales
- Launder money from drug-trafficking
- Stop labor strikes
- Supply needed campaign contributions at all levels of government
- Fix elections in the United States
- Spy on enemy submarines, plan the invasion of Sicily during World War II, and help the allies run military government in Italy after the allied victory there

Likewise, certain legitimate business and entertainment interests have long used crime syndicates for a variety of purposes:

- Chemical firms have used the Mafia to cheaply dispose of hazardous waste.
- Businesses have long hired crime families to stop labor unions from forming, while certain unions (like the Teamsters) have allied themselves with the Mafia in order to win union recognition from employers.

- Corporations and crime syndicates have formed business partnerships in the United States and offshore islands to build gambling casinos and resorts. Sydicate members have also been used to train pit bosses and dealers in casinos (Kohn, 1976).
- Disreputable landlords have hired mob-controlled arson rings to burn down slum buildings whose insurance value has exceeded their assessed property value.
- Organized crime has also been a proven customer of legal goods and services, such as long-distance phone calls to operate illegal gambling bets, traffic in narcotics, and legally invest capital in market securities and new businesses (King, 1975).
- Organized crime families are consumers of a large variety of everyday products and services: pagers, cellular phones, chemicals for processing illegal drugs, and office supplies (computers, stick-up note pads, writing implements, and the like).
- Organized crime has served as an alternative employment source in poor neighborhoods, and its drug trafficking in these areas may distract residents from political discontent (McIntosh, 1973; Spitzer, 1975; Tabor, 1971).
- Banks, wholesale jewelers, check cashing services, major investment houses, and many other businesses have been handsomely paid to launder profits from drug trafficking (see below).
- Stolen cargo (cigarettes, gasoline, and numerous other stolen products) can be bought from smugglers at prices substantially below wholesale, and sold for large profits.
- For businesses and individuals with bad credit, Mafia loan sharks have long served as a source of badly needed cash. (See also Pearce, 1976, 140.)

Let us look at some real life examples of these relationships.

Consider corruption, long an embarrassment to politicians and members of the criminal justice system. Politicians running for office are always in need of cash for their political campaigns. Members of the criminal justice system are usually not nearly as well paid as drug cartel operators or local drug dealers.

Retired FBI agent William Roemer has put the matter succinctly: "Corruption goes hand in glove with organized crime. The mob which can't corrupt can't operate" (Roemer, 1995, 354). Roemer uncovered all manner of alliances between the Chicago "outfit" and so-called public servants during his long career. Patterns of corruption in Chicago were cemented in the Prohibition Era (1919–1933) during the reign of Al Capone.

- In 1930, the police raided the hotel room of one of Capone's gangsters. To their astonishment, the room contained a copy of a secret Chicago police department memo calling for the arrest of 41 members of Capone's mob. Shockingly, so close was the relationship between Capone and the police that the memo had been given to Capone himself. "Big Al" promptly deleted the names of eight of his most trusted lieutenants from the list of those to be arrested. Thus the outfit was practically in charge of the police department.
- By 1934, there were 7,500 illegal gambling operations all operating under the protection of the Kelly-Nash political machine in Chicago. The mayor's office and ward politicians made sure that no police captain was assigned to any area paying protection to the politicians unless the officer was also corrupt (Roemer, 1995, 50).

Lest you think such corruption is merely an unpleasant memory left over from a bygone era, consider the following:

* In the 1960s, the FBI gave the Chicago Police Department evidence of corruption among 49 of its officers. The report was never used by the Department, and not a single officer was prosecuted (Roemer, 1995, 205).
* In the 1990s, nearly 100 judges and court personnel in Chicago's Cook County were convicted of accepting bribes from the outfit in an effort to fix criminal cases (Roemer, 1995, 359).

Likewise, the former underboss of New York's Gambino crime family was Sammy ("The Bull") Gravano. He was, in the early 1990s, the highest ranking member of La Cosa Nostra ever to turn state's evidence against his former family. Gravano's testimony was crucial in convicting Gambino family "dapper don" John Gotti, as well as dozens of key Cosa Nostra captains, a corrupt juror, and eight high-ranking union officials (for labor racketeering) (Maas, 1997, 474).

Equally interesting, as well, are Gravano's recollections concerning cooperation of various business executives and corrupt members of the criminal justice system. One stronghold of the New York City mob families was the construction industry. Gravano owned a cement pouring business, and one of his partners was Joe Madonia, who was not a mob member, but who owned a legitimate company, Ace Partitions. More important, concrete pouring on every major construction contract in New York City—meaning $2 million or more—could not take place until it received the approval of four of the City's five crime families. (The Bonanno family was excluded from construction considerations due to its dispute with the other families.) Colombo family member Ralph Scopo was president and business manager of the local cement and concrete workers union.

All the New York City concrete pouring firms under mob control would take turns being low bidder on the projects. The prices of the contracts were immediately increased by the cement pouring firms, so much so that the price of a cubic yard of poured cement in Manhattan became the highest in the nation. Legitimate builders, contractors, and developers, who also worked on the projects, would follow the mob's lead by jacking up their prices as well. The legitimate firms knew full well that the Cosa Nostra was their silent partner, but went along with the mob's scam because the profits on non-mob firms also increased! After all, all costs were passed on to those who bought or leased office space or condos in these projects (Maas, 1997, 271).

Finally, Ovid Demaris's biography of Jimmy ("the Weasel") Fratianno is loaded with episodes of collusion between the mob and large numbers of professional entertainers, business executives, and politicians. Here are just a few examples:

Fratianno's relationship with Frank Sinatra began in 1947. In Cuba, it is known that dictator Batista allowed Mafia financier Meyer Lansky to set up gambling casinos in Havana in 1933. Following Castro's closing of the casinos in the early 1960s, organized crime figures were recruited by the CIA to aid in assassinating Castro. In Vietnam in the 1960s and early 1970s, organized crime figures cooperated with the CIA in setting up Asia's Golden Triangle, Southeast Asia's center for heroin distribution. This triangle stretches for some 150,000 square miles across northeast Burma, northern Thailand, and northern Laos. The CIA's involvement included transporting opium using their own airline, Air America.

Organized crime has long served as a source of campaign funds for political elites on virtually every level of U.S. politics—local, state, and national. By the early 1970s, Southeast Asia's Golden Triangle had become a major new heroin source for the U.S. organized crime syndicate of Santos Trafficante, Jr., a Lansky rival in heroin trade. Trafficante had ties to both the Nixon White House and the Laotian Chiu Chow syndicate, a major opium source in Southeast Asia and the owner of the Laotian Pepsi Cola Company, whose U.S. counterpart had longtime ties to the Nixon organization (Lyman & Potter, 1997, 368–370; Simon, 1996, 132ff).

These illustrations have led some criminologists to conclude that organized crime has served and continues to serve the domestic and foreign political goals of the U.S. political and economic elites. Finally, it is important to understand that, despite recent convictions of aging godfathers in New York and Sicily, organized crime is in key aspects stronger than ever. Virtually all the illegal gambling and drug trade remain intact.

There is ample evidence now of links between traditional Italian/Sicilian organized crime and international drug smugglers from Colombia and Mexico, who import cocaine and heroin. Nontraditional organized crime groups in the United States, including the Japanese Yakuza, Hell's Angels motorcycle gang, Jamaican and Chinese-American vice groups, and numerous street gangs, make up of a host of minority groups who also have ties to the Mafia through illegal drug trade, prostitution, and gambling (Brandt, 1995).(These links are further explored in Chapter 7.)

Certainly, illegal drug trafficking has proven much more intractable than nearly anyone had surmised. A chief reason for the tenacity of the drug trade is the very corruption of and cooperation with legitimate political and at times economic elites by organized criminal syndicates, who are now an integral portion of the higher immorality.

Fratianno was a member of the U.S. Cosa Nostra from 1947 to 1978, at which time he entered the federal witness protection program. During his long career he associated with large numbers of legitimate businesspeople, lawyers, and entertainers. His various relationships demonstrate the intertwined network between the criminal underworld and legitimate elites:

- One of the Weasel's friends was Hollywood attorney Sidney Korshak. Korshak was one of the nation's highest paid attorneys. His client list included the L. A. Dodgers, San Diego Chargers, Diner's Club, and Hilton and Hyatt hotel chains. His close friends included people such as studio heads from MGM, Paramount Pictures, as well as the mega-agent firm MCA. Ironically, it was mob lawyer Korshak that was able to get Al Pacino released from his exclusive contract at MGM so he could star in the quintessential organized crime movie. Korshak was a master negotiator, and was used by organized crime for years to mediate disputes between and within crime families (Demaris, 1981, 373).
- Another of Fratianno's friends was bank owner, attorney, and mayor of San Francisco, the late Joseph Alioto. So notorious were Alioto's mob ties that they were the subject

of a story in *Look Magazine*. The story, published in 1969, claimed that Alioto was engaged in alliances with at least six Cosa Nostra members, and had provided mob members with bank loans, business counsel, and a respectable front which the mobsters used to begin new businesses. In return, Alioto was paid various fees, business profits, campaign contributions, and political support. So popular was Alioto in 1968 that Democratic presidential candidate Hubert Humphrey considered choosing him as his vice presidential running mate.

Alioto was so outraged by the article that he filed a $12.5 million lawsuit against the magazine. Alioto eventually won a $350,000 settlement against *Look,* but not because the basic facts were wrong. One minor paragraph of the story described meetings between Alioto and mob members at the Nut Tree Restaurant between San Francisco and Sacramento. The authors' source for that part of the story turned out to be unreliable, so Alioto used legal sleight of hand to dispute the entire story, and won.

- Fratianno first met Frank Sinatra in 1947, and is in a famous picture along with mob boss Carlo Gambino and numerous other mobsters. The photo was taken at a 1967 concert Sinatra performed at the request of Fratianno and other gangsters, who needed profits from the affair (Demaris, 1981, 404ff).
- Sinatra also convinced scores of his show business pals to perform at mob-owned Las Vegas casinos in the 1960s and '70s. At one point in his career, Cosa Nostra nightclub owners were the only people willing to hire Sinatra because of his adulterous behavior with actress Ava Gardner, and he remained grateful for the favor throughout his career. The casinos were built by organized crime with huge loans from the International Brotherhood of Teamsters Central States Pension Fund. So corrupted were the Teamsters that every one of their presidents from the 1950s to the 1990s was sent to prison on corruption and racketeering charges. In 1997, the election of the latest Teamster president, Ron Carey, was overturned by the government because of illegal campaign contributions.
- Another of the Weasel's friends was Mark Anthony, President of Bob Hope enterprises. Fratianno was to gain free use of Hope's mansion one afternoon in order to have sex with a nightclub singer he had met while serving a prison sentence!

What was true about crime syndicate–power elite cooperation in the 1960s is equally true in the 1990s, and it is the same all over the world:

- In February, 1997, former Mexican anti-drug unit commander General Jesus Robollo was forced to resign his post under suspicion that he was doing business with Mexican drug syndicate heads. The general had just attended high-level meetings in which the drug war activities of the United States were discussed. A few days after Robollo resigned the *New York Times* reported that two Mexican governors had been directly linked to drug traffickers with whom they had made millions of dollars (Wright, 1997, 8). The Robollo case was just one more in a series of money laundering and drug-trafficking incidents involving high-level Mexican officials. In 1995, U.S. Customs officials discovered that former Mexican prosecutor Mario Ruiz possessed a $7 million secret bank account in a Texas bank (L. A. Times, 1995, A-1). The brother of Mexico's former president used secret bank accounts to launder money for the Cali cocaine cartel through secret bank accounts at Citibank, one of the largest U.S. banks. Citibank purposely distracted its own investigator from looking into the matter (*The Wall Street Journal,* 1996, June, A-3.

- Recent cases demonstrate that respected members of various legitimate professions have been involved in money laundering. The list includes attorneys in the United States and in a variety of Latin American and European nations, including former U.S. prosecutors, car dealers, stock brokers and bankers, and even interior designers and rabbis (*Los Angeles Times,* 1997, June, A-1; *The New York Times,* 1997, August, A-1.

Types of Organized Crime

While the general picture of organized crime consists of traditional crime syndicates such as the American Mafia, a variety of other types exist (Hagan, 1998, 372–373), including traditional crime syndicates; nontraditional syndicates; semiorganized crime groups; local, politically controlled organized crime groups; and national, politically controlled organized crime groups. These are not intended to be mutually exclusive categories.

Traditional organized crime syndicates are comprehensive criminal organizations that exhibit the highest degree of characteristics of organized crime. They have hierarchy, restricted membership, secrecy, make use of or threaten violence, provide illicit services in public demand, are profit oriented, and obtain immunity of operation through corruption and enforcement. Groups such as the American Cosa Nostra, Japanese Yakuza, and Chinese Triads serve as examples. Nontraditional syndicates are less comprehensive criminal groups that exhibit less development on the organized crime continuum. Large-scale narcotics smuggling groups such as the Colombian cartels, white-collar fraud groups, independent local vice operators, and rural organized crime networks (Potter & Gaines, 1992) are illustrations. Black, Hispanic, Jamaican, Russian, and other ethnic-based groups are also examples.

Semiorganized crime syndicates are smaller and less sophisticated, with a narrower range of operations. Outlaw biker gangs such as the Pagans and Hell's Angels provide examples. Professional burglary, arson, and robbery rings possess some of the characteristics of organized crime. Local, politically controlled organized crime groups are ones in which the local political power structure is not simply corrupted, but is an actual partner in organized crime operations. Block and Chambliss (1981, 112–113) even go so far as to claim that in many U.S. cities those running criminal investigations are members of business, political, or law enforcement communities. Finally, national, politically controlled organized crime syndicates are operated in partnership with members of the national power structure; such authorities help in planning and executing criminal activity. On July 1, 1997, the British crown colony of Hong Kong was delivered back to China after over a century of control by the British, who had won it in the Opium Wars in which European countries forced China to accept trafficking in opium. Both the U.S. and France in Indochina encouraged local tribes to grow and traffic in opium in order to fund the war against communism (McCoy, 1972). Russia and Mexico serve as more recent examples.

Contemporary Global Crime Syndicates

Unquestionably the most important contemporary organized crime phenomenon is global organized crime (Viviano, 1995, 17ff.) The end of the Cold War created new opportunities for transnational organized crime. "Transparent national borders, fewer trade restrictions, and truly global financial and telecommunications systems provide significant opportunities for criminal organizations to expand operations beyond national boundaries" (Kerry, 1997b, 161). Russian organized crime has formed an unholy alliance with Sicilian, Asian, Mexican, and Colombian syndicates, and the results are devastating.

- In Russia, thousands of poorly guarded nuclear warheads and hundreds of unsafe reactors (20,000 safety violations during 1993 inspections and 78 shutdowns for safety reasons) are rusting away on the Soviet fleet, many with nuclear fuel aboard. The Russian Academy of Sciences estimated in 1995 that the Russian Mafiya now owns 50 to 80 percent of all voting stock in Russia's legitimate corporations (Kerry, 1997a, 160).
- Drug cartels from Columbia, Russia, Italy, Japan, and China instantly transfer huge sums around the world with "wire" (actually satellite) transfers, using offshore banks. The cartels manipulate accounts drawn in the names of "shell" corporations. The economies of a number of tiny sovereign nations, such as the Cayman Islands, are completely dependent on laundering transactions.

    Organized crime groups from the former Soviet Union, Asia, and Italy are forming partnerships among themselves as well as with the drug barons of Latin America. All syndicates are engaging in corruption on a grand scale,

- In 1995, more than 6,000 Italian bureaucrats, corporate executives, and politicians (among them a staggering 438 deputies and senators) were under investigation or have been indicted on various corruption charges. One estimate is that the Mafia has paid $40 billion in bribes to executives and officials over the past decade. On March 2, 1995, seven-time Prime Minister Giulio Andreotti was indicted for being a "made member" of the Italian Mafia (Kerry, 1997a, 73).
- The Colombian cartels now trade cocaine to the Italian Mafia in exchange for heroin. The Columbian Cali cartel boss now earns $4 billion annually from cocaine, and has invested hundreds of millions in banks in Russia, Europe, and the United States.
- In Mexico, the former Mexican Federal Deputy Attorney General Eduardo Valle Espinosa resigned his official post in frustration in May 1996, and it is estimated that at least half of Mexico's federal police chiefs and attorney generals receive illegal payoffs from drug dealers. Some police chief candidates now pay $1 to $2 million just to get hired. From 1988 to 1994, the brother of the former president of Mexico transferred over $80 million from a Citibank (a U.S. bank) branch in Mexico through Citibank's New York headquarters to a secret Swiss bank account. Mexico's chief drug czar had to resign in 1997 when it was learned that he had ties to Mexico's drug cartel (Kerry, 1997a, 100–153, 159–161).
- Of the approximately 1.5 million U.S. vehicles stolen each year, several hundred thousand are illegally exported out of the country to Central America and Eastern Europe. One Columbian criminal, Gabriel Taboada, testified at a U.S. Senate committee hearing that he bribed diplomats, who are exempt from paying duty on imported cars, "to import cars in their name" (Kerry, 1997a, 72).

Approximately $500 billion in currency is laundered annually utilizing various global financial institutions, making money laundering the third largest industry in the world. Federal law requires that banks report all cash deposits of $10,000 or more to the Internal Revenue Service (IRS). In 1975, there were only 3,000 such activities reported. By 1988, there were 5.5 million reported annually. It is now estimated that the total amount of drug money laundered each year is an immense $300 billion, about half of all funds connected to the worldwide drug trade. Of this amount, $100 billion is laundered in the U.S. Nine-tenths of this amount ends up overseas, often in secret Swiss accounts, where it can then be freely moved. This outflow of money contributes substantially to the nation's foreign trade deficit (Simon, 1996, 140ff.)

The largest money laundering operation ever uncovered took place in 1989. U.S. banks were used to ship $1 billion a year to cocaine traffickers. The drug profits were disguised as proceeds from phony front businesses—wholesale gold and jewelry—run largely out of Los Angeles. Another money laundering investigation in 1990, Operation Polar Cap, resulted in the freezing of hundreds of accounts in 173 American banks, more than half of which were in New York and Florida. The accounts contained some $400 million in Colombian drug profits. Another source of laundered money are storefront check-cashing and money-transmitting services, most of which are unlicensed and run by newly arrived or illegal immigrants. Most of these are in states with few regulators, who are unable to keep up with the growth of such businesses. This is especially true of Florida, Texas, New York, and California. Each year, such operations take billions in cash from drug dealers and send it overseas. These storefront operations defraud honest customers by failing to send their money to requested addressees. Many customers cannot complain because they are either newly arrived immigrants ignorant of the law, or illegals (Kerry, 1997a, 157–160).

Russian Organized Crime

Mafiya groups in Russia inherited a unique survival skill in the Soviet Communist system that put them in a position to take advantage of the new, weak, and yet unorganized fledgling democracy in Russia or the more liberal democratic system to be found in Western Europe and the United States. Kenney and Finckenauer (1995, 274) note:

> All the emigres from the former Soviet Union share a common heritage—a state-run, centrally planned Soviet command economy that produced massive shortages as well as widespread bribery and thievery. No area of life in the Soviet Union was exempt from pervasive, universal corruption. Scarce goods and services unavailable through normal channels could usually be gotten through blat (connections) or na lev (on the left). An illegal second or shadow economy arose to operate in tandem with the official economy.

Konstantin Simis in *USSR, The Corrupt Society* (1982) claims that the Soviet system bred corruption on a massive scale. This did not readily decline with the demise of the Soviet Union. The young Russian democracy is now threatened by the breakdown of law enforcement, the growth of private armies, and protection rackets that regularly resort to violence. The Russian Interior Ministry reported in 1994 that 70 to 80 percent of private businesses and banks had been forced to pay protection money (Brunker, 1997). Russian gangs in the United States have been particularly involved in health care fraud, insurance scams, antiquities swindles, forgery, and gas tax evasion. In March 1997 a Russian group (Globus) was arrested for a fraudulent stock scheme bilking investors out of millions by convincing them to invest in a fraudulent Internet company. Between 1993 and 1996, 400 business executives and politicians were killed in Russia after challenging organized crime or official corruption, and 90 percent of the businesses in St. Petersburg were paying protection money (Payton, 1997). Parallels might be drawn with America's early robber barons; the boundary between legality and illegality is blurred.

> *In the early years of reform, managers and bureaucrats illegally used Communist Party money or state assets to set up banks or launch businesses. Now it's difficult to distinguish these Soviet survivors from true entrepreneurs who pulled themselves up by their bootstraps. Nearly everyone broke the law in some way. But, some want to go legitimate. They've amassed big enough fortunes that they now want to be seen as legitimate businesspersons. Some may even run for parliament.... (Kranz, 1995).*

With the collapse of the Soviet Union and the end of the Cold War, writers such as Claire Sterling and U.S. Senator John Kerry (1997b) warned of a "pax mafiosa," the evolution of global organized crime. In *Thieves World, The Threat of the New Global Network of Organized Crime,* Sterling (1994) claims that the growing interdependence of countries and financial institutions finds crime syndicates also cooperating internationally. With an estimated $120 billion of laundered criminal money a year moving internationally, she sees cooperation among Sicilian, Colombian, Japanese, and Russian groups (see also Sterkuy, 1994). While such a world conspiracy is an exaggeration, cooperation certainly has taken place. John Kerry (1997b) indicates,

> *A decade ago, my committee investigators and I began to uncover portions of a common international infrastructure for crime. We interviewed criminals inside various U.S. prisons and found that they had remarkable access to political figures in countries all over the world. This work led me to the drug network of Manuel Noriega and eventually to the place he laundered his money, the Bank of Credit and Commerce International (BCCI).... The new global criminal axis is composed of five principal powers in league with a host of lesser ones. The Big Five are the Italian Mafia, the Russian mobs, the Japanese yakuza, the Chinese triads, and the Colombian cartels. They coordinate with smaller but highly organized gangs with distinct specialties in such countries as Nigeria, Poland, Jamaica and Panama, which remains a significant transshipment and money-laundering point even after the arrest of General Noriega. Various alliances among these groups are still in the formative stage, but all indications are that those relations are rapidly becoming more complex and coordinated.*

Kerry then gives a number of examples to support his claims (1997b),

> *In the summer of 1982 the leaders of the Russian and Italian mobs held a series of secret summits in Prague, Warsaw, and Zurich to form a drug trade alliance.*

> *A hit man was flown in from Moscow to kill an uncooperative store owner in New York for the Organizatsiya (a Russian organized crime group). His fake papers were supplied by the Sicilian Mafia in return for Soviet Army surplus ground-to-air missiles which were supplied to the Bosnian Serbs.*
>
> *Colombian cartels produce cocaine and exchange it with Chinese groups for heroin that is smuggled into the U.S. The triads bring cocaine to Japan, which is then distributed by the yakuzas. Then the drug money is laundered in Europe.*
>
> *Triad groups run extortion and loan-sharking operations in Great Britain; heroin in Rotterdam; prostitution, gambling, robbery, and contract murder in Germany; money laundering in Prague; weapons trafficking in Romania; and alien smuggling in Moscow.*
>
> *The Camorra supplied Russian groups with counterfeit $100 bills in exchange for property such as banks and arms shipments.*

In November 1994, the United Nations sponsored a conference in Naples, Italy, of 138 nations on transnational crime to counteract what was described as costing a staggering $750 billion a year (Cowell, 1994). The conference noted that the scope of organized crime had broadened beyond traditional crimes such as extortion, narcotics, and vice to money laundering, into legitimate businesses as well as illegal trade in nuclear weapons, toxic waste disposal, smuggling of illegal immigrants, and illicit organ transplants.

Electronic money transfers contain the possibility of major problems in monitoring money laundering operations or following paper trails. Note the following description from the web pages for European Union Bank, a favorite of Russian Mafiya groups for banking services. Note also that for $995 U.S. one can set up an Antiguan international business corporation, a convenient means of making "dirty money" appear legitimate. If the authors could be so bold as to coin a new term, this might be called "money dry cleaning" since it involves a new, more modern method of electronic laundering.

> *Until recently, the only barrier to offshore banking was the remoteness of the bank from its clients. Modern technological advances and world telecommunication improvements have removed that barrier. Now clients of European Union Bank can communicate with the bank at anytime from anywhere via the Internet. From the convenience of their office or home, account holders can check balances, wire money, or take out a loan as easily as if they had been transported to Antigua. With an Internet connection, you can also take advantage of the financial rewards of offshore banking with the European Union Bank. Modern computer communications make this way of banking the easiest, least expensive, and most secure means of client-bank interaction ever (http://www.eubank.ag/abouteub.htm).*

Money Laundering

Phil Williams (1997, 18) indicates:

> *Money laundering provides one of the most important junctures between what Alex Schmid has termed the "upperworld and the underworld." Money laundering is*

one of the major ways in which criminal organizations penetrate the licit economy and often involves the co-option of supposedly reputable members of society such as bankers and lawyers. Allowing money laundering to go unchallenged, therefore, would have a corrosive impact on the integrity of financial institutions.

The repositories for crime syndicates, enabling them to reinvest their ill-gotten riches in legitimate businesses, are tax haven banks such as in the Bahamas, Cayman Islands, the Netherlands Antilles, Switzerland, Luxembourg, Austria, and Cyprus. The Cayman Islands has one bank for every 53 citizens. Criminal organizations often transfer money to and from shell corporation accounts. Instant electronic transfers make the old technique of traveling with suitcases full of money obsolete and law enforcement detection more difficult. Williams (1997, 19) notes that simply transferring money from one country to another often creates legitimate money *de facto*. In a "safe haven" all money becomes "clean."

Some examples well illustrate the interconnections with legitimate society as well as the cross-national nature of such operations. "Operation Dinero" was a joint international sting operation against the Cali Cartel involving the Drug Enforcement Agency (DEA), the Internal Revenue Service, Immigration and Naturalization Service, the Federal Bureau of Investigation, and law enforcement agencies from Canada, Italy, Spain, and the United Kingdom. The DEA set up an offshore bank in Anguilla that advertised its willingness to launder money for drug traffickers. By 1994, the Cali Cartel had become so established that the bank was asked to sell famous art masterpieces (a favorite money laundering investment) for them. The network included Colombia, Mexico, Southern California, Canada, the United States, and the Pasquale Locatelli organization which operates in Canada, France, Greece, Spain, and Romania. Also involved was the Severa organization in Italy, which also laundered money through legitimate businesses. The operation netted 88 arrests, seizure of about 9 tons of cocaine, and over $50 million in cash and property (Williams, 1997).

The Spence money laundering network in New York City, which was busted in 1994, involved an honorary consul general for Bulgaria, a New York City police officer, two lawyers, a stockbroker, an assistant bank manager at Citibank, two rabbis, a firefighter, and two more bankers in Zurich. Directed by a law firm and using a trucking business and beer distributorship as a front, couriers picked up drug proceeds throughout Manhattan, and two lawyers put it in the bank with the help of the Citibank contact. The money was then wired to Europe and transferred to the accounts of the drug traffickers. In a two-year period the group laundered up to $100 million (Williams, 1997, 20). Even when the operations are broken, the money is often beyond the reach of U.S. law enforcement. One significant development in examining money laundering is the emergence of a new class of white-collar criminal—the professional money broker, specialists who, for a fee, manage money for crooks. Drug traffickers buy import-export firms and manufacturing firms to produce products for export, inside which they can hide drugs or money. Casinos, restaurants, and food delivery establishments remain excellent cover for laundering. The use of nations in transition whose financial system is insecure is a growing trend. As indicated previously, it is estimated that the majority of the Russian banking system is controlled by organized crime.

The BCCI, Bank of Credit and Commerce International, was a Third World bank that was involved in the largest international bank collapse in history. Those involved in the scandal included intelligence agencies, governments, terrorist groups, drug traffickers, and organized criminals. Nikos Passas (1994, 2) explains,

> *BCCI's illegal activities covered an impressive range, Ponzi schemes, deceitful accounting, frauds against depositors, money laundering, financing of illegal arms deals and nuclear programs, corruption of politicians and other influential individuals, illegal control of financial institutions and assistance to intelligence agencies for illicit purposes.*

Controlling Money Laundering

While the cross-national crime of money laundering has initially exceeded the ability of international law enforcement to keep pace, there are some signs of progress. In the United States alone a series of legislation beginning with the Bank Secrecy Act of 1970 has been instrumental. This required a currency transaction report for deposits or exchanges over $10,000, reports on similar amounts leaving or entering the country, and that citizens holding foreign bank accounts report these on their federal tax returns (Albanese, 1996, 201). The Financial Crime Enforcement Network, established in 1990 in the Treasury Department, was designed to support law enforcement agencies in tracking money launderers. These and additional pieces of legislation in the U.S. have been mirrored internationally, particularly in the creation of the Financial Action Task Force, which in 1990 made 40 recommendations for action.

The increasing level of law enforcement experience is illustrated by the use of highly sophisticated software by the Australian Transaction Reports and Analysis Center (Austrac). This software, originally developed to track incoming intercontinental ballistic missiles, is now being used to identify patterns in money transfers. Despite all of these efforts, Williams (1997, 25) is of the opinion that the gap between money launderers and enforcers has widened rather than closed, particularly with the unregulated financial environment created in the former Soviet Union as well as in much of the developing world. The impact of electronic financial transactions (money dry cleaning) and cyber-money (electronic currency) present an expanding challenge. "Tacit connivance" (Willaims, 1997, 27), in which bankers and legitimate operators rationalize their cooperation with drug traffickers with the theme that, if they do not do it, rival institutions will, will be a continuing problem. Connivance quickly becomes collusion.

Potter and Gaines (1996, 43–44) point out how it has been common in U.S. history for the under- and upperworlds to develop ongoing corrupt relationships. Shearson/American Express, Merrill, Lynch, the Miami National Bank, Citibank, and others eagerly laundered money for organized crime syndicates (Lernoux, 1984b; Moldea, 1978). In the famous "Pizza Connection Case," in which Sicilian gangsters used U.S. pizza parlors to sell heroin, millions of dollars were laundered through New York City banks with the Merrill, Lynch brokerage firm depositing huge amounts of small-denomination bills on their behalf. Further, $13.5 million was laundered through E. F. Hutton.

Asia

International examples of organized white-collar deviance abound. The Japanese yakuza, now called "Boryokudan" ("violent ones") by the Japanese police, is according to Fenton Bresler (1992) the top business in Japan, earning 5.6 billion pounds sterling in 1990, or more than second-ranked Toyota. In addition to illegal enterprises such as extortion, gambling, prostitution, and drug running, about one-fifth of their earnings are from legitimate businesses. Incredibly, there were an estimated 87,000 yakuza in Japan in 1990. By comparison, the U.S. Cosa Nostra at its peak was never estimated to have more than 5,000 made members. In 1991 the presidents of two of Japan's top stockbrokerages (Nomura Securities and Nikko Securities) resigned when it was learned their firms loaned two billion yen to Susumu Ishii, the boss of Inagawa Kai, the second-largest yakuza group. In 1996, it was revealed that an additional two billion yen had been loaned by 17 other financial institutions to Yamaguchi Gumi, the largest yakuza group. These firms covered any losses the yakuza may have experienced when the stockmarket took a dive. Political parties and corporations have long used yakuza as muscle men (security) at stockholder meetings.

An expert on Taiwanese organized crime, Lin Chung-cheng, estimates that 20 percent of the country's economy is "underground" and much of that is mob linked. He expresses concern with the mob's influence in presidential political campaigns (Shaw, 1997). A recent crackdown on United Bamboo, Taiwan's largest organized crime group, led Zhang An-la (a.k.a. White Wolf), the honorary godfather, to remark, "These brothers may not use conventional or legal methods in the construction industry. But, politicians involved in construction also rig bids. So why sweep the brothers out?... They're sweeping out the brothers while covering up their own crimes" (Cheng, 1997). Nearly $26 billion in public works project funds are estimated to have been siphoned off by organized crime and crooked officials and politicians between 1990 and 1996. An estimated 10 percent of the national legislature are believed to have criminal links.

Product Counterfeiting

A continuing hallmark of organized crime operations has been "illegal enterprise." What could be more natural for organized crime groups to get involved in than product counterfeiting, particularly since it involves supplying an illicit product in public demand? Officials have recently found at least three triad groups in Los Angeles involved in a counterfeit software ring (IACC, 1997). The Vietnamese gang Born to Kill (BTK) uses extortion to convince merchants in New York's Chinatown to sell BTK-made counterfeit Rolex and Cartier watches.

The movement of legitimate business into such product counterfeiting is well illustrated by the black market pirate culture of knock-offs in Italy (Tagliabue, 1997). Industrial piracy is increasing within one of the most skilled sectors of the Italian economy, the manufacturers of luxury handbags, shoes, skirts, and scarves. Ironically, these bogus products are indistinguishable from real Chanel, Prada, and Dior products because they are illegally made by the same producers, even competing against themselves on the world market. Competing with other pirating centers such as Hong Kong, Taiwan, and Thailand, everything from fake Gucci bags and belts to American software, recordings, and books racked up an estimated $6 billion in 1996. The countries of the worst industrial pirates in 1995 were Turkey, China, Thailand, Italy, and Colombia, according to the European Brands Association (Taglibue, 1997). The largest producers of illegal software in 1996 were to be found in the U.S., Japan, China, and South Korea, says the Business Software Alliance. In 1995, illegal video production was highest in Russia, Italy, China, Britain, and Japan, according to the Motion Picture Association of America, while the International Federation of the Phonographic Industry found the highest number of illegal copies of CDs and cassettes in Russia, China, India, Pakistan, and Mexico.

Discussion

Traditionally in criminology "organized crime/deviance" has been viewed as a separate category of wrongdoing from "white-collar crime/deviance" such as occupational and corporate crime. In this chapter we have documented the increasing interrelationships and similarities of these categories. Organized and white collar crime/deviance promise to become increasingly blurred, multinational, and symbiotic in the twenty-first century.

Critical Thinking Exercise 6-1: Criminal Interconnections

One of the central points of this chapter is that organized crime is not an alien conspiracy, allowed to bully its way into wherever it pleases. Rather, organized criminal syndicates exist in interrelationship with corrupt political organizations and corporations. Go to a data base like Info Track, Proquest, or the Reader's Guide. Do a search on a global organized crime topic such as corruption, money laundering, or a related topic (yours or instructor's choice). List all cases in which organized crime syndicates were involved in a criminal act with law enforcement personnel, judges, politicians, and/or corporate executives. Do you notice any patterns of corruption in your study?

Chapter 7

A Theory of
White-Collar Deviance

Why White-Collar Deviance?

- On October 23, 1989, Charles and Carol Stuart were on their way home from a Boston hospital childbirth class. When Charles pulled the car over to allegedly check some problem, he pulled a gun on his wife (who was eight months pregnant) and shot her at point-blank range. Initially, Stuart told police his wife had been killed by a black gunman. Two months later, Charles confessed that he shot his wife because he stood to collect hundreds of thousands of dollars in life insurance, with which he could realize his American Dream of owning a restaurant (Derber, 1992, 8).

- In 1987, a poll was taken of 200,000 college freshmen by the American Council on Education. Of those polled, 76 percent said that it was very important to be financially well off. Twenty years earlier, only 44 percent of freshmen held such materialistic views. In 1976, 83 percent of respondents felt it important to develop a philosophy of life. In 1987, only 39 percent of students expressed such a wish. A 1990 report by the Carnegie Foundation for the Advancement of Teaching complained of a breakdown of civility on the nation's college campuses. Especially alarming were epidemics of cheating by students, racial attacks, hate crimes, and rapes on campus. Studies at the University of Tennessee and Indiana University found that a majority of students at each campus admitted to submitting papers that were written by others, or to copying large sections of friend's papers (Derber, 1992).

- Elite universities, including Stanford, Harvard, MIT, Cal Tech, and others have all recently experienced scandals involving the unlawful expenditure of research funds. Some of the illegal purchases included country club memberships, yachts, going-away parties for administrators, and flowers.

The problem that runs through these examples has many names: "social breakdown" (Dissent, 1991), the rise of "the morally loose individual" (Nisbet, 1988), instrumental and expressive "wilding" (Derber, 1992), and the "ethical crisis of Western civilization" (Lipson, 1993). Whatever one chooses to call it, the problem of moral decline is a major cause of white-collar deviance as well as many other types of deviant behavior.

White-Collar Deviance and the Sociological Imagination, A Paradigm for Analysis *(Simon, 1995; 1997)*

We began our discussion of white-collar deviance with a look at the power structure of American society. The power elite model was developed by C. Wright Mills in the 1950s (Mills, 1956). As our examination reveals, a great deal of evidence exists to support this notion of interrelated corporate, media, political, and military elites. Further, in Chapter 2, we explored the existence of the so-called "higher immorality," the set of deviant practices that Mills claimed goes on in elite circles. Again, our examination demonstrated case after case of the higher immorality that has taken place since Mills wrote in the 1950s. We have also noted how the nature of the higher immorality has changed, with scandal now an institutionalized phenomenon within the Executive Office of the President, Congress, and the National Security state's intelligence apparatus. What remains is to account for the theoretical causes of white-collar deviance.

Again, we turn to one of Mills's conceptions, the sociological imagination (Mills, 1956). The sociological imagination is a paradigm, a model for looking at social reality, in this case social problems like white-collar deviance. Paradigmatic models can be used to develop a number of scientific theories. "What is important," Mills notes, "is the fact that neither the correctness nor the inaccuracy of any of the specific theories necessarily confirms or upsets the usefulness of the adequacy of the models. The models can be used for the construction of many theories" (Mills, 1960, 3).

Thus, in this chapter we will first lay out the paradigm for constructing a theory of white-collar deviance, and then proceed to make various theoretical statements derived from the model.

The paradigm raises questions regarding three levels of social analysis. These include:

1. **The macro level of analysis.** Here we must explain how the institutional structures and the cultural values of a given society contribute to white-collar deviance.

2. **The immediate milieu.** Here we must explain how the immediate environment of everyday life, especially the structure and characteristics of the bureaucratic organizations in which people work, contribute to the planning and commission of acts of white-collar deviance.

3. **The individual level.** Here we must explain how individual personality characteristics of elites and those in their employ figure in the planning and commission of acts of white-collar deviance. Specifically, how do issues of character structure and alienation contribute to the commission of white-collar deviance?

We move to an analysis of macro level concerns, specifically values and institutional structures.

White-Collar Deviance and American Values, The American Dream

Messner and Rosenfeld (1994, 6) argue that the causes of crime lie within the same values and behaviors that are usually viewed as part of the American version of success. "The American Dream" is defined as a "broad cultural ethos that entails a commitment to the goal of material success, to be pursued by everyone in society, under conditions of open individual competition." The power of the American Dream comes from the widely shared values that it includes:

An achievement orientation. This includes pressure to "make something " of oneself, to set goals and achieve them. Achieving material success is one way that personal worth is measured in America. While this is a shaky basis for self-esteem, it is nevertheless true that Americans view their personal worth much like a stock, one that rises or falls with the realization of money making.

Individualism. This refers to the notion that Americans possess not only autonomy, but basic individual rights. Americans make individualistic decisions regarding marriage and career choices, religion, political outlook, and probably thousands of other issues. The result is that individualism and achievement combine to produce anomie, because fellow Americans often become rivals and competitors for rewards and status. Intense personal competition increases pressure to succeed (Horney, 1938). Often this means that rules by which success is obtained are disregarded when they threaten to interfere with personal goals. The case of Charles Stuart, described above, offers an extreme example of anomie and the American Dream.

Universalism. This includes the idea that the American Dream is open to all. Universalism means that the chances of success and failure are possibilities that are open to everyone. Fear of failure is intense in America, and it increases the pressure to abandon conformity to rules governing proper conduct in favor of expedience.

The "fetishism" of money. Money has attained an almost sacred quality in American life. It is the way Americans keep score in the game of success, and, as noted, there are no rules that tell us when enough is enough. What is stressed in the American Dream are ends over means. As Elliott Currie (1991) notes in his discussion of a market society, the pursuit of private gain has become the organizing principle for all of social life. Charles Derber (1992) argues that, during the Reagan-Bush era, increasing inequality, along with an ethic of "greed is good," combined to give the American character an element of narcissism. Narcissism is a personality disorder, a mental illness, characterized by distorted self-love and, most important, selfishness coupled with a lack of guilt. The Reagan-Bush ideology of self-reliance stimulated large numbers of upper-world crooks to engage in a quest for power, status, and attention in a "money culture." The result was an unrestrained quest for personal gain.

Sociologist Robert Merton (1994) pointed out over a half century ago that the great contradiction of American culture concerned its stress on winning and success, but a lack of opportunity to achieve such success. A portion of this contradiction is due to what sociologist Emile Durkheim (1966) described as anomie, a social situation where norms are unclear. Success in America has no official limits, the private accumulation of wealth is without "a final stopping point" (Merton, 1994). No matter what their income level, people want about 50 percent more money (which, of course, becomes 50 percent more once it is achieved).

Achieving success via force and fraud has always been considered smart, so smart that for a number of decades our culture has lionized gangsters. Beginning with Al Capone, we have come to admire Mafia dons who do not hesitate to take shortcuts to success. Thus *People* magazine's 1989 cover story on Gambino family godfather John Gotti pictured the don as so tough that he could punch his way through a cement block. A multimillionaire, with plenty of charisma, *People* noted, Gotti is also a loyal family man, who has never cheated on his wife. The fact that he personally has murdered a number of rivals is largely accepted as being an occupational requirement.

Merton (1994, 116) noted that crime "is a very common phenomenon" among all social classes in the United States. A study of 1,700 middle-class New Yorkers in 1947 indicated that 99 percent of them admitted to committing crimes violating one of New York's 49 criminal offenses, for which they could have been imprisoned for at least a year. Moreover, 64 percent of the men and 29 percent of the women reported committing felonies. Thus one of the myths about crime is that America is divided into two populations, one law abiding, the other criminal.

Social critic James Adams (1929, 38), who coined the term "The American Dream," once remarked that many people coming to America's shores were relatively law abiding before they arrived here. People "were made lawless by America, rather than America being made lawless by them." It has been American elites that have served as role models (examples) to ordinary people. Thus white-collar deviance provides an excuse for nonelites to engage in crime without feeling guilty. White-collar deviance also sends the message that it is stupid not to commit crime if one has the opportunity. Many drug dealers and street gang members have remarked that they are just doing what the Rockefellers, Carnegies, and other robber barons did in the nineteenth century—establishing monopolies.

Aside from the values associated with the American Dream, white-collar deviance is also related to the social structure of American society.

Social Structure, The Dominance of Elite Institutions

The structure of American society is that of a mass society. A mass society is characterized by a capitalistic economy dominated by huge multinational corporations. Corporate elites (owners and managers) frequently take temporary positions in government and its military establishment.

In the United States, the economic institution has always taken precedence over other institutions in American life. This has immense implications for the nature of America's social problems.

America is the only nation in the history of the world whose founding creed involved the inalienable right to pursue happiness. The American concept of happiness has always involved the unlimited accumulation of profit and property. The goal of making money has been widely accepted as the definition of happiness and success, a central feature of what is called The American Dream.

So important has the goal of accumulating wealth, of achieving The American Dream, become that profit in America has frequently taken place without the restraints placed on capitalist economies in other nations. In the United States, attempts to regulate the excesses of business have been criticized as government interference, or socialism.

Second, other institutions in American life have had to accommodate to the needs of business. Thus most people go to college, not because they are fascinated by learning, but because it leads to a middle-class occupation afterwards. America has always been the most anti-intellectual nation in the Western world—precisely because its primary definition of success has involved making money. Thus colleges and universities offer evening and weekend programs, many of them in business, because people's jobs take precedence over the needs of educational and other institutions. The requirements of work also take precedence over the needs of family life. The United States remains the only advanced industrial democracy without paid family leave, without national health care, and without an extended family vacation policy, precisely because the needs of business are given precedence over everything else in the American institutional order. Moreover, despite all the political rhetoric about the importance of the American family, it is nearly impossible to support a family in this country if parents are unemployed.

Government, too, has historically been subservient to the needs of business. Now that the government is a central part of the economy, the primary responsibility of modern government is not to provide for the needs of its citizens, but to assure economic growth. Much of American foreign and defense policy is about protecting the holdings of multinational corporations, not in assuring that human rights and democracy are encouraged in other nations. The United States has a long history of supporting oppressive regimes that are friendly to American business interests. Moreover, American government at all levels grants generous subsidies, tax breaks, loans and loan guarantees, as well as government contracts to American businesses in the hope of stimulating economic growth. This is one reason that American federal government has spent over $4 trillion on defense since 1947, much of it on expensive weapons systems. For all these reasons it is now more appropriate to speak of a political economy in which political and economic activity have become interrelated in a myriad of ways.

Likewise, white-collar deviance often requires the explicit coordination of a number of bureaucratic institutions in order to be planned and executed, yet remain undetected and unpunished. Thus, the Farben case required the participation of the Nazi government in order for slave labor to be utilized in the building of synthetic chemical plants. Similarly, throughout this book we have cited numerous additional examples, illustrating how white-collar deviance involved interorganizational cooperation.

- For years, government and business groups have employed organized crime to perform illegal and unethical acts. In the early 1960s, the Central Intelligence Agency (CIA) hired Mafia members to assassinate Fidel Castro. Mafia-generated drug money is routinely laundered through banks in Miami, often with the bankers' full knowledge (Lernoux, 1984b, 186–198).
- In Chapter 2, we described the cozy relationship between Pentagon employees and defense industry consultants. Promises of positions in the defense industry for retiring Pentagon employees sometimes resulted in their providing insider information to defense contractors.
- In Chapter 2, we described further episodes of Mafia–CIA ties in money laundering through a variety of savings and loans. In Chapter 3, we noted the possible ties between CIA and Mafia personnel in execution and alleged coverup of the assassination of Pres-

ident John F. Kennedy. Also in Chapter 3, we explored more fully the implications and history of this so-called secret government (Moyers, 1988).

These examples show that white-collar deviance often involves links between business, government, and, at times, other institutions, such as organized crime syndicates. And because of these interorganizational ties, white-collar deviance has a great chance of going undetected and unpunished (or at least lightly punished). As we have discussed, economic elites regularly participate in political processes involving candidate selection, monetary contributions to candidates and parties, and lobbying. This means that elites have great influence over the content and character of the law. As a result, many acts that might otherwise become crimes are prevented from becoming illegal in the first place. Thus, drug company Hoffman-LaRoche successfully kept amphetamines out of federal control by paying a Washington law firm three times the amount of the annual budget of the Senate subcommittee seeking legislation for tighter controls. Moreover, when white-collar deviance is made illegal, it is often treated quite differently than nonwhite-collar deviance. For instance, a number of the environmental protection laws require corporations to monitor the pollution levels at their own factories. Other laws only address breaking regulations per se; what happens as a result of the infraction is ignored. In England, a company was found to be responsible for an accident that resulted in the deaths of five workers. The firm was prosecuted for not properly maintaining or inspecting the equipment; it was not charged with the deaths of the workers. Such laws focus on intention in order to substantiate guilt, which makes it virtually impossible to prove fault in the case of worker injury or fatality (Box, 1983). Under these circumstances, it is little wonder that many acts of white-collar deviance constitute violations of civil or administrative law, rather than criminal law. Moreover, the penalties for such violations—barring a serious public outcry or a request by elites themselves for government regulation—tend to remain relatively lenient.

Other institutions in American life have been penetrated by the language, ethics, and requirements of American business. Terms like "bottom line" and "cash flow" have become part of everyday language. Many politicians believe the way to solve the problems of government is to run government like a business. Thus, in 1992 Ross Perot ran for president, promising to bring the principles that had made him a billionaire businessman to bear on governmental problems. Moreover, many individuals from the private sector are appointed to cabinet-level positions in America.

The causal links between the macro-level variables of the American Dream and institutional dominance by the political economy are numerous. Several possible hypotheses related to the sociological imagination paradigm follow from this macro-level theory:

1. Rates of elite and nonelite deviance are not constant. They wax and wane in response to changes in the U.S. value system and changing institutional conditions. Thus both elite and nonwhite-collar deviance will be higher in those historical periods when there is more emphasis placed on the values associated with The American Dream than in periods when the culture emphasizes values such as community, teamwork, spirituality, and so on.

2. Likewise, now that the government has become a central part of the economy, and that the ethics of business dominate governmental institutions, both corporate crime and political scandals will occur at the same time, and frequently be interrelated.

Rates of deviance are influenced not only by macro considerations, but by organizational considerations as well.

The Characteristics of Bureaucratic Structures

We agree with those who insist that white-collar deviance is explained by examining the nature of the actors' roles within an organization, as well as the bureaucratic structures (characteristics) that shape such roles (Ermann & Lundman, 1982). Bureaucracy, as a form of social organization, possesses certain structural characteristics that account for both its amoral ethical nature and potential to generate acts of great harm.

Modern bureaucracies are characterized by several things, including (1) centralization of authority, (2) creation of specialized vocabularies and ideologies, and (3) fragmentation and routinization of tasks. Each of these characteristics in turn often produces a number of social and psychological processes, all of which help create the environment for white-collar deviance.

Centralization of Authority

Obedience to elite authority is of central importance to the study of organizations and the deviance they commit. Orders, decisions, and plans that are unethical or illegal are often carried out by underlings, in part because they feel they have no choice; they feel powerless to disobey, regardless of the intent of the order. Examples of such cases are numerous, including the My Lai massacre, Watergate, and the General Electric price-fixing case of 1961.

Surprisingly, those who seem most powerless include both those "far removed from the centers of power and...those relatively close" Kelman (1976, 308). Thus, while such perceived powerlessness is usually characteristic of the lower-middle and lower classes, Kelman (1973) found a striking degree of such conformity among high-level military officers and bureaucratic functionaries, as well. Kanter and Kanter (1988) have discussed the existence of widespread feelings of powerlessness at both top and middle levels of organizations. However, the empirical study of such powerlessness and its relationship to organizational and interorganizational deviance remains understudied. We do know that conformity among those in the higher circles of the power elite results for a variety of reasons.

One important structural condition that perpetuates white-collar deviance is the massive centralization of power in the hands of the elite themselves. Such centralization tends to guarantee the conformity of underling bureaucrats, either corporate or governmental, for two reasons. Because they possess such overwhelming power, elites can often secure nonelite cooperation by giving direct orders to engage in deviant acts. Refusal to conform to such directives may result in severe sanctions for potential dissidents, including being fired, court-martialed, blacklisted, demoted, or not promoted. Still other sanctions might include transfer to a less desirable assignment or geographic location, or forced early retirement. (Glass, 1976)

Thus, the distinction often made between those deviant acts committed by workers for their personal enrichment versus those committed on behalf of their employer is misleading (Edelhertz et al., 1977, 8). That is, given the centralization of power in organizations, acts committed on behalf of an organization often involve personal rewards for nonelites, as well as the threat of sanctions for noncompliance with elite directives. Moreover, people who occupy positions in bureaucratic organizations play roles for which they have been trained. As such, they are acutely aware that, as people, they are replaceable, interchangeable parts, mere occupants of bureaucratic positions (MacCoby, 1976). This is certainly a dehumanizing realization for the individuals involved. Nonetheless, such conformity is the rule rather than the exception.

Quite clearly, much conformity is due to feelings of powerlessness. On the other hand, no organization operates by the threat of sanction alone. Elite authority—especially that of a national president or an upper corporate manager—is obeyed in large measure because it is recognized as legitimate. Such authority is seldom questioned. This legitimacy is part of another aspect of white-collar deviance, the higher immorality. As we discussed in Chapter 2, the higher immorality includes many forms of deviance that are not considered to be particularly wrong by the elites who engage in them (e.g., antitrust violations). A number of social psychological factors account for elite approval of such deviance.

Specialized Vocabularies and Ideologies

From a social-psychological perspective, the higher immorality consists of a subculture that forms at the top of bureaucratic organizations. A small group of power holders tends to develop precepts and customs delicately balanced between conventional and criminal (deviant) behavior, as well as objectives that may be obtained through both deviant and non-deviant means. Part of this subculture of elite behavior consists of norms and sentiments that make deviance permissible. That is, deviant acts are filtered through a sanitizing, ideological prism, which gives them the appearance of not being criminal or deviant.

Part of this sanitizing ideology involves the adoption of special vocabularies of motive. A number of recent case studies of white-collar deviance report the construction of an elaborate vocabulary designed to provide both motive and neutralization of guilt (Janis, 1971). Janis made this observation of the Johnson administration's Vietnam policy group:

> *The members of the group adopted a special vocabulary for describing the Vietnam war, using such terms as body count, armed reconnaissance, and surgical strikes, which they picked up from their military colleagues. The Vietnam policy makers, by using this professional military vocabulary, were able to avoid in their discussions with each other all direct references to human suffering and thus to form an attitude of detachment similar to that of surgeons. (Janis, 1971, 73)*

Likewise, the Nazi SS, in their extermination of the Jews, adopted such a policy in dealing with "the Jewish problem." Special language rules were adopted. Terms like *special treatment,* and *clearing up fundamental problems,* were utilized as euphemisms for mass murder (Arendt, 1964). Moreover, such vocabularies are symptomatic of the alienation, stereotyping, and dehumanization involved in white-collar deviance.

A final aspect of the vocabulary of motives involves a series of mechanisms specifically designed to neutralize guilt. While such mechanisms are found in almost all deviant subcultures, in the case of the elite, their adoption is more direct and absolute, since the elite themselves have generated and established the ideology of deviance, as discussed earlier.

When applied to white-collar deviance, the general ideology of deviance becomes interlaced with a number of guilt-reducing "techniques of neutralization" or rationalizations (Sykes & Matza, 1957).

1. *Denying responsibility.* The rationalization here is that what went wrong was not the organization's fault. Mechanical malfunctions in the workplace resulting in employee deaths are termed "accidents." Likewise, consumers are blamed for their ignorance in "misusing" products that cause harm. Or blame may be shifted to other officials or organizations, as when businesses blame a problem on a lack of government regulations.

2. *Deny victimization/dehumanization.* This guilt-reducing mechanism functions to convince interested parties that no real person was or is being victimized. Such denials usually take one of two forms. The first may be *object-directed dehumanization;* it involves the perception of others as statistics or commodities in a vast numbers game. People are no longer viewed as human beings but as a portion of a less than human collectivity (e.g., the enemy, the market, the competition, or the government).

Janis has described the presence of a second denial mechanism at work in elite circles. Termed *groupthink,* it refers to "a mode of thinking that people engage in where they are deeply involved in a cohesive in-group, where the members' striving for unanimity overrides their motivations to realistically appraise alternative courses of action" (Janis, 1972; Bernard et al., 1971). Groupthink reduces individual capacity for moral judgment, enhancing the formation of stereotyped thought by in-group members. Thus, during the Vietnam era, members of the Johnson inner circle of policy makers created stereotypes portraying the poor of the world as wanting to take from the rich and espousing Asian disregard for human life. The Vietnamese were also the subject of racial stereotypes developed by U.S. troops, who used terms like *mooks, gooks, slopes,* and *dinks,* and described the people as barbaric and uncivilized, deserving of ruthless slaughter.

3. *Authorization/higher loyalties.* Another rationalization technique, termed authorization, stems directly from the legitimacy of elite power. Authorization is an ideological device involving the creation of some transcendent mission whereby elites stake claim to supposedly higher purposes that are clearly outside legal and ethical boundaries. In the case of government, such purposes usually relate to the national interest, executive privilege, or fighting the Communist menace or other foreign threat. In the case of corporate deviance, such notions usually involve meeting profit targets or protecting the interests of the stockholders. Such amoral justifications have been propagated for decades by conservative social critics. Milton Friedman (1972, 133), for example, has long argued that businesses possess virtually no social responsibility for their acts:

> *There is one and only one social responsibility of business: to use its resources and engage in activities designed to increase its profits so long as it stays within the rules of the game . . . [and] engages in open and free competition, without deception or fraud. . . . Few trends could so thoroughly undermine the very foundations of our free society as the acceptance by corporate officials of a social responsibility other than to make as much money for their stockholders as possible. This is a fundamentally subversive doctrine. If business people do have a social responsibility other than making maximum profits, how are they to know what it is?*

Such statements can easily be interpreted to mean that any profit-making behavior in which businesses engage is morally acceptable, as long as no laws are broken.

4. *Condemning condemners.* This mechanism is used to handle critics of deviant behavior. Namely, attention is diverted away from the real issue and focused on another topic or even the critics themselves. For instance, corporations often attack proposals involving further government regulation as being opposed to free enterprise. Governments, in turn, often view critics of civil rights abuses or war crimes as "Communist sympathizers."

These neutralization techniques, along with an official ideology of deviance accepted by general society, ensure that elites may commit deviant acts without guilt or damage to their respectable self-images. Moreover, underlings will come to share these ideological visions and adopt the Adolf Eichmann excuse of elite authorization (i.e., "only following orders").

Finally, these ideological constructions allow elites to attribute real deviance and crime to the lower classes, thus mystifying themselves as to their own deviance and misdirecting perceptions of the distribution of societal harm in general. The dimensions of such harm are even greater when committed by organizations because of the nature of modern organizational life.

Fragmentation and Routinization

Decisions to commit deviant acts—even murder—are carried out within established routines. Such routines not only involve filling out forms, reports, and schedules. Indeed, a number of scholars maintain that the large, complex nature of modern organizations encourages deviance, for two reasons: (1) specialized tasks involve the same routines, whether they are deviant or legitimate; and (2) elites both discourage being informed by lower functionaries of scandals within organizations and also hide acts of white-collar deviance from functionaries and the public (Silver & Geller, 1971).

Related to the specialization of tasks found in modern organizations is alienation, which denotes "a mode of experience in which the person experiences him/herself [and other people] as alien" (Fromm, 1955, 111). Within bureaucratic organizations, alienation is manifested partially through distance. For example, workers engaged in producing dioxin never witnessed the effects of the chemical on the residents of Love Canal in Niagara Falls. Similarly, pilots serving in the Vietnam War convinced themselves that they were bombing geographic targets on maps, not killing civilians in their homes. In modern society, technology has produced a world of such extreme distances that victimization becomes impersonal.

Image Construction and Inauthenticity: Front Activities

The centralization of power and fragmentation of tasks in large organizations creates still another important aspect of white-collar deviance, a world of image construction that masks acts of deviance behind a smokescreen of "front" activities.

A number of scholars have commented on the subject of front activities involved in white-collar deviance. Yet the term is vague and has come to include everything from making deceptive or false statements about a deviant act (or series of acts) to the creation of pseudoevents and phony crises by news media, public relations firms, and governmental agencies (Boorstin, 1961). Quite simply and directly, front activities may be described as management via image manipulation.

During the Watergate era, for example, a number of commentators observed that the White House staff felt that the basic problem was successfully managing public opinion (Simon, 1978). And during the Carter era, White House staffers commonly complained that the confidence gap between the White House and the public was due to an image problem.

Front activities to camouflage deviance is a common and accepted practice of virtually all types of bureaucratic entities. Turk believes that lying within government agencies is "a routine tactic" and that its use is limited only by expediency (Turk, 1981). Such lying is accompanied by many front activities: (1) providing only the information requested by investigating officials or citizens, (2) destroying or conveniently misfiling incriminating items before they have to be produced, (3) fragmenting information so it appears incomplete and out of sequence, and (4) depicting deviant acts as the work of "bad apples" or even past leaders. Another common ploy is to deny access to information on the basis of "need to know," "national security," or other justifications to hide embarrassing secrets (Bernstein, 1976).

The discussion in this chapter has centered around the structural causes of white-collar deviance. A central portion of this discussion has emphasized that the causes and consequences of white-collar deviance are hidden—even mystified—from both elites and non-elites, from victimizers, as well as from victims (Thio, 1988).

This mystification of white-collar deviance via an official ideology and a host of guilt-neutralizing techniques and front activities has serious implications for those who occupy positions in bureaucratic hierarchies. The alienation and dehumanization that characterizes white-collar deviance produces a condition that has been described as *inauthentic* (Etzioni, 1968; Baxter, 1982; Seeman, 1966). As an objective social condition, inauthenticity refers to maintaining overt positive appearances, despite the presence of negative underlying realities (Etzioni, 1968). Within powerful organizations, inauthenticity is indicated by the amount of resources spent on various front activities, as the organization tries to convince workers, clients, and the general public of its positive attributes in the face of negative, often tightly held secrets.

Given these central variables regarding modern organizations, bureaucratic concerns may be hypothesized to cause white-collar deviance in a number of respects:

- Hypothesis: The more centralized authority within an organization, the more secrecy, and the more white-collar deviance will be committed.
- Hypothesis: Organizations that engage in one type of white-collar deviance (e.g., price-fixing or environmental law violations) will also tend to engage in other types of white-collar deviance (e.g., sexual harassment or other civil rights violations).
- Hypothesis: Organizations that engage in high levels of inauthentic front activities (e.g., public relations and image-enhancing advertising) will also be engaging in high levels of deviant activity.

Finally, it is likewise important to understand the types of personality traits that are likely to characterize individuals who engage in deviant acts within organizations.

White-Collar Deviance and "Individual" Characteristics

Certain people who work in organizations also possess unique personality characteristics that lead them to engage in deviant acts of various kinds. Presthus has noted that one type of personality is particularly successful in making it to the top of bureaucratic organizations (Presthus, 1978). Such an individual exudes charisma via a superficial sense of warmth and charm. He or she is able to make decisions easily because matters are viewed in black-and-white terms. This requires the ability to categorize and thus dehumanize individuals as entities for the purpose of making decisions concerning layoffs, firings, plant closings, and advertising campaigns.

Clinard's study (1983) of managers of large corporations found that those executives likely to engage in acts of organizational deviance were often recruited from outside the companies they administered. These executives were interested in getting publicity in financial journals, showing quick increases in profits, and moving on to higher positions, usually within two years.

Recent studies of work alienation demonstrate that people with such high extrinsic needs also tend to be workaholics, displaying what are called type-A personality characteristics. Such traits involve "free floating hostility, competitiveness, a high need for socially approved success, unbridled ambitions, aggressiveness, impatience, and polyphasic thought and action" (i.e., trying to do two things at once) (Kanungo, 1982, 157). Such persons also frequently exhibit the lowest scores on mental health measures in such studies. Thus, victimizers in white-collar deviance often turn into victims, in a sense, dehumanizing both their victims and themselves.

Finally, there is evidence that, within single organizational hierarchies, many of the same people who execute deviance on behalf of the organization also commit acts against it for their own personal gain. In a Canadian study, Reasons (1982) noted that supervisory personnel accounted for approximately two-thirds of the business dishonesty over the last decade. Furthermore, within the organizations that commit deviant acts, those individuals who participated were likely to engage in acts of deviance for personal gain against their employers. This may be true because such employees resent being asked to engage in deviant acts and thus strike out against their employers in revenge. Or perhaps, having demonstrated their corrupt moral nature to their employees, such organizations invite acts of deviance against them by providing an untrustworthy role model. Again, we come to a similar conclusion regarding conformity within bureaucratic organizations.

One useful concept in explaining the deviant behavior of some individuals is *attachment disorder,* a condition that effects 30 million children in the United States (Keough, 1993). These children are frequently the victims of incest, abuse, or neglect. They are unable to bond—to become attached—to other human beings. As children they often strangle animals, start fires, try to drown their playmates, and steal, lie, and inflict physical damage on other people's belongings.

The symptoms associated with attachment disorder involve severe forms of inauthenticity and dehumanization. Disordered children do not treat themselves or other people as human beings with needs for love and recognition. Consequently, their symptoms reflect extreme forms of alienation, as follows:

- Self-destructiveness is common. Disordered children often stab themselves with knives, and they exhibit no fear of dangerous heights or other risky situations (like reckless driving, or robbing convenience stores).

In adulthood, these people become the salespeople who sell unsafe used cars, the bosses who steal their subordinates' ideas, the consumers who fail to pay their debts, or the serial killers (like Ted Bundy or Charles Manson). Attachment-disordered children exposed to phoniness (personal inauthenticy) have no idea how to relate to other people. Consequently, they tend to behave insincerely when expressing love, or other emotions. They tend to be perceived as untrustworthy, and come across as manipulators. One parent of an attachment-disordered child remarked that it was like living with a "robot" (Keogh, 1993, 56).

- Stealing, hording, and gorging of food and possessions is common among attachment-disordered children. Not knowing how to form attachments to other people, disordered children experience severe unmet emotional needs. As a substitute for needs involving love and human contact, disordered children often steal and hoard items like food, even if they are not hungry.
- Conning behavior is also common. Acts of deception take place in both childhood and adulthood. As children, disordered persons often feign helplessness, act loving or cute, smart or beguiling, whatever suits their need at the time to obtain what they want. In adulthood, such behavior many manifest itself as fraud and con games.
- A final symptom of attachment disorder involves what is termed "crazy lying" (Keough, 1993, 55–56). Such children lie even under the most extreme circumstances, especially when they are caught directly in the act of misbehaving. Crazy lying means that lies will be told even when they are obvious.

Organizational Conditions and the Production of Deviant Personalities

It is much too facile to argue that white-collar deviance is caused by deviant personalities—people who were predisposed to deviant acts before they arrived at the organization's doorstep. Reality, unfortunately, is a good deal more complicated but much more interesting than this. There are instances when organizations can and do influence workers to commit deviant acts. Such motivations are frequently associated with the presence of alienation within organizations.

Thus Boston University professors Donald Kanter and Philip Mirvis (1989, 34) have substantiated that alienation is surprisingly widespread in America. In their analysis of a national sample of data, about half of their respondents agree with the statement that "most people are only out for themselves and that you are better off zapping them before they do it to you." Among their most important findings are that many people in American now take a cynical approach to the work they do, and that this cynicism extends from the very top to the lowly bottom of the American occupational structure.

White-collar workers often suffer from self-estrangement and other feelings of alienation associated with inauthenticity, as well. One of the most interesting studies in this regard is Jan Halper's *Quiet Desperation* (1988). Dr. Halper is a humanistic psychologist and organizational consultant. She interviewed 4,126 *Fortune 500* executives, middle mangers, and other professionals. She also intensely interviewed and provided free therapy to a sub-sample of executives.

To advance in their firms, these men must go along, sacrificing for the sake of their careers and companies. What Halper discovered was that a large proportion of these successful men were self-estranged, cut off from their feelings, wishes, wants, and needs. Their socialization both within their families and at work has taught them to deny their feelings, and to conform to the demands of job and family.

Halper found that a large portion of these men, almost two-thirds, are tired of being dutiful, loyal employees with no control over their jobs. Many suffer from reactions to denying their feelings for so long. Depression, feeling out of control, and other stress reactions are common. Some commit suicide.

Moreover, many of these men suffer the ill effects of not knowing who they are. They confuse the roles they play with who they are as people. Often they see themselves as a group of titles, "hero, breadwinner, lover, husband, father, warrior, empire builder, or mover-and-shaker" (Halper, 1988, 66). Relinquishing a role or two, through dismissal, retirement, or divorce, often leads to an identity crisis in which they feel they are nothing without their roles.

The credo these men are taught is that they are responsible for other's needs over and above their own. Often they avoid thinking about their own needs in order not to feel anticipated guilt—that they have violated the male credo. Despite their considerable accomplishments in many cases, a large number of these professionals suffer from low self-esteem. Frustrated at work, not intimately related to their wives, many of these men lead rich fantasy lives, preferring to see themselves as what they want, rather than who they really are. No matter how accomplished they are, many feel that they've not achieved success.

Many people have made a tacit bargain with the capitalist system, exchanging their work time for escapist consumption and leisure. Alienation at work was soon transformed into reification in the marketplace. It is often rendered in a reluctant, incomplete, and psychologically stressful manner. Moreover, such conformity is related to a number of types of more personal deviance, even among elites themselves. This is especially true when front activities fail and organizations are implicated in deviant acts. For instance, Eli Black, chairman of United Brands, committed suicide when it was revealed that his company was involved in a bribery scandal designed to hold down taxes on bananas. Similarly, Japanese executive Mitsushiro Shimada killed himself when his company was proven to be involved in the Grumman bribery scandal (Fisse & Braithwaite, 1983, 240). We can conclude then that, if official ideologies of deviance were fully accepted, embarrassed organizational elites would probably not resort to such desperate acts.

Taken together, this body of evidence leads to the following hypotheses:

- Hypothesis: Those individuals likely to engage in acts of white-collar deviance will tend to exhibit weak attachments to friends, family, and coworkers. Elite deviants are thus likely to suffer from all of the symptoms that accompany attachment disorder, including the ability to freely lie and manipulate and the inability to delay any sort of gratification.
- Hypothesis: Organizations headed by people suffering from alienation and attachment disorder will likely be "polyoffenders." As we have seen with General Electric

(Chapter 3), corporations that commit deviant acts in one area (e.g., defrauding the government in defense contracting) will likely commit deviant acts in other areas (e.g., ecological crime).

White-Collar Deviance and Victimization

A great deal of attention has been paid by sociologists in recent years to the effects of class, race, gender, and age on human behavior. Nowhere are these variables more relevant than in the study of the victims of white-collar deviance. Consider the following.

- In 1993, a Defense Department report found that 83 women and seven men were assaulted during the 1991 Tailhook Association convention at the Las Vegas Hilton. (The association's members are present and former navy fliers.) The 300-page report was based on more than 2,900 interviews. The report said that victims were "groped, pinched, fondled" and "bitten" by their assailants and that oral sex and sexual intercourse performed in front of others contributed to a "general atmosphere of debauchery" (World Almanac & Book of Facts, 1994, 52). Ultimately, Navy Secretary John Dalton asked for the removal of Admiral Frank Kelso, Chief of Naval Operations, and three other admirals were censured. Then 28 other admirals and one marine general received letters of caution. None of the officers involved ever went to prison.
- In November 1996, an Army sexual misconduct scandal broke at the Army's Aberdeen Proving Ground, Maryland, where Company Commander Captain Derrick Robertson was charged with rape; violation of the Ordnance Center and School Regulation that prohibits improper student/cadre relationships; conduct unbecoming an officer (fraternization); adultery; and obstruction of justice; and related charges. Staff Sergeants Nathanel Beach and Delmar Simpson, both drill sergeants, were charged with a variety of charges including rape, forcible sodomy, adultery, and obstruction of justice. As part of the investigation, the Army established an 800 number for receiving calls from victims, parents, and anyone with information regarding the sexual misconduct investigation (*Army News Service,* 1996).
- In April 1997, one drill instructor was convicted of raping six trainees (Associated Press, 1997a). The Aberdeen Proving Ground incident was the most serious case arising from a sexual deviance scandal that spread to U.S. military bases worldwide. The same former drill instructor had already been sentenced to 32 years in prison for having consensual sex with 11 trainees, a violation of army rules.
- Immediately following the former drill instructor's conviction, General John Longhouser, the Aberdeen Proving Ground's base commander, announced his retirement, admitting he had had an adulterous affair in 1992, while separated from his wife. The general reportedly became the subject of a Pentagon inquiry after an anonymous tip was received over a telephone hot line, established because of the charges leveled at Aberdeen drill sergeants. Other sexual harassment complaints were leveled against Air Force Lt. Kelly Flinn, the air force's only female bomber pilot. Kelly was given a general (less than honorable) discharge and forced to resign from the service. The incident touched off national debate over a sexual double standard wherein women charged

with sexual misconduct are forced to resign under less than honorable conditions, while males charged with similar behavior simply retire without penalty.

The debate intensified when Air Force Gen. Joseph Ralston, vice chairman of the Joint Chiefs of Staff, admitted to an adulterous affair, but President Clinton refused to accept his resignation, noting that he wanted the general to become his new top military advisor. Likewise, retired Sgt. Maj. Brenda Hoster accused the army's highest-ranking enlisted man, Sergeant Major McKinney, of grabbing her and demanding sex during a business trip. Hoster made her charges public after learning that Sgt. McKinney had been appointed to a panel investigating sexual misconduct in the army.

As usual, the Tailhook scandal and the 1997 army sexual harrassment scandals are symbolic of a much more widespread condition. In March 1994, four women serving in the military told a House committee that sexual harassment in the military is very common and that complaints about it often go unheeded. While stronger harassment rules have been issued by all branches of the armed services, and sensitivity training initiated, the female personnel claim that complaints of sexual harassment are met with disdain, ostracism, and in some cases transfer to a dead-end job (Associated Press, 1997a).

Sexual harassment has long been part of the organizational culture of the military, but it is certainly not limited to the armed services. Such harassment is most heavily centered in male-dominated occupations and organizations, and its toleration depends on the behavior of the elites in charge. If vigorously opposed, its prevalence can be overcome. The same is true of the denial of civil liberties to gays, over 10,000 of whom have been forcibly discharged from the U.S. military in the last 30 years, and there exist many forms of institutional discrimination against homosexuals and lesbians in American life (D'Emilio, 1993; Blumfield & Raymond, 1993).

Moreover, the Tailhook scandal points up one additional facet of organizational life, but this time the organization concerns the discipline of criminology itself. Recent literature has pointed out that women as victims of "white-collar crime" have gone unstudied, as indeed all such victims have (Szockyj & Fox, 1996). As this book has pointed out for a decade, many of the victims of international corporate dumping are women and children, but their victimization does not stop there.

- In 1991, 25 people were killed in a fire in a North Carolina chicken processing plant. Over 75 percent of the victims were female, in a plant where doors were locked to prevent workers from stealing chickens.
- The Dalkon Shield intrauterine birth control device which caused sterilization, infections, and sometimes death was a scandal that victimized women, as was Ovulen, an oral contraceptive—information about the dangerous side effects of which was withheld by it manufacturer, Searle Company. Likewise, carpal tunnel syndrome (an atrophication of thumb muscles) primarily effects female assembly-line workers and typists, who are primarily female. The same is true for conditions related to the use of video display terminals in offices, which can cause a variety of neck, back, and shoulder problems, as well as eyestrain and carpal tunnel syndrome. Likewise, in the textile industry, women make up from 62 to 89 percent of the workers in some of the various occupations that

are in danger of contracting "brown lung" disease from exposure to cotton dust (Gerber & Weeks, 1992).

Finally, the elderly suffer very high rates of victimization from white-collar crimes, especially scams (confidence games) and frauds.

- Over 10,000 elderly residents of Arizona alone are victims of fraudulent auto repairs and other consumer frauds, and the same is true nationwide (*60 Minutes,* 1994).
- The elderly are among those prone to cons by televangelist hucksters. In 1990, Reverend Jim Bakker received a 45-year prison sentence for mail fraud and related offenses when he misappropriated moneys supposedly raised to support his PTL ("Praise the Lord") ministries. Bakker's $150 million-a-year "Church" was well connected to the Reagan and Bush administrations, and to large corporations. One firm, Wedtech (later bankrupted in a scandal involving defense contracting fraud), paid thousands to silence Jessica Hahn, a secretary who was forced to engage in sex with Bakker and an associate. Many of the people who mailed money to Bakker were elderly, some of whom went without heat during the winter, and whose only incomes were their Social Security checks.
- The elderly's cost of living continues to rise faster than that of other consumers. This is because the elderly spend a higher proportion of their incomes on medical care and shelter than do other groups. Throughout the 1980s, a special consumer price index (cpi) for the elderly rose 19.5 percent compared with an 18.2 percent cpi rise for nonelderly persons living in urban areas (Simon, 1997, 421).

All these examples point to the fact that the most powerless people in American society and around the world are the leading victims of white-collar deviance of all kinds, and part of their continuing victimization includes a lack of attention to this serious social problem.

Symbiosis between White-Collar Deviance and Nonwhite-Collar Deviance

Another critical and often overlooked aspect of white-collar deviance when the subject is confined to so-called corporate criminality or political deviance involves the mutually dependent (symbiotic) relationship between certain types of elite and nonwhite-collar deviance. This point stems from an additional aspect of the sociological imagination that holds that society, as Mills put it, is "a network of rackets" (Mills, 1960, 17). Such rackets arise because of institutional contradictions, permanent conflicts within social structures (Simon, 1995; 1997). The symbiotic relationship between elite and nonwhite-collar deviance exists on two levels, tangible (involving money, products, and/or services) and symbolic (involving the construction of ideological and social structural variables) (Thio, 1988, 88–96).

Tangible Links
The tangible links between elite and nonwhite-collar deviance are represented in Figure 7.1. As the figure shows, the great bridge between elite and nonwhite-collar deviance is organized crime.

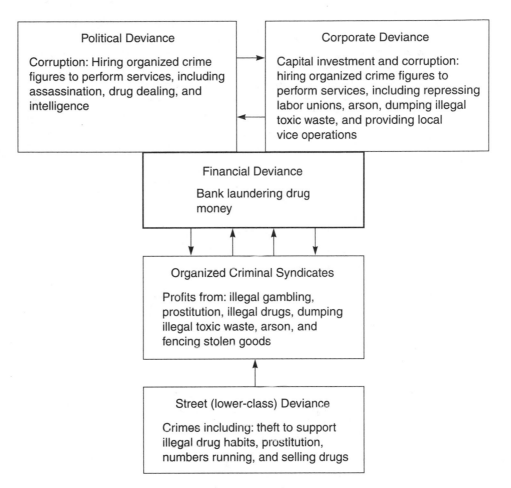

FIGURE 7.1   Links among Tangible Forms of Deviance

Profits from the activities of organized criminal syndicates are made from various types of street crime, including prostitution, illegal gambling, and selling drugs, which includes moneys obtained by burglars and robbers who need to support drug habits. Such proceeds, totaling some $150 billion in annual gross revenues, generate an estimated $50 billion in net profits, profits that must be reinvested in order to grow (Smith, 1980; 1982; Cook, 1980). At times, such profits have been invested in partnership ventures with legitimate corporations, as when Pan Am and Mafia interests opened gambling resorts in the Caribbean following Castro's expulsion of the Mafia from Cuban casinos.

Likewise, business dealings between organized crime and legitimate corporations include the use of racketeers to suppress labor unions and the laundering of Mafia drug funds through banks and other legal enterprises. In addition, there are numerous financial links between organized criminal syndicates and the government, from campaign donations of Mafia moneys to outright bribery of politicians (not to mention the infamous activities of the CIA).

Finally, as mentioned above, numerous legitimate and illegitimate financial links exist between political and economic elites, political lobby groups, government contracts, bribery, and corporate efforts to influence governmental behavior overseas. This is not to say that all legitimate corporations working with legitimate politicians are also automatically linked to organized criminal syndicates. It is merely to say that such three-way links do exist. And obviously, many of the links between legitimate corporations and Mafia-owned businesses are of a customer-retailer nature. This includes phone calls made by bookies using AT&T lines, Mafia-owned automobile dealerships, syndicate influence in the legitimate gambling industry (i.e., Las Vegas and Atlantic City), and relationships among the Mafia-dominated Teamsters Union, legitimate corporations, and politicians. (See Chapter 9 for further examples.)

Symbolic Links

As discussed in Chapters 1 and 2, the United States's most powerful elites have access to the nation's great socializing institutions, especially the mass media and the schools. Such access has been utilized in part to create an ideological view of deviance. This view holds that the U.S. crime problem is the fault of a supposedly dangerous lower class that is criminal in nature, deserving of its poverty and moral inferiority, and in need of increased social-control measures by the state. Such deviants are typically viewed as the products of certain individual pathologies (e.g., "evil, subculture of poverty"). The notion that justice is blind in its fairness, ignoring race, class, and power is completely overlooked.

Because many people in the United States are convinced that the deviance of the powerless is a greater harm to society than that of elites, both moral indignation and financial resources are focused there. This further serves to convince elites of their own moral superiority, reaffirming that their acts do not constitute the real deviance of common criminals. Thus, the official (elite) ideology of deviance serves to convince elites of the rightness of their own conduct, even if unethical or illegal. It also serves to keep the attention of law from the deviance of elites, focusing instead on the apprehension, processing, and punishing of so-called street criminals.

Finally, the official ideology of deviance gives rise to a situation in which the deviance of the powerless reinforces the inequality between the powerless (nonelites) and powerful (elites). This occurs in part because the victims of nonelite street criminals are disproportionately members of the same powerless lower class. Such deviance tends to keep the lower class divided within itself, destroying any sense of community that might result in a united lower-class movement for social change.

For its part, the deviance of elites has both direct and indirect impacts on the deviance of nonelites. First, elites, under certain circumstances, may order relatively powerless people to commit deviant acts. We observed this in the Farben case, where the cruel capos were ordered to oversee the slave-labor inmates of Nazi concentration camps. Second, as we have already noted, white-collar deviance often has a trickle-down effect, providing a standard of ethics and behavior by which nonelites can justify their own deviant acts. Finally, white-collar deviance often victimizes nonelites financially and in other ways. Such exploitation serves to reinforce the inequalities of power and wealth that are in large measure responsible for this symbiotic relationship between elite and nonwhite-collar deviance. To understand the causes of white-collar deviance, one must first understand the symbolic and symbiotic dimensions of the structure of wealth and power, in U.S. society and elsewhere.

Constructionist and Objectivist Positions on White-Collar Deviance

Throughout this book, we have presented a view of white-collar deviance that is admittedly controversial. Rather than take a safe position, involving only white-collar criminal acts, we have argued for a definition that encompasses both illegal and immoral acts. But, one may ask, whose morality is to be used as a basis in deciding what may be termed white-collar deviance?

In general, two answers may be offered to this question. First, there is the constructionist position, which views all deviance as acts occurring in a particular context, a given historical period, a specific culture, and even an isolated situation within a specific culture (Eitzen, 1984). Thus, a murder committed during peacetime may become a heroic act in war. But not all societies condone all wars or even war in general.

In this chapter, we have stressed the importance of reality as a social construction in our discussion of the official, elite ideology of deviance. This official ideology has several negative effects: (1) it blinds both elites and nonelites to the greater harms generated by white-collar deviance, (2) it focuses attention and resources on the less harmful deviance of the powerless, and (3) it serves as a basis for guilt-reducing rationalizations used by powerful individuals engaged in deviance. We have also examined the question of who possesses the power to construct such definitions or, conversely, to prevent competing definitions of deviance from being constructed. Finally, we have assessed the harmful consequences that follow from defining deviance in this way.

A central problem with the constructionist position is that it treats all moral positions as relative, denying the existence of any absolutes as well as the reality of human pain and suffering. Erich Goode's argument in his otherwise excellent text, *Deviant Behavior* (1997, 354–356), is characteristic of the constructionist view on this point. Like most constructionists, he argues that human suffering is nothing but a social construct, thus implying that there is no human suffering until such misfortunes are officially defined as such. Moreover, just because new practices (such as various human rights violations) come into existence, and old ones (like slavery) disappear, does not mean that the pain of physical injury or death, or theft, or rape or any other practice that causes suffering is less painful. Goode also seems determined to limit the definition of white-collar deviance to violations of human rights, thus overlooking all our discussions of the higher immorality, the interrelated nature.

Ideologically, the constructionist position is safe because it easily excuses one from taking sides and advocating solutions, which leads to the implicit acceptance of the dominant ideology concerning social problems, including various forms of deviance. Thus, the constructionist position supports the stance that nothing matters, which for us is unacceptable.

An alternate position is that of the objectivists, which holds that there are moral absolutes regarding social problems.

> *There are social structures that induce material or psychic suffering for certain*
> *segments of the population; there are structures that ensure the maldistribution*
> *of resources within and across societies; . . . there are corporate and political*

organizations that waste valuable resources, that pollute the environment, that are imperialistic, and that increase the gap between the "haves" and "have nots" globally and societally (Eitzen, 1984, 7).

The objectivist (or normative) approach, unlike that of social constructionism, argues for the adoption of moral imperatives and human needs that are universal and ahistorical. To describe violation of these norms by elites as "wrongs," "deviance," or social problems" is merely to state such universals using another label. Stated in the positive, such universals provide a coherent view of basic human needs that may serve as a foundation for policies designed to address the causes and consequences of the types of deviance we have described in this book. Among these basic needs are essential physical requirements (food, clothing, shelter, and medical care), as well as a host of nonmaterial needs, including the basic human rights discussed in Chapter 3.

More important, however, is the realization that dangers are involved with adopting any set of basic "rights," "wrongs," and "shoulds," or causes and solutions. Objections can be offered to any position, as seen in the following examples.

1. The only reason most of the examples that make up this book are here is because they constitute what Simon and Hagan believe to be deviance. They are just being self-righteous.

This charge is profoundly untrue. The examples in this book constitute a case-by-case series of deviant acts that have offended the sensibilities of many leading social critics, muckrakers, and social scientists. The ethical foundation rests on the same moral principle on which the Judeo-Christian, as well as many other non-Western ethical systems, are founded, namely, the Golden Rule, which holds that one should treat others as he or she would like to be treated. What society would sanction the behavior related in this chapter's examples? Even I. G. Farben's use of slave labor would have been disapproved of by the mass of the German people, had they known about it and been free to render a judgment.

2. How dare you speak of the salaries of corporate executives, war crimes, antitrust violations, and pollution as if they all constitute equal wrongs? All you do is open up a Pandora's Box! Now virtually anything elites do can be considered deviant by someone writing on the subject. As a result, the issue of criminal white-collar deviance is lost in the process.

Such an argument forgets that we have introduced a standard by which to measure deviance and harm, including physical loss (death and injury), financial loss, and the destruction of public trust. Our argument is not that all deviant acts cause the same kind and degree of harm. Instead, we find that such acts, whether technically criminal or not, are harmful in some way. For instance, the three-martini lunch and other special privileges given the elite executives cause harm by furthering massive federal deficits, as wealthy individuals and corporations legally evade paying taxes. In addition, citizens lose faith in taxation, thus destroying public trust. Those $3,000-per-day executive salaries and perks further contribute to many social inequalities, which are in turn related to many social ills, including crime at all societal levels. So yes, not all the wrongs we discuss are of equal dimension. Nonetheless, they are still wrongs and are symbolic and symptomatic of yet greater problems.

3. Calling some practices "deviant" when they are not considered to be so by those who commit them is irrational. Practices such as corporate dumping, even if dangerous, are still legal and justified by those individuals involved. They have their reasons. Your approach completely rules out any understanding of the people involved.

Yes, and juvenile delinquents, Nazis, I. G. Farben executives, rapists, and all other criminals have their reasons, too. Deviant individuals erect ideologies and rationalizations to reduce the guilt they feel. Further, they feel that what they do is quite rational, according to their own value systems.

Still, just because corporate dumping in foreign countries is profitable and legal does not make the harm it causes any less serious for those who lose their lives to pesticide poisoning or suffer birth defects due to faulty contraceptives. And the fact that they are not Americans should not matter; they are still human beings. Calling such behavior "rational" misses the point. The harm is intrinsically real and empirically measurable, as this book documents.

Moreover, the rational pursuit of profit may not be as rational as we sometimes think. Practices like corporate bribery actually have very negative consequences for many of the companies and officials involved. Therefore, in the long run, they may be viewed as irrational.

It is impossible to account for every individual rationale when trying to define white-collar deviance. So instead, should we limit our definition to include only criminal acts? Doing so would be unfortunate. Many great harms would go neglected—harms that, if properly understood, would aid in our knowledge of how and why white-collar deviance works.

Discussion

The discussion in this chapter has analyzed how rationalizations for white-collar deviance are constructed and maintained through the use of front activities, and how they fail due to the emergence of scandal and opposing beliefs. Based on this analysis, we conclude that white-collar deviance is understandable from the deviant's perspective. In addition, we feel that white-collar deviance is empirically testable. To establish such empiricism, the following hypotheses must be verified:

1. *Hypothesis:* Public distrust and alienation are increased by elite acts that are considered to be immoral/unethical, as well as by those that are clearly illegal.
2. *Hypothesis:* Major corporations involved in scandals (such as pollution or dangerous working conditions) are likely to suffer from distrust among their employees, the result of which will be deviance, stealing from the workplace, absenteeism, and perhaps drug and alcohol abuse.
3. *Hypothesis:* Employees asked to participate directly in acts of organizational deviance may comply with such directives. But in some cases, especially when scandal occurs, intense psychological strain will result in acts of personal deviance (e.g., drug addiction,

mental illness, suicide) and resentment against the organization (causing white-collar crime).

Each of these hypotheses may be tested via interviews. Thus, we see little incompatibility between our so-called ideological stance and the canons of empirical science. The factor that white-collar deviance is empirically testable is one of the major strengths of our view of deviance.

The discussion in this chapter has illustrated the complexity of the subject, white-collar deviance. It is quite clearly a product of our complex society, as a number of forces work together to provide the motive, the opportunity, and the structure necessary for deviance to occur (see Figure 7.2).

Perhaps the most basic cause of white-collar deviance is the structure and intraworkings of the contemporary political economy. Assigning structural causes requires one to examine solutions that are structural, as well. Not to include solutions in a text such as this does little more than contribute to the feelings of powerlessness and alienation that already plague U.S. society, not to mention much of social science. Not to propose such changes would be, we feel, intellectually dishonest. Unfortunately, we find that a double standard operates in this area. When so-called objective social scientists offer reformist solutions to the problems plaguing society, their work is labeled as "policy study," "social policy," "foreign policy," or some other pseudoscientific label. Most important, it is believed to be unbiased, scientific, and value free. On the other hand, when anyone proposes change that involves the basic distribution of wealth, power, and structural changes, that work is labeled as "utopian," "unscientific," "social criticism," or even "subversive."

To this arbitrary approach to social problems we suggest that the time for labels is past. To avoid making proposals leaves students with a sense of hopelessness and fatalism that merely serves to perpetuate such problems. To label our approach as being more ideologi-

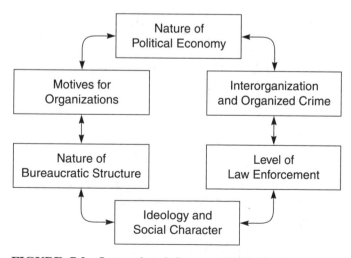

FIGURE 7.2   Interrelated Causes of Elite Deviance

cally biased than reformist in nature is to deny the pluralistic nature of the U.S. political and intellectual landscape. However, to criticize our beliefs as being utopian does us great honor, for we, with Kenneth Keniston, hold that positive utopian visions are essential as a source of hope in an increasingly cynical, alienated, and negative world (Keniston, 1965).

Critical Thinking Exercise 7-1: White-Collar Deviance and the Sociological Imagination

Write a short paper (three to five pages, double-spaced) stating your opinion in response to the following questions. Be sure to make a copy of your paper. What's important now is your impressions of the issues raised here.

  1. *Social Problem.* Select a magazine or newspaper article about a topic currently in the news—a murder in a high school, say, or an indictment of a politician on corruption charges, a kidnapping, a terrorist bombing incident, or a shoot-out between rival drug gangs. Does the article's topic indicate a more widespread problem in America? What types of harm result from this socially patterned problem? Consider the following dimensions of the sociological imagination.
  2. *Contradiction.* What are the institutional contradictions surrounding the problem? For example, do some institutions in American society approve of drug use, either legal or illegal, while other institutions condemn it? What contradictions are inherent in American institutions that may cause the problem you selected?
  3. *Historical Epoch.* What events in the recent past have raised concern about this problem?
  4. *Immediate Milieu.* To what extent is this problem a part of your immediate environment? For example, do you know other students who abuse alcohol or illegal drugs? Has someone ever attempted to sell you illegal drugs? Have you experienced any direct contact with the problem you chose to analyze?
  5. *Personal Troubles.* Have you or members of your family experienced problems with the issue you chose? Are any of your friends experiencing problems with it? If so, what sorts of trauma have you experienced because of this social problem? Is the problem resolvable within your immediate environment, or do you believe that some larger effort is necessary, perhaps a private effort in your local community, or governmental legislation, or public service education by the mass media? If so, what kinds of efforts do you believe are necessary to rid your everyday life of this problem?

Chapter 8

White-Collar Deviance: Policies and Directions

Bertram Gross (1980, 110, 113–115), in his book *Friendly Fascism*, tells us about the "dirty secrets of crime":

> *We are not letting the public in on our era's dirty little secret, that those who commit the crime which worries citizens most—violent street crime—are, for the most part, products of poverty, unemployment, broken homes, rotten education, drug addiction, alcoholism, and other social and economic ills about which the police can do little if anything. . . . But, all the* dirty little secrets *fade into insignificance in comparison with one* dirty big secret. *Law enforcement officials, judges as well as prosecutors and investigators are soft on corporate crime. . . . The corporation's "mouth pieces" and "fixers" include lawyers, accountants, public relations experts and public officials who negotiate loopholes and special procedures in the laws, prevent most illegal activities from ever being disclosed and undermine or sidetrack "over zealous" law enforcers. In the few cases ever brought to trial, the penalties amount to gentle taps on the wrist.*

What explains this leniency with white-collar offenders? Until recently, American business has followed "caveat emptor" (let the buyer beware) and "laissez faire" economics (the doctrine of government noninterference in business). Many laws related to environmental and occupational health and safety have been passed only since World World II. It was not until the twentieth century that restraint of trade, patent violations, and false advertising were considered criminal matters. Only recently has the general public begun to express resentment against white-collar criminals. This may be related in part to the fact that in the past there was less publicity given in the media to white-collar crime, which appeared complicated and boring compared to violent street crime. In some instances the media might be owned by corporate offenders or reliant on them for advertising. There was hardly any coverage during the eighties of the biggest public policy failure of the eighties, the savings and loan scandal, in part due to the fear of being sued.

Elite white-collar criminals share the same social class and background as those who make and enforce the law and do not fit the public stereotype of a criminal. The system of campaign financing and political pressure groups blocks enforcement and lawmaking. Many offenders lack an official history of wrongdoing and, therefore, are first offenders who are usually treated with greater leniency; and they also tend to cooperate with the law, once again warranting more lenient consideration. Prosecution, particularly of corporate offenders, tends to be a protracted process and often an uneven one in which the legal talent and staff available to offenders exceeds that of the government. In the final analysis, it is easier for politicians, public officials, and moral entrepreneurs to attack the crimes of the poor, the young, and minorities than those with greater power.

Regulatory agencies are the "white-collar crime cops" and are armed with a variety of esoteric sanctions that are generally not available for street offenders. Warnings, recalls, consent decrees and agreements, injunctions, and monetary penalties are available and usually preferable to criminal penalties. If it appears that the government has a good case, corporations are permitted to plead "nolo contendere" (no contest) to charges. This enables the corporation and its offenders to avoid the stigma or label of being criminal. Consent decrees merely indicate that the offenders promise to quit violating the regulation in question. As cited previously, Clinard and Yeager (1980, 96) note, "One may well wonder why such small budgets and professional staffs are established to deal with business and corporate crime when billions of dollars are willingly spent on ordinary crime control, including 500,000 policemen, along with tens of thousands of government prosecutors and officials."

The front line of defense against corporate crime is federal regulatory agencies. Such agencies have been barely effective for a number of reasons. Most agencies are understaffed and underbudgeted, making sufficient investigation of corporate wrongdoing difficult. They often must rely upon the very records of the agencies that they are investigating in order to detect wrongdoing. The penalties attached to corporate offenses are often insignificant and hardly a deterrent; they often amount to the equivalent of a "crime tax" or "license to steal." Imprisonment of corporate offenders is rare and, when it occurs, tends to involve "Club Fed" facilities or less onerous prisons than those available for traditional offenders. Many enforcement divisions of regulatory agencies have been cut back during various periods of deregulation. The directors of these agencies are often appointed from the very industries to be regulated, and many ex-regulators, upon retirement, accept positions with the very companies that they used to regulate. Besides more utopian, fundamental changes to be suggested later in the chapter, a proximate mechanism for fighting corporate crime is simply to call for more strict enforcement and harsher punishment. Ironically, while such "conservative" measures have not been uniformly successful solutions with street criminals, they are considered a radical suggestion when applied to elite criminals where such measures have had a history of success.

Professional White-Collar Crime/Deviance

Sutherland's "differential association theory" (Sutherland & Cressey, 1978, 80–83) argues that crime is learned behavior; that individuals become predisposed to crime due to an excess of contacts which advocate criminal behavior. Professional criminals, particularly cannons (professional pickpockets), con artists, and professional burglars, appear to fit this pattern. They participate in informal apprenticeship of jobs, learn specific skills, and make contacts with fences and fixers. Letkemann (1973) calls this "crime as work," in which professional criminals learn not only technical skills but social and organizational skills. This shared subculture is often an indispensable part of occupational socialization.

Traditional professional crimes, such as those of pickpockets and safecrackers, are becoming rare, while modern versions, such as telemarketing "slammers," have increased. Most experts on the subject feel that professional crime has declined since its heyday during the Great Depression of the 1930s. Inciardi (1975) points to the decline as beginning in the 1940s with the acceleration of the application of scientific methods and modern communications to criminal investigation. This included computers, fingerprints, regional cooperation in law enforcement, and greater professionalization within the field of criminal justice. Other writers (Staats, 1977; Chambliss, 1975; Hagan, 1991) see professional crime as undergoing a transition; that is, the traditional professional crime of an industrial society is rapidly transforming itself into "white-collar professional crime" of the postindustrial society.

Professional criminals have been successful in the past due to their invisibility and ability to forestall action by "putting in the fix" (gaining the cooperation of corrupt officials). A steady demand for stolen goods has also aided such criminals. State attorneys generals' offices and state departments of consumer affairs have been the most active in going after professional criminals. The U.S. Chamber of Commerce as well as the Federal Bureau of Investigation have also been active; however, in the past the FBI tended to view "white-collar crime" as primarily professional crime (scams and con artist operations). While a serious concern, such activities are relatively minor compared to the persistent and economically more momentous illegal activities of legitimate enterprises. Most professional criminals turn out to be not all that clever after all, once federal and state agencies begin collaborating, studying their operations, and attacking them with multijurisdictional specialists. The National White Collar Crime Center (Morgantown, West Virginia) now provides experts to assist local prosecutors in both investigation and courtroom expertise in such cases, and the F.B.I. and state and local police have conducted a number of very successful sting operations against professional criminals.

Occupational and Corporate Crime/Deviance

Compared to professional criminals, occupational and corporate offenders do not perceive of themselves as criminals. They maintain a commitment to conventional society even though they violate its laws because they usually enjoy the informal support of occupational and corporate subcultures that sanction such behavior (Frank & Lombness, 1988). Occupational and corporate offenders are participants in what Al Capone called "the legitimate rackets." Mel Weinberg, the professional criminal who helped set up the Abscam sting for the FBI, claims, "I'm a swindler... the only difference between me and the congressmen I met on this case is that the public pays them a salary for stealing" ("The Man behind Abscam," 1980, 1A).

Corporate deviance is affected by the corporate environment and its market structure. Leonard and Weber (1970) in their study of crime in the auto industry indicated that price-fixing requires two elements, a few suppliers and inelasticity of demand (people have to buy the product regardless of the price). Corporate concentration has also had an impact. The market structure of advanced capitalistic societies has moved from competitive capitalism of companies to shared monopolies by huge corporations, conglomerates, and multinational corporations. In 1979, nearly 80 percent of the assets and 72 percent of the profits were controlled by 450 firms in the U.S. (Simon, 1996, 15). Shared monopolies (fewer than five companies controlling a market) result in prices about 25 percent higher than they should be, according to the Federal Trade Commission (Simon, 1996, 19). Such companies have power and huge assets that exceed those of most states and even national government.

While the cost of corporate crime far exceeds that of street crime, the likelihood of conviction of upper-level white-collar criminals remains rare. When convictions do occur, the penalties remain mild. Even "serial white-collar offenders" or high recidivists remain able to beat the system. The Great Savings and Loan Scandal of the 1980s cost the American public $500 billion dollars, while property crime as measured by the FBI's *Uniform Crime Reports* is less than $20 billion a year and robberies less than $100 million a year. The S&L losses equalled 25 years of property crime or 5000 years of robberies. Despite this, by 1994 the average sentence given to S&L crooks was 36 months compared to 38 months for car thieves and 56 months for burglars (Pontell, Calavita, & Tillman, 1994).

White-collar crime is clearly one type of crime for which the classical theory of crime and rational choice models apply. The offenders are generally not poor, deprived, subjects of discrimination or lacking in legitimate opportunity. Those who call for "three strikes and you're out" and mandatory sentences for street crimes often find no impact or deterrence. However, with white-collar crimes such punishment appears to act as a clear deterrent. The reason for leniency seems to have more to do with the social class and power of the defendant than the potential usefulness of harsh punishments. The low apprehension and negligible penalties negate the deterrence model (Cullen, Makestaad, & Cavender, 1987). Guilty verdicts and harsher penalties do appear to inhibit recidivism (Simpson & Koper, 1991). Heavier use of organizational probation rather than merely fines also appears to hold promise (Lofquist, 1992). Nolo contendere pleas, consent decrees, warnings, and cease and desist orders all provide nicer ways of applying sanctions without criminal stigma. Most pleas are permitted because the legal staffs of regulatory agencies are shorthanded, underfinanced, and unable to prosecute most cases (Clinard & Yeager, 1980). The antitrust division of the Department of Justice has historically filed few criminal cases, and the few cases won have resulted in ridiculously weak penalties. Between 1890 and 1969 the two percent of the corporate violators convicted by the antitrust division and serving prison terms did so for labor violations (McCormick, 1977).

The Racketeer Influenced and Corrupt Organizations (RICO) provision of the 1970 Organized Crime Control Act has been used by the Justice Department to prosecute and civilly sue companies that have committed two or more crimes within a ten-year period. This has represented a powerful, if not controversial, tool against organizational crime.

Political White-Collar Crime/Deviance

Political criminals are motivated neither by greed nor anger, but by ideological motivations. They do not view their behavior as criminal, but deny the legitimacy of existing laws or view their activities as essential in either bringing about change in the existing system (crime against government) or as preserving the existing system (crime by government). Operating within subcultures that define their behavior as appropriate, political criminals feel that they have the support of their peers, whether it be theories of racial supremacy (the Ku Klux Klan), preservation of the state (illegal police violence), terrorist activities, nonviolent civil disobedience, or political assassinations (Hagan,1997).

Governmental political criminals are ideologically committed to preservation of the status quo, and this is separate from the aggrandizement of power (which is more an example of occupational crime). Many governmental criminals justify their actions using the doctrine of *raison d'etat* (reason of state), a concept developed by 16th-century Italian philosopher Niccolo Machiavelli. This assumes that state officials may, of necessity, violate the law in order to achieve a nobler, higher goal such as preservation of the state. Machiavelli's notion, "the end justifies the means," becomes a rationalization for political offenders of all types—governmental, religious, or political.

Those involved in illegal activities, such as what Austin Turk (1982) calls "political policing," shroud incidents under the labels "official" secrets, "national security," and "reasons of state." Intelligence agencies in particular may involve themselves in covert activities that challenge congressional oversight and defy our own values. In the Iran-Contra case, the conspirators availed themselves of "plausible deniability," being able to lie that one did not know about something because one was not exactly made aware of the means by which the policy was carried out.

The definition of acts as political crime varies by time, place, and observer. Spies or terrorists, for instance, may be condemned in one country as traitors yet celebrated as heroes in another. The lack of ideological consensus internationally has stymied attempts to obtain unitary condemnation of global terrorism or human rights violations by organizations such as the United Nations. While reactions to crimes against government are generally quite strong, until recently, reactions to crimes by the government have been relatively mild. The watershed in this regard was Watergate. Since the break-in at Democratic National Headquarters, public response to crimes by government in the United States has been less tolerant—on the part of both the press as well as the general public.

Organized White-Collar Crime/Deviance

By the 1980s, law enforcement in the United States began to become quite effective in going after organized crime, particularly the Cosa Nostra. A variety of investigative procedures have been used, including financial analysis, electronic surveillance, use of informants and undercover agents, citizens' commissions, and computer assistance (Albanese, 1996, 105–120). Financial analysis employs classic Internal Revenue Service procedures such as following paper trails (records of transactions) and analyzing net worth (to see if one's lifestyle and spending match one's annual income). Electronic surveillance (use of bugs and wiretaps) is the single most effective tool against organized crime. Informants and undercover agents have also been indispensable. The conviction of the "teflon don" John Gotti was possible due to information supplied by his underboss, Sammy "The Bull" Gravano. Citizens' commissions can supply a valuable, independent watchdog and voice while computer-assisted investigation and crime analysis (compstats—computer statistics) have also been invaluable.

An arsenal of laws have been used in prosecuting organized crime. The Hobbs Act, an antiracketeering act, makes it a federal offense to interfere with interstate commerce to any degree; hence, a gambling device produced in another state could be interpreted as a violation. The single, most significant piece of legislation ever passed against organized crime was the Organized Crime Control Act of 1970 and, particularly, the RICO (Racketeer Influenced and Corrupt Organizations) provision of the act. The Organized Crime Control Act contains a number of important provisions, including authorization for the creation of special grand juries to investigate organized crime activity and the ability to grant general immunity for witnesses, which abrogates the right to self-incrimination in return for protection against the use of compelled information in a criminal procedure. Recalcitrant witnesses who refuse to provide information once immunized can be incarcerated, individuals can be convicted of perjury for irreconcilably inconsistent declarations under oath, and protected facilities for housing government witnesses are provided. The act also permits the prosecution to introduce depositions (testimony given under oath outside the courtroom), prohibits any challenge to the admissability of evidence due to its being the product of an unlawful government act that took place five years before the event under consideration, and makes gambling a federal offense.

As previously indicated, the most important feature of the act is the RICO statute. RICO permits federal prosecutors to seize legitimate operations if they have been purchased with the fruits of illegal activities. Assets seizure (forfeiture) has emerged as a major tool in attacking criminal enterprises. It curtails their ability to continue criminal operations. Prosecutors are given wider latitude in presenting previous patterns of racketeering. The very sweeping nature of the law has made it controversial, particularly when applied to more traditionally white-collar crimes. It uses a more generic definition of organized crime, which covers "organized lawbreaking," including white-collar crime and political corruption. Holding that target organizations need not be wholly corrupt, the law could apply to business, unions, government, and even criminal justice agencies. If illegal funds are obtained from, or used to acquire an interest in, or used to conduct, an enterprise, then it is eligible for RICO. RICO has been used against the Macon County (Georgia) Sheriff's Department, a Florida state judge, a hospital equipment business, a pornography operation, a construction company, Michigan mayor, crooked pharmacists, nursing home operators (Press, Shannon, & Simons, 1979, 82–83), and brokerage firm Drexel, Burnham, Lambert for insider trading.

Civil RICO proceedings permit victims of fraud to sue with or without the Justice Department. While critics view RICO as out of control, forcing threatened companies to settle lest they be branded racketeers, others see it as a powerful means of controlling both white-collar and organized crime (Boucher, 1989; Waldman & Gilbert, 1989).

Fundamental Changes

Crime can be viewed as a "presenting problem," the tip of the iceberg, that represents a symptom of deeper, more underlying problems.

Our examination of the white-collar deviance plaguing America and much of the world indicates that the causes of this immense social problem are systemic—stemming directly from the institutional arrangements and value system of the nation's political economy. Given these realities, we believe that only sustained changes at the systemic level will help to remedy the problem of white-collar deviance. Therefore, we recommend the following as much-needed changes in the American social structure:

1. *Reorganize large corporations democratically to meet human needs.* Multinational corporations are a primary barrier to progressive change. They possess no local or national loyalties, and are unconcerned with their role in causing inflation, unemployment, pollution, and the perpetuation of gross inequalities—inequalities that inherently corrupt democracy. One of the best ways to extend democracy and community responsibility to corporations is to have workers invest their pension funds in them until they own a majority of the company's stock. This would not only ensure worker ownership and control, but would take away the layers of secrecy, from which so much corporate scandal grows. Worker-owned companies appear less likely to experience strikes, as well as the problems that accompany worker alienation, especially drug abuse, absenteeism, and sabotage. Consumer activist Ralph Nader has long advocated the appointment of consumer and worker representatives on corporate boards of directors.

2. *Reduce the government's size in the United States.* This change appears at first to be a near political and economic impossibility. For most Americans, the greatest problems represented by government concern deficit spending, high taxes, unfair welfare programs, and gridlock. The system now in place has degenerated into government by special (business) interests, with reelection campaigns of politicians financed by such groups. Overcoming these problems is a complex task, but it is not impossible, as evidenced by the Clinton administration's downsizing of the federal government. Care must be taken, however that "reinventing government" not cut core regulatory enforcement.

The writers of the American Constitution never dreamed there would be a class of professional politicians who made being in office a life's work. The Constitution says nothing about political parties. Our current pathologies suggest the need for (1) campaign finance reform (federally financed congressional elections), (2) strong consideration and study of term limitations for senators and representatives, and (3) the abolition of "welfare" for able-bodied people of working age. Perhaps the best way to reduce the debt and the deficit is to pare down all possible expenditures, including welfare and corporate subsidies, and increase government receipts without raising taxes on working people. Welfare reform must be accompanied by commitment to creating jobs. Full employment is the best medicine for our economic woes.

3. *Bring about full employment.* This may require issuing new tax write-offs to employee-owned corporations to expand factories and jobs here in the United States. It may also require making government the employer of last resort if not enough corporate-sector jobs are available. There is no question that government is capable of playing such a role, as Roosevelt's New Deal demonstrated with the Works Progress Administration (WPA), Civilian Conservation Corps (CCC), and similar programs. Moreover, attached to every job ought to be cradle-to-grave benefits, health and dental insurance, life insurance, and family leave, and some system of day care for children of employees. Day care centers go back at least as far as World War II in America, and there is no reason that such facilities at job sites could not experience a rebirth. Why not finance these benefits through a combination of government sponsorship, employer contribution, and employee payroll deduction? The vast majority of other industrial democracies already sponsor such programs as paid family leave and national health care. Are Americans any less valuable than citizens of other democracies? Such reforms are, of course, greeted with staunch resistance by special-interest groups, as evidenced by President Clinton's ill-fated national health plan.

The financing of such programs could also take place through increased taxes on the those Americans who possess the greatest wealth and who earn the greatest income. It is now the case that the richest 2.5 million Americans earn more income than the poorest 100 million. Clearly this situation is incompatible with the growth of democracy in a nation where money buys access and influence. The framers of the Constitution assumed that America would be an upper-middle-class society and Jefferson, himself, warned that if the United States became an urban, manufacturing nation, class conflict and the growth of a few rich and many poor would follow. "He believed that almost all Americans should continue farming to avert social ills, class distinctions, and social conflict" (Etzkowitz, 1980, 3). And Jefferson said all this decades before Karl Marx was born. As historian Charles A. Beard once noted, one does not have to be a Marxist to know that wealth and power go hand and hand. Americans have always believed in the unlimited accumulation of wealth. It is part of The American Dream, as well as part of our conception of individualism. The notion that a few ought to fairly sacrifice for the benefit of all has not become part of the American character. Would there be much harm to Americans' motivation if their wealth were limited to $100 million? One billion? For 98 percent of the population, such a limitation would be of no consequence. A national debate on such limits ought to begin soon.

4. *Establish a program of social reconstruction.* Rarely has there been such unmet need in America. Trillions of dollars worth of streets, roads, and bridges are in disrepair. Millions of first-time home buyers cannot afford a home. There is a need for better schools and smaller classes, more family doctors (and fewer specialists), more nurses, teachers, computers in education and in homes, police and fire personnel, libraries, and drug-treatment facilities (to name just a few). What seems reasonable is a domestic Marshall Plan for America, one similar to the one that rehabilitated the economic stability of European nations after World War II.

The question is, of course, how to pay for these programs. Aside from the tax changes discussed above, there is a need to drastically reduce spending on defense weapons systems, and to engage in economic conversion to meet these needs. Many corporations can convert their plants to engage in badly needed peacetime activities—creating mass transit systems, manufacturing prefabricated housing units, and the development of future technology (like interactive video and virtual reality systems).

While economic democracy is a necessity in America, government also suffers from concentrated power within organizations. For example, secretive organizations can lead the nation into war without a congressional declaration—proof enough of democracy's erosion in America. Many proposals exist for extending democracy in America. Dr. Michael Lerner has advocated making extensive use of legislative initiatives (proposals for law or changes therein that come from citizens and appear on ballots after the proper number of petition signatures have been collected). People then vote the proposal(s) up or down in the next general election. Lerner also advocates more extensive use of the recall, where a majority of voters can vote a politician out of office. One of Lerner's more provocative notions concerns the use of television to extend democracy: Voters express their preferences through voting devices attached to their television sets. They would vote after an electronic town hall meeting that debated the issue(s) in question; representatives would consider the results of the vote (Lerner, 1973). Lerner's ideas are not the last word concerning how to expand democracy in America. The need to do so, however, remains paramount.

Foreign Policy and Population Crisis: Social Action

Because we live in an interdependent world, whatever happens elsewhere is a matter of concern everywhere. The United States has political and economic relations and commitments everywhere. Consequently America's true interest and moral principles lie in promoting peace, democracy, and prosperity/full employment wherever possible.

The United States is, after all, only one nation in a world composed of nearly 150 nations. America can, nevertheless, do more than it is doing now. One valuable policy the United States could promote is to have as many Third World nations as possible coalesce into common market trading partners. Such arrangements can serve indirectly to promote freedom of travel and other human rights. The arrangement has worked so well in Europe that much of that continent is on the verge of forming a united, super economic power, complete with multiple citizenship privileges, a common currency, and many additional advantageous features.

Given the depth of the global population and environmental crises, organized groups of people must engage in nonviolent action to oppose shortsighted corporate and governmental environmental policies.

Suggested Readings and Resources on New Directions for U.S. Society

The following is a list of articles, books, and organizations concerned with transformation issues.

Articles

BankCheck. 1847 Berkeley Way, Berkeley, CA 94703. World Bank and I.M.F. activities and opposition campaigns. Web site, http://www.irn.org.

The Ecologist. c/o M.I.T. Press, Journals, 55 Hayward St., Cambridge, MA 02142. Europe's leading journal on social and environmental issues; emphasizes effects of globalization and grassroots resistance movements. E-mail, theecologist@gn.apc.org.

Multinational Monitor. P.O. Box 19405, Washington, DC 20036. Reports on corporate activity, emphasizing accountability, trade, worker health, indigenous rights, and environment and consumer issues. Web site, http://www.essential.org.

Third World Resurgence. Third World Network, 228 Macalister Road, 10400 Penang, Malaysia. Deep analysis of north-south economic, social and environmental issues from perspectives of southern activists and governments.

Books

Maude Barlow and Bruce Campbell. *Straight Through the Heart, How the Liberals Abandoned the Just Society.* HarperCollins, 1995. Documents Canadian Liberal Party's dismantling of the world's most effective social welfare programs.

Richard J. Barnet and John Cavanagh. *Global Dreams, Imperial Corporations and the New World Order.* Simon & Schuster, 1994. How 200 companies are weaving webs of production, consumption, finance, and culture leading to social, environmental, and political disintegration.

Walden Bello with Shea Cunningham and Bill Rau. *Dark Victory, The United States, Structural Adjustment, and Global Poverty.* Pluto Press, 1994. Reports on multilateral development banks and their effects on the poor.

Clifford Cobb, Ted Halstead, and Jonathan Rowe. "If the GDP Is Up, Why Is America Down?" *The Atlantic Monthly,* October 1995. Offers blistering critique of G.N.P. and other current economic measurements, and suggests new measurements that account for social and environmental effects.

Herman E. Daly. "The Perils of Free Trade." *Scientific American,* November 1993. The inherent flaws of free trade; why it cannot possibly promote equity or ecological sustainability.

Herman E. Daly and John B. Cobb, Jr. *For the Common Good, Redirecting the Economy toward Community, the Environment, and a Sustainable Future.* Beacon Press, 1994. Critique of current economic theory, practice; promotes alternative economic values for sustainability, not growth.

Carlos A. Heredia and Mary E. Purcell. *The Polarization of Mexican Society, A Grassroots View of World Bank Economic Adjustment Policies.* The Development GAP, 1994. Study of the effect of World Bank policies on Mexico's small farmers and the urban poor.

David C. Korten. *When Corporations Rule the World.* Kumarian Press, 1995. How the rules of the global economy were created by and for transnational corporate gain, while devastating the environment and social equity; also offers a relocalizing strategy.

Jerry Mander and Edward Goldsmith. *The Case against the Global Economy.* Sierra Club Books, 1998. Forty-three authors bring comprehensive analyses of globalization's effects, the corporations and theories that drive it, and some ideas for localizing alternatives.

Chakravarthi Raghavan. *Recolonization, GATT, the Uruguay Round, and the Third World.* Third World Network, 1990. Analysis of the latest round of global trade talks.

Jeremy Rifkin. *The End of Work*. Putnam's, 1994. Scary study of how new technologies are destroying jobs in industry, agriculture, and service sector globally.

Vandana Shiva. *Monocultures of the Mind, Perspectives on Biodiversity and Biotechnology*. Third World Network, 1993. Analysis of effects of new technologies on Third World cultures.

Lori Wallach, Peter Cooper, Chris McGinn et al. "NAFTA's Broken Promises, The Border Betrayed." *Public Citizen,* January 1996. Examines environment and health decline of the U.S.–Mexico border in NAFTA's first two years.

Organizations

Council of Canadians. 904–251 Laurier Ave. W., Ottawa, Ontario K1P 5J6, Canada. Leading battler against NAFTA; works to safeguard Canada's social programs and the environment and advocates alternatives to free trade.

Development Group for Alternative Policies (D-GAP). 927 15th St. N.W., 4th Floor, Washington, DC 20005. Brings Southern grassroots voice into international economic policy making. Web site, http://www.igc.apc.org/dgap.

Earth Island Institute. 300 Broadway, Suite 28, San Francisco, CA 94133. Environmental group has led resistance to GATT challenge of Marine Mammal Protection Act, other wildlife issues. Publishes excellent journal. Web site, http://www.earthisland.org/ei/.

Fifty Years Is Enough, US Network for Global Economic Justice. 1025 Vermont Ave. N.W., Suite 300, Washington, DC 20005. International coalition challenging World Bank/I.M.F. economic model. E-mail, wb50years@igc.apc.org.

Friends of the Earth. 1025 Vermont Ave. N.W., Suite 300, Washington, DC 20005. Leading environmental group campaigns against globalization and current economic policies. Web site, http://www.foe.org.

Global Exchange. 2017 Mission St., Suite 303, San Francisco, CA 94110. Books and publications on globalization; builds links between international organizing efforts. E-mail, globalexch@igc.apc.org.

Institute for Agriculture and Trade Policy. 1313 5th St. S.E., Suite 303, Minneapolis, MN 55414. Pioneer campaigner and publisher against NAFTA and GATT, and for preservation of small and indigenous farms. Web site, http://www.iatorg/iat.

Institute for Food and Development Policy (Food First). 398 60th St., Oakland, CA 94618. Think tank and publisher supporting citizen action on issues of food, poverty, development, and globalization. E-mail, foodfirst@igc.apc.org. Web site, http://www.netspace.org/hungerweb/FoodFirst/index.htm.

Institute for Local Self-Reliance. 1313 5th St. S.E., Suite 306, Minneapolis, MN 55414. Develops alternative economic and technological policies for local production, consumption, and political control. Web site, http://www.ilsr.org.

Institute for Policy Studies. Working Group on the World Economy, 1601 Connecticut Ave. N.W., Washington, DC 20009. Progressive think tank produces books, studies, articles, and films on globalization and strategies for citizen responses. E-mail, ipscomm@igc.apc.org.

International Forum on Globalization. P.O. Box 12218, San Francisco, CA 94112. New alliance of activists from twenty countries presenting public education events and publications against globalization. E-mail, ifg@igc.org.

International Labor Rights Fund. 110 Maryland Ave. N.E., Suite 101, Washington, DC 20002. Pioneered international worker rights through legislative, consumer, corporate, labor, and social charter strategies. E-mail, laborrights@igc.apc.org.

International Society for Ecology and Culture. 850 Talbot Ave., Albany, CA 94706. Workshops and publications on counterdevelopment strategies, antiglobalization, and preservation of local cultures.

People-Centered Development Forum. International alliance seeking sustainable and equitable community-based economies. Web site, http://iisd1.iisd.ca/pcdf.

Program on Corporations, Law, and Democracy. P.O. Box 806, Cambridge, MA 02140. Educational programs on corporate dominance; organizing strategies for challenging corporate charters. E-mail, poclad@aol.com.

Public Citizen/Global Trade Watch. 215 Pennsylvania Ave. S.E., Washington, DC 20003. Policy development, organizing, and legal action on issues of trade and food safety, public health, the environment, and democracy.

Rainforest Action Network. 450 Sansome St., Suite 700, San Francisco, CA 94111. Focuses on threats that global trade rules pose to tropical and temperate forests, and on native peoples. E-mail, rainforest@ran.org. Web site, http://www.ran.org/ran/.

Redefining Progress. One Kearny St., 4th Floor, San Francisco, CA 94108. Think tank challenging economic assumptions and measurements that ignore social and environmental costs. E-mail, info@rprogress.org.

Sierra Club. 85 2nd St., 2nd Floor, San Francisco, CA 94105. Mainstream environmental group opposing GATT and NAFTA. Web site, http://www.sierraclub.org.

Southwest Network for Environmental and Economic Justice. P.O. Box 7399, Albuquerque, NM 87194. Grassroots organization of people of color promoting regional strategies on environmental degradation and corporate behavior.

References

Abadinsky, Howard. 1997. *Organized Crime.* 5th ed. Chicago: Nelson-Hall.

ABC. "Nightly News." Broadcast, August 17, 1987.

Abramson, Jill. 1990. "Thrift Aide Says Pressure by Senators Helped Delay Action on Lincoln S&L." *Wall Street Journal,* 6 December, A18.

———. 1991. "Cranston Is Only 'Keating Five' Member Who Is Charged with Ethical Misconduct." *Wall Street Journal,* 28 February, A14.

Adams, J. R. 1929. *Our Business Civilization.* New York: Holmes & Meier.

"Affluenza," (1997). PBS (15 Sept).

Albanese, Jay. 1982. "What Lockheed and La Cosa Nostra Have in Common, The Effect of Ideology on Criminal Justice Policy." *Crime and Delinquency* 28, 211–232.

———. 1995. *White Collar Crime in America.* New York: Prentice Hall.

———. 1996. *Organized Crime in America.* 3rd ed. Cincinnati: Anderson.

Albini, Joseph. 1971. *The American Mafia: Genesis of a Legend.* New York: Appleton-Century-Crofts.

American Bar Association. 1952. *Report on Organized Crime.* New York: American Bar Association.

Anderson, Annelise. 1979. *The Business of Organized Crime, A Cosa Nostra Family.* Stanford, CA: Hoover Institution Press.

Anderson, Jack, and Leo Whitten. 1997. "Mafia Chieftan." *Erie Times News,* 24 March, 3B.

Anderson, John W. 1997. "Scandal Exposes Mexican Military's Corruptibility." *Washington Post,* 20 February, A25.

Anspach, Donald F. 1990. *Door to Door Mutual Funds, The Legal Taking of Other People's Money.* Paper presented at the American Society of Criminology Meetings, Baltimore, Maryland, November.

"A.R. Baron and 13 Employees Charged in $75 Million Fraud." 1997. May 13, *http://www.foxnews.com.*

Arendt, H. 1964. *Eichmann in Jerusalem: A Report on the Banality of Evil.* New York: Viking.

Army News Service. 1996. November 8.

Associated Press. 1997a. 29 April.

Associated Press. 1997b. "U.S. Turning Legal Tables on Drug Cartel's Lawyers." *Washington Post,* 5 May, A8.

Babcock, C. R., and A. Devroy. 1992. "The Uncertain Intersection, Politics & Private Interests," 34–39. In *Society in Crisis, The Washington Post Social Problems Companion,* edited by the Washington Post Writer's Group. Boston: Allyn & Bacon.

Balz, Dan. 1998. "The Story So Far in Week Two, a Survival Strategy Emerges," *Washington Post,* 1 February, A01.

Bandow, Doug. 1991. "Robert Gates: A Case Worth Investigating." *Wall Street Journal,* 12 September, A12.

Barlas, Pete. 1997. "Sexual Misconduct by Physicians on the Increase." *The Business Journal,* 14 April, *www.amcity.com,80/sanjose/stories/041497.*

Barnet, R. J. 1993. "The End of Jobs." *Harpers,* October, 47–52.

Barnett, H. 1994. *Toxic Debts and the Superfund Dilemma.* Chapel Hill: University of North Carolina Press.

Bartlett, D. L., and J. Steele. 1992. *America, What Went Wrong?* Kansas City: MO: Andrews & McMeel.

Bassis, M., R. J. Gelles, and A. Levine. 1982. *Social Problems.* New York: Harcourt, Brace.

Bastone, William. 1997. "Mob Bell, They're All Connected at Gotti Jr.'s Telephone Card Company." *The Village Voice,* http://www.villagevoice.com,80/ink/bastone.html.

Bates, J. 1991. "BCCI, Behind the Bank Scandal." *Los Angeles Times,* July 30, D-1.

Beaty, J., and S. C. Gwynne. 1991. "The Dirtiest Bank of All." *Time,* July 29, 42–47.

Behar, Richard. 1990. "The Underworld Is Their Oyster." *Time,* 3 September, 54–57.

Bell, Daniel. 1953. "Crime as an American Way of Life." *Antioch Review* 13, 131–154.

Bell, D. 1993. "Downfall of the Business Giants." *Dissent* 40 (Summer), 316–323.

Bergier, Jacques. 1975. *Secret Armies, The Growth of Corporate and Industrial Espionage.* Translated by Harold J. Salemson. Indianapolis: Bobbs-Merrill.

Bernard, V. et al., 1971. "Dehumanization," in *Sanctions for Evil,* Eds. N. Sanford and C. Comstock. San Francisco: Jossey-Bass, 102–124.

Bernstein, B. 1976. "The Road to Watergate and Beyond: The Growth and Abuse of Executive Authority since 1940." *Law and Contemporary Problems* (Spring), 57–86.

Bernstein, B., and Howard, L. 1994. "Reagan Aid Linked to Drug Running Says Former DEA Agent." *San Francisco Weekly,* May 18, 6.

Better Business Bureau. 1997. "Phony Invoice Schemes." February 26, http://www.bbb.org/library/ba-inv.html.

Blakey, G. Robert, and Richard Billing. 1981. *The Plot to Kill the President: Organized Crime Assassinated JFK.* New York: New York Times Books.

Blankenship, Michael, ed. 1995. *Understanding Corporate Crime.* New York: Garland.

Bloch, Herbert A., and Gilbert Geis. 1970. *Man, Crime and Society.* 2nd ed. New York: Random House.

Block, Alan, and William J. Chambliss. 1981. *Organizing Crime.* New York: Elsevier.

Block, Alan, and Constance Weaver. 1997. "State Organized Crime: A Consideration of the National Intelligence Service." Paper presented at the American Society of Criminology Meetings, San Diego, California, March.

Bluestone, B., and B. Harrison. *The Deindustrialization of America.* New York: Basic Books.

Blumberg, Abraham. 1967. "The Practice of Law as a Con Game." *Law and Society Review,* 1, 15–39.

Blumfield, W., and Diane Raymond. 1993. *Looking at Gay and Lesbian Life.* Updated ed. Boston: Beacon Press.

Boorstin, D. 1961. *The Image: A Guide to Pseudo-Events in America.* New York: Harper and Row.

Boucher, Rick. 1987. "Trying to Fix a Statute Run Amok." *New York Times,* 12 March, 4E.

Box, Steven. 1983. *Crime, Power, and Mystification.* London: Tavistok, 58–60.

Brandt, D. 1995. "As Criminal Capitalism Replaces Communism, Organized Crime Threatens the New World Order," *NameBase NewsLine,* No. 8 (January–March).

Braun, D. 1993. *The Rich Get Richer.* Chicago: Nelson-Hall.

Bresler, Fenton. 1992. *Interpol.* London: Penguin Books.

Brooks, J. 1988. "Waste Dumpers Turning to West Africa," *The New York Times,* 17 July, A-1.

Browning, Frank, and John Gerassi. 1980. *The American Way of Crime.* New York: G. P. Putnam's Sons.

Brunker, Mike. 1997. "Russians Shine at White-Collar Crime." *MSNBC,* http://ww.msnbc.com,80/news/66789.as.

Buncher, J. F., ed. 1977. "Excerpts of the Final Act of The 1975 Helsinki Conference," New York: Facts on File, 11–17.

Caldicott, H. 1992. *If You Love This Planet, To Heal the Earth.* New York: Norton.

Cameron, Mary Owen. 1964. *The Booster and the Snitch, Department Store Shoplifting.* New York: The Free Press.

Caplow, T. 1991. *The Forest and the Trees.* Fort Worth: Harcourt Brace.

Carey, Joseph. 1988. "From Revival Tent to Mainstream." *U.S. News and World Report,* 19 December, 52–61.

Carland, S., and M. Lewin. 1990. "Centrust, the Saudi, and the Luxembourg Bank." *Business Week,* 27 August, 36–7.

Carman, John. 1998. "Media Can't Help Chasing the Story," *San Francisco Chronicle,* 4 February, A-1, A-11.

Carter, David L., and Andra J. Katz. 1996. "Computer Crime, An Emerging Challenge for Law Enforcement." *FBI Law Enforcement Bulletin,* December, 1–7.

Cary, Peter. 1987. "Dial-a-dupe on Con Man's Coast." *U.S. News and World Report,* 21 December, 62–63.

Cass, V. 1994. "The International Toxic Waste Trade." Presented at the 1994 Meeting of the American Society of Criminology.

CBS. 1990. "Mile Busters." *60 Minutes.* Telecast December 9.

Chambliss, William J., with Harry King. 1984. *Harry King, A Professional Thief's Journey.* New York: John Wiley and Sons.

"Charles Keating." 1990. *Frontline* (Public Broadcasting System). Aired May 1.

"Cheating Medicare 'Easy' Doctor Says." 1981. *Erie Morning News,* 10 December, 4A.

Cheng, Allen T. 1997. "Taiwan's Dirty Business." *Asia, Inc. Online,* May, http://www.asia-inc.com/archive/1997/9704taiwan.html.

"Chrysler Fined for Violations." 1990. *Erie Morning News,* 11 August, 2A.

Clarke, M. 1990. *Business Crime, Its Nature and Control.* Cambridge: Polity Press.

Clinard, M. B. 1983. *Corporate Ethics and Crime, The Role of Middle Management.* Beverly Hills: Sage.

Clinard, Marshall B., and Richard C. Quinney. 1986. *Criminal Behavior Systems, A Typology.* 2nd ed. Cincinnati: Anderson.

Clinard, Marshall B., and Peter C. Yeager. 1978. "Corporate Crime, Issues in Research." *Criminology* 16, 255–272.

———. 1980. *Corporate Crime.* New York: Macmillan.

Coleman, James W. 1989. *The Criminal Elite.* 2nd ed. New York: St. Martin's Press.

Coleman, James. 1994. *The Criminal Elite.* 3rd ed. New York: St. Martin's Press.

Commoner, B. 1994. "Achieving Sustainability." In *The State of the Union 1994,* edited by R. Caplan and J. Feffer. Boulder, CO: Westview, 134–150.

Conklin, M. 1997. "Terror Stalks a Columbian Town." *The Progressive,* February, 23.

Cook, J. 1980. "The Invisible Enterprise." *Forbes,* 29 September, 60–71.

Cook, William J., Jr. 1995. "Corruption and Racketeering in the New York City School Boards." In *Handbook of Organized Crime in the United States,* edited by Robert J. Kelly, Ko-Lin Chin, and Rufus Schatzberg. Westport, CT: Greenwood Press, 269–288.

Corn, D. 1988. "The Same Old Dirty Tricks," *The Nation,* 27 August, 158.

Council for a Livable World. 1996. "Pentagon Follies." Washington, DC: Council for a Livable World.

Cowell, Alan. 1994. "138 Nations Confer in Italy on Rise in Global Crime." *New York Times,* 22 November, A1.

Cressey, Donald. 1953. *Other People's Money.* New York: The Free Press.

Croal, Hazel. 1992. *White Collar Crime.* Buckingham, England: Open University Press.

Crock, Stan, and Jonathan Moore. 1997. "Corporate Spies Feel a Sting." *Business Week,* http://www.businessweek.com,80/1997/28/63535116.html.

Crovitz, L. Gordon. 1991. "The More Lawsuits the Better and Other American Notions." *Wall Street Journal,* 17 April, A17.

Cullen, Francis T., William Makestaad, and Gray Cavender. *Corporate Crime Under Attack: The Ford Pinto Case and Beyond.* Cincinatti: Anderson.

Curran, R. 1995. "Too Hot To Handle." *S.F. Bay Guardian,* 29 March–4 April, 15–17.

Currie, Elliott. 1991. "The Market Society," *Dissent,* Winter, 255–258; elaborated in a speech, "The Market Society," at the 1994 Meeting of the Academy of Criminal Justice Sciences, Chicago, IL.

Dahl, R. 1967. *Pluralist Democracy in the United States, Promise & Performance.* 3rd ed. Chicago: Rand McNally.

Danaher, Kevin, ed. 1996. *Corporations Are Gonna Get Your Mama.* Monroe, ME: Common Courage Press.

Davis, L. J. 1990. "Chronicle of a Debacle Foretold." *Harpers,* September, 64.

———. 1995. "Medscam, A Mother Jones Investigation." *Mother Jones,* May, www.mojones.com/Mother-Jones/MA95/davis.html.

Demaris, Ovid. 1981. *The Last Mafioso: The Treacherous World of Jimmy Fratianno.* New York: Bantam.

D'Emilio, J. 1993. "All That You Can Be." *The Nation,* 7 June, 806–808.

Derber, Charles. 1992. *Money, Murder, and The American Dream, Wilding From Wall Street to Main Street.* New York: Faber & Faber.

Dickey, Christopher. 1989. "Missing Masterpieces." *Newsweek,* 29 May, 65–68.

Dissent, 1991. Winter (Special Issue).

Domhoff, G. W. 1967. *Who Rules America?* Englewood Cliffs, NJ: Prentice-Hall.

———. 1970. *The Higher Circles.* New York: Random House.

———. 1998. *Who Rules America: Power and Politics in the Year 2000,* 3rd ed. Mountain View, CA: Mayfield.

———. 1993. "The American Power Structure." In *Power in Modern Societies* edited by M. E. Olsen and M. Marger. Boulder, CO: Westview Press, 170–182.

Donahue, J. 1992. "The Missing Rapsheet, Government Records of Corporate Abuses." *Multinational Monitor,* December, 17–19.

Dowd, D. 1993. *Capitalist Development Since 1776.* New York: M.E. Sharpe.

Draper, Theodore. 1989. "Revelations at The North Trial," *New York Review of Books* 27 (17 August), 54–59.

Draper, Theodore. 1991. *A Very Thin Line: The Iran-Contra Affairs.* New York: Hill and Wang.

"Drug Raid Conducted at Pa. Prison." 1995. *Erie Morning News,* 24 October, 2A.

During, A. 1992. *How Much Is Enough?* New York: Norton.

Durkheim, E. 1966. *Suicide.* New York: Free Press.

Dye, T. 1990. *Who's Running America, The Bush Years.* Englewood Cliffs, NJ: Prentice-Hall.

Dye, Thomas, and Harmon Zeigler. 1996. *The Irony of Democracy, An Uncommon Introduction to American Government.* 8th ed. Pacific Grove, CA: Brooks/Cole.

Edelhertz, Herbert. 1970. *The Nature, Impact and Prosecution of White-Collar Crime.* Washington, DC: National Institute of Law Enforcement and Criminal Justice, Government Printing Office.

Edelhertz, Herbert, et al., 1977. *The Investigation of White-Collar Crime.* Washington, DC: U.S. Government Printing Office.

Eitzen, D. S. 1984. "Teaching Social Problems, Implications of the Objectivist-Subjectivist Debate." Paper presented at the 1984 Meeting of the Society for the Study of Social Problems, San Antonio, Texas, August, 23–26.

Epstein, Edward J. 1983. "Edwin Wilson and the CIA, How Badly One Man Hurt Our Nation." *Parade,* 18 September, 22–24.

Ermann, M. D., and R. J. Lundman, eds., 1982. *Corporate and Governmental Deviance: Problems of Organizational Behavior in Contemporary Society.* 3rd ed. New York: Oxford University Press.

Etzioni, A. 1968. "Basic Human Needs, Alienation, and Inauthenticity." *American Sociological Review,* 33 (December), 870–84.

———. 1969. "Man and Society, The Inauthentic Condition," *Human Relations,* 22 (Spring), 325–332.

———. 1990. "Is Corporate Crime Worth the Time?" *Business and Society Review* 36 (Winter), 33–36.

Etzkowitz, H. 1980. *Is American Possible.* 3rd ed. St. Paul: West.

Evans, D. 1993. "We Arm the World." *In These Times,* 15–28 November, 14–18.

"Everybody Does Not Do It, and You Know It." 1991. *Wall Street Journal,* 31 January, A14.

Farnham, A. 1990. "The S & L Felons." *Fortune* 5 November, 90–108.

Fialko, John. 1997. *War by Other Means, Economic Espionage in America.* New York: Norton.

Fisher, Marc. 1997. "In a Class All by Themselves." *Washington Post National Weekly Edition,* 2 June, 29–30.

Fisse, B., and J. Braithwaite. 1983. *The Impact of Publicity on Corporate Crime.* Albany: SUNY Press, 240.

Fox, K., and T. Lutgen. 1992. "Today on the Planet." *Los Angeles Times,* 25 May, H 6–7.

Francis, D. 1988. *Contrepreneurs.* Toronto: Macmillan of Canada.

Frank, Nancy, and Michael Lombness. 1988. *Controlling Corporate Illegality.* Cincinnati: Anderson.

Frank, Nancy, and Michael Lynch. 1992. *Corporate Crime, Corporate Violence.* New York: Harrow & Heston.

Freedman, David H., and Charles C. Mann. 1997. "Cracker." *U.S. News and World Report,* 2 June, 57–65.

Freitag, 1975. "The Cabinet & Big Business." *Social Problems* 23, 137–152.

Friedman, Milton. 1972. *Capitalism and Freedom.* Chicago: University of Chicago Press.

Friedrichs, David O. 1996. *Trusted Criminals, White Collar Crime in Contemporary Society.* Belmont, CA: Wadsworth.

Fritz, S. 1991. "Lax Rules Blamed in Bank Schemes." *Los Angeles Times,* 28 April, A-20, A-22.

Fritz, S., and Joel Havemann. 1991. "Early Signs of BCCI Scandal Were Ignored." *Los Angeles Times,* 4 August, A-1, 10–11.

Fromm, E. 1955. *The Sane Society.* New York: Holt, Rinehart and Winston.

Fry, Fran, Jr. 1990. "Postal Officials Investigating Telemarketing Firms." *Erie Times News,* 29 April, 1C.

"FTC Telemarketing Fraud, Spread the Word." 1997, http://www.ftc.gov/telemarketing/scams.htm.

Fuller, John G. 1962. *The Gentlemen Conspirators, The Full Story of the Price-Fixers in the Electrical Industry.* New York: Grove Press.

Fund, John H. 1991. "The Gilded Ages BCCI and Charles Keating." *Wall Street Journal,* 2 August, A6.

Galbraith, J. K. 1992. *The Culture of Contentment.* Boston: Houghton Mifflin.

Geis, Gilbert. 1974. "Upperworld Crime." In *Current Perspectives on Criminal Behavior,* edited by Abraham S. Blumberg. New York: Alfred A. Knopf, 114–137.

Geis, Gilbert, and Robert Meier, eds. 1977. *White Collar Crime, Offenses in Business, Politics and the Professions.* Revised ed. New York: The Free Press.

General Accounting Office. 1989a. "Failed Thrifts, Internal Control Weaknesses Create an Environment Conducive to Fraud, Insider Abuse, and Related Unsafe Practices." Statement of Frederick D. Wolfe, Assistant Comptroller General before the Subcommittee on Criminal Justice, Committee on the Judiciary, House of Representatives, March 22.

———. 1989b. "Troubled Thrifts, Bank Board Use of Enforcement Actions." Briefing Report to the Honorable Henry B. Gonzales, Chairman, Committee on Banking, Finance, and Urban Affairs, House of Representatives, April.

———. 1989c. "Thrift Failure, Costly Failures Resulted from Regulatory Violations and Unsafe Practices." *Report to Congress.* June.

Gerber, Jerg, and Susan Weeks. 1992. "Women as Victims of Corporate Crime, A Call for Research on a Neglected Topic." *Deviant Behavior* 13, 325–347.

Gilbert, D., and J. A. Kahl. 1993. *The American Class Structure, A New Synthesis.* 4th ed. Belmont, CA: Wadsworth.

Glass, J. 1976. "Organizations in Action," *Journal of Contemporary Business* (Autumn), 91–111.

Glassman, J. 1990a. "The Great Bank Robbery, Deconstructing the S&L Crisis." *New Republic,* 6 October, 16–21.

———. 1990b. "Looking for New S&L Culprits." *Newsweek,* 26 November, 55–56.

Glastris, Paul, et al. 1997. "Hang on to Your Wallet." *U.S. News and World Report,* 14 April, 26–31.

Goode, Erich, 1997. *Deviant Behavior.* 5th ed. Upper Saddle River, NJ: Prentice-Hall.

Gore, Al. 1993. "From Red Tape to Results: Creating a Government That Works Better and Costs Less." Washington, DC: U.S. Government Printing Office.

Goulden, J. C. 1984. *The Death Merchant, The Rise and Fall of Edwin Wilson.* New York: Simon and Schuster.

Gozan, J. 1992. "Wealth for the Few." *Multinational Monitor,* December, 8.

———. 1993. "The Tortures' Lobby." *Multinational Monitor,* April, 6–7.

Greenberg, E. S. 1985. *Capitalism & the American Political Ideal.* New York: M.E. Sharpe.

Greenwald, J. 1991. "Feeling the Heat." *Time,* 5 August, 44–46.

Greider, W. 1992. *Who Will Tell the People?" The Betrayal of American Democracy.* New York: Simon & Schuster.

Gross, Bertram. 1980. *Friendly Fascism, The New Face of Power in America.* New York: M. Evans and Co.

Gross, Martin. 1996. *The Political Racket: Deceit, Self-Interest and Corruption in American Politics.* New York: Ballentine.

"Hacker Traced to Argentina." 1996. *Erie Morning News,* 30 March, A1–A2.

Hagan, Frank E. 1983. "The Organized Crime Continuum, A Further Specification of a New Conceptual Model." *Criminal Justice Review* 8 (Fall), 52–57.

———. 1987. "Book Review, James Mills," *The Underground Empire, Where Crime and Governments Embrace. American Journal of Criminal Justice* 99, 128–130.

———. 1990. *Introduction to Criminology, Theories, Methods, and Criminal Behavior.* 2nd ed. Chicago: Nelson-Hall.

———. 1991. "The Professional Criminal in the Nineties." Paper presented at the Academy of Criminal Justice Sciences Meetings, Nashville, Tennesseee, March.

———. 1996. "Varieties of White Collar Crime, Corporate, Organizational, Occupational, Organized, Political and Professional." In *Proceedings of the Academic Workshop, Definitional Dilemma, "Can and Should There Be a Universal Definition of White Collar Crime?"* edited by James Helmkamp, Richard Ball, and Kitty Townsend, Morgantown, WV: National White Collar Crime Center, 243–261.

———. 1997. *Political Crime, Ideology and Criminality.* Boston: Allyn and Bacon.

———. 1998. *Introduction to Criminology, Theories, Methods and Criminal Behavior.* 4th ed. Chicago: Nelson-Hall.

Hagan, Frank E., and Peter J. Benekos. 1990. "The Biggest White Collar Crime in History, The Great Savings and Loan Scandal." Paper presented at the Annual Meetings of the American Society of Criminology, Baltimore, Maryland, November.

———. 1992. "What Charles Keating and 'Murph the Surf' Have in Common, A Symbiosis of Professional, Occupational and Corporate Crime." *Criminal Organizations* 7 (Spring), 3–27.

Hagan, F., and D. R. Simon. 1994. "Elite Deviance in the Bush Era." Paper presented at the 1994 Meeting of the American Society of Criminology.

Hagedorn, Ann, and Paul M. Barrett. 1991. "Securities Panel's Decision is Overturned." *Wall Street Journal,* 20 December, B5.

Halper, Jan. 1988. *Quiet Desperation, The Truth about Successful Men.* New York: Warner Books.

Hamilton, Peter. 1967. *Espionage and Subversion in an Industrial Society.* London: Hutchinson.

Handelman, Stephen. 1994. "Making the World Safe for Crime." *New York Times,* http://search.nytimes.com/book/se . . . v+17058+56.

Haugaard, L. 1996. "Torture 101." *In These Times,* 14 October, 14–15.

Hedges, S., and G. Witkin. 1990. "The Bulletproof Villains." *U.S. News and World Report,* 23 July, 18.

Hellenger, D., and D. Judd. 1992. *The Democratic Facade.* Belmont, CA: Wadsworth.

Hellerman, Michael, with Thomas Renner. 1977. *Wall Street Swindler.* New York: Doubleday and Company.

Helmkamp, James, Richard Ball, and Kitty Townsend, eds. 1996. *Proceedings of the Academic Workshop, Definitional Dilemma, "Can and Should There Be a Universal Definition of White Collar Crime?"* Morgantown, WV: National White Collar Crime Center.

Henderson, Joel H., and David R. Simon. 1994. *Crimes of the Criminal Justice System.* Cincinnati: Anderson.

Herbert, B. 1993. "No Job, No Dream . . ." *Oakland Tribune,* 10 September, A-15.

Herling, John. 1962. *The Great Price Conspiracy, The Story of the Antitrust Violations in the Electrical Industry.* Washington, DC: Luce.

Hersh, Seymour. 1997. *The Dark Side of Camelot.* New York: Random House.

Hilts, J. 1993. "50,000 Deaths a Year Blamed on Soot in Air." *San Francisco Chronicle,* 19 July, A-1, A-15.

Holstein, William J. 1997. "With Friends Like These, Is JETRO Helping U.S. Companies or Snooping on Them." *U.S. News and World Report,* 16 June, 46–48.

Hopkins, J. 1993. "How the Cold War Ended, Defeat for Everybody." *San Francisco Examiner,* 27 August, A-11.

Horney, Karen. 1938. *The Neurotic Personality of Our Time,* New York: W.W. Norton.

Howe, Kenneth. 1997. "Blue Shield Pays Fine for Fraud." *San Francisco Chronicle,* 3 May, B1.

Hubbard, L. Ron. 1963. *Dianetics.* New York: Paperback Library.

IACC (International Anti Counterfeiting Coalition). 1997. "Organized Crime and Product Counterfeiting," http://www.ari.net/iacc/organized_crime.html.

Ianni, Francis. 1972. *A Family Business, Kinship and Social Control in Organized Crime.* New York: Russell Sage.

Icove, David, Karl Seger, and William VonStorch. 1995. *Computer Crime, A Crimefighter's Handbook.* Sebastopol, CA: O'Reilly and Associates.

Inciardi, James. 1974. "Vocational Crime." In *Handbook of Criminology,* edited by Daniel Glaser. Chicago: Rand, McNally.

———. 1975. *Careers in Crime.* Chicago: Rand, McNally. Internet Corruption Ranking. 1997. http://www1.gwdg.de/~uwvw/rank-96.htm.

Jackson, Jerome. 1994. "Fraud Masters, Professional Credit Card Offenders and Crime." *Criminal Justice Review* 19 (Spring), 24–54.

Jacoby, Tamar. 1988. "A Web of Crime Behind Bars." *Newsweek,* 24 October, 76–81.

Jamieson, Katherine M. 1995. *The Organization of Corporate Crime, An Inquiry into the Dynamics of Antitrust Violation.* Beverly Hills: Sage.

Janis, Irving. 1972. *Victims of Groupthink.* Boston: Houghton Mifflin, 9.

———. 1971. *Groupthink among Policy Makers.* In *Sanctions for Evil,* edited by N. Sanford and C. Comstock. San Francisco: Jossey-Bass, 102–124.

Jensen, C., and Project Censored Staff. 1993. *Project Censored, 1993.* Chapel Hill, NC: Shelburne.

———. 1997. *20 Years of Project Censored.* New York: Seven Stories.

Johnson, H. 1987. "Casey Circumvented the CIA in 1985 Assassination Attempt." *Washington Post* 26 September, A-1.

Johnson, Haynes. 1991. *Sleepwalking through History, America in the Reagan Years.* New York: W.W. Norton.

Jones, Del. 1997. "48% of Workers Admit to Unethical or Illegal Acts." *USA Today,* 3 April, 1–4.

Joyce, J. A. 1978. *The International Bill of Rights.* In *The New Politics of Human Rights,* edited by J. Joyce. New York: St. Martin's Press.

Kane, Edward J. 1989. *The S&L Insurance Mess, How Did It Happen?* Washington, DC: The Urban Institute Press.

Kanter, Donald, and Philip Mirvis. 1989. *The Cynical Americans.* San Francisco: Jossey-Bass.

Kanter, R. M. 1977. *Men and Women of the Corporation.* New York: Basic Books, 189–205.

Kanter, R. M., and B. A. Stein, eds. 1979. *Life in Organizations.* New York: Basic Books, 80–96.

Kanungo, R. N. 1982. *Work Alienation, An Integrated Approach.* New York: Praeger.

Kappeler, V., et al. 1997. *The Mythology of Crime and Criminal Justice.* 2nd ed. Prospect Heights, IL: Waveland.

Kappeler, V., et al. 1993. *The Mythology of Crime and Criminal Justice.* New York: Harrow & Heston.

Kelly, M. 1993. "Free Trade & the Politics of Toxic Waste." *Multinational Monitor,* October, 13–17.

Kelman, H. 1976. "The Social-Psychological Context of Watergate," *Psychiatry* 39 (Winter), 308.

Kelman, H. 1973. "Violence without Moral Restraint: Reflections on the Dehumanization of Victims and Victimizers," *Journal of Social Issues* 29 (Fall), 25–61.

Keniston, Kenneth. 1965. *The Uncommitted.* New York: Dell, Chapter 2.

Kenney, Dennis J., and James O. Finckenauer. 1995. *Organized Crime in America.* Belmont, CA: Wadsworth.

Keough, R. 1993. *Attachment Disorder.* New York: Dell.

Kerbo, H. 1993. "Upper Class Power." In *Power in Modern Societies,* edited by M. E. Olsen, and M. N. Marger. Boulder, CO: Westview Press, 223–237.

Kerry, John. 1997a. *The New War.* New York: Simon & Schuster.

———. 1997b. "Organized Crime Goes Global While the U.S. Stays Home." *Washington Post,* 11 May, C1.

Kessler, Ronald. 1996. *Inside the White House.* New York: Bantam.

King, R. 1975. "Gambling and Crime," In *An Economic Analysis of Crime,* edited by L. J. Kaplan, and D. Kessler. Springfield, IL: Charles C. Thomas, 40.

Klein, John F. 1974. "Professional Theft, The Utility of a Concept." *Canadian Journal of Criminology and Corrections* 16, 133–144.

Knight, Jerry. 1990. "Like Finding a Trapdoor to Stolen Treasure," *Washington Post National Weekly Edition,* 26 February–4 March, 19.

Kohn, George C. 1989. *Encyclopedia of American Scandal.* New York: Facts on File.

Kohn, H. 1976. "The Nixon-Hughes-Lansky Connection," *Rolling Stone,* 20 May, 41–50, 77–78.

Kramer, R. C. 1982. "Corporate Crime: An Organizational Perspective." In *White Collar and Economic Crime,* edited by P. Wickman and T. Daley. Lexington, MA: D.C. Heath, 75–94.

Kranz, Patricia. 1995. "Organized Crime Is Shooting Its Way into Big Business." 14 August, *http://www.nd.edw/~astrouni/zhiwriter/spool/izi.htm.*

Krulak, V. H. 1993. "Time to Get Tough on Terrorists," *San Diego Times Union,* 13 July, B6

Kwitny, Jonathan. 1979. *Vicious Circles: The Mafia in the Marketplace.* New York: W.W. Norton.

Lang, C. 1989. "Blue Sky & Big Bucks." *Southern Exposure* 1 (Spring), 24–32.

Lapham, L. 1988. *Money and Class in America.* New York: Ballantine.

Lee, Martin. 1997. "The Co The Gangster and The Beauty Queen," *In These Times,* 28 April, 18–20.

Leonard, A. 1994. "Dumping Pepsi's Toxic Waste," *Multinational Monitor,* September, 7–10.

Leonard, William N., and Marvin G. Weber. 1970. "Automakers and Dealers: A Study of Criminogenic Market Forces." *Law and Society Review.* February, 407–424.

Lernoux, 1984a. *In Banks We Trust.* Garden City, NY: Anchor Press.

———. 1984b. "The Miami Connection." *The Nation,* 18 February, 186–198.

Letkemann, Peter. 1973. *Crime as Work.* Englewood Cliffs, NJ: Prentice-Hall.

Lipson, Leslie. 1993. *The Ethical Crisis of Civilization.* Newbury Park, CA: Sage.

Lloyd, Holly. 1995. "Zedillo's Choice." *Mother Jones,* May/June, http://www.mojones.com/mother-jones/MJ95/mafia-mexico.html.

Lofquist, William S. 1997. "A Framework for Analysis of the Theories and Issues in Corporate Crime." *Deterring Corporate Crime,* edited by William S. Lofquist, Mark Cohen, and Gary A. Rabe. Cincinnati: Anderson, 1–29.

———. 1992. "Corporate Sentencing and the United States Sentencing Commission: The Development of Organizational Probation." Paper presented at the Academy of Criminal Justice Sciences meetings. Pittsburgh, Pennsylvania, March.

L.A. Times. 1995. 8 March, A-1.

———. 1997. 19 June, A-1.

Lowenthal, Max. 1950. *The Federal Bureau of Investigation.* New York: William Sloane Associates.

Lutterbeck, Deborah. 1994. "License to Deal, How Uncle Sam Helps Weapons Merchants Arm the World." *Common Cause Magazine,* June, 9.

Lyman, M. D., and G. W. Potter. 1997. *Organized Crime.* Upper Saddle River, NJ: Prentice-Hall.

Maas, Peter. 1986. *Manhunt, The Incredible Pursuit of a CIA Agent Turned Terrorist.* New York: Random House.

———. 1997. *Underboss: Sammy The Bull Gravano's Story of Life in the Mafia.* New York: Harper Paperbacks.

MacCoby, Michael. 1976. *The Gamesman.* New York: Simon and Schuster.

Magdoff, H. 1992. "Globalization—To What End." In *The Socialist Register, 1992, New World Order,* edited by R. Miliband and L. Panitch. London: Merlin Press, 44–75.

Males, M. 1993. "Infantile Arguments." *In These Times,* 9 August, 18–20.

"The Man behind Abscam." 1980. *Erie Morning News,* 12 February, 1A.

Maurer, David W. 1940. *The Big Con.* Indianapolis: Bobbs-Merrill.

———. 1964. *Whiz Mob.* New Haven: College and University Press.

Mayer, Martin. 1990. *The Greatest-Ever Bank Robbery, The Collapse of the Savings and Loan Industry.* New York: Charles Scribner's.

McCombs, Phil. 1990. "The Unrepentant Charles Keating." *Washington Post National Weekly Edition,* 12–18 March, 6–7.

McCormick, Albert E., Jr. 1977. "Rule Enforcement and Moral Indignation, Some Observations on the Effects of Criminal Antitrust Convictions upon Societal Reaction Process." *Social Problems* 25 (January), 30–39.

McCoy, Alfred W. 1972. *The Politics of Heroin in Southeast Asia.* New York: Harper and Row.

McIntosh, M. 1973. "The Growth of Racketeering." *Economy and Society* 2, 63–64.

"Men of God." 1991. *Prime Time Live.* ABC Television Broadcast, November 21.

Merton, Robert. 1994. "Social Structure and Anomie." In *Theories of Deviance,* 4th ed., edited by S. Traub and C. Little. Itasca, IL: Peacock, 114–148.

Messner, S. F., and R. Rosenfeld. 1994. *Crime and the American Dream.* Belmont, CA: Wadsworth.

Miller, Nathan. 1976. *The Founding Finaglers.* New York: David McKay.

Mills, C. Wright. 1956. *The Power Elite.* New York: Oxford University Press.

———. 1960. *Images of Man.* New York: Braziller.

Mills, James. 1986. *The Underground Empire, Where Crime and Governments Embrace.* New York: Doubleday.

Milton, Pat. 1997. "FBI Director Sees Growing Danger of Computer Crime." *New York Times* Cybertimes, 6 March, http://search.nytimes.com/search/d...ime.

Mitford, Jessica. 1963. *The American Way of Death.* New York: Paperback Library.

Mock, Lois F., and Dennis Rosenbaum. 1988. *A Study of Trade Secret Theft in High-Technology Industries.* Washington, DC: National Institute of Justice.

Moldea, D. E. 1978. *The Hoffa Wars, Teamsters, Rebels, Politicians, and the Mob.* New York: Paddington.

Mother Jones. 1993. January, Pullout.

Moyers, Bill. 1988. *The Secret Government, The Constitution in Crisis.* Berkeley, CA: Seven Locks Press.

Multinational Monitor. 1996. October, 23ff.

"Museum Jewel Robbery." 1964. *Time,* 6 November, 23.

Myers, Gustavus. 1936. *The History of Great American Fortunes.* New York: Modern American Library.

National Advisory Committee on Criminal Justice Standards and Goals. 1976. *Organized Crime, Report of the Task Force on Organized Crime.* Washington, DC: Law Enforcement Assistance Administration.

National Consortium for White Collar Crime Research. 1997. "Inaugural Economic Crime Summit." *NCWCCR News,* 1 (Summer), 1–3.

Neergard, Lauren. 1994. "Consumer Group Claims U.S. Doctors Performing Unnecessary C-Sections." *Erie Morning News,* 14 May, 1, 8C.

Neff, Joseph. 1991. "Recession 'Prime Market' for Con Artists." (Associated Press). *Erie Morning News,* 11 June, 11A.

Nelan, Bruce W. 1997. "The Ponzi Revolution." *Time,* 17 March, 32.

Nettler, Gwynn. 1974. "Embezzlement without Problems." *British Journal of Criminology,* 14 January, 70–77.

New York Times. 1975. 30 January, 1.

———. 1993. October, A-1, A-8.

———. 1994. 10 March, A-1, A-11.

———. 1996. 29 October, A1, B19.

———. 1997. 2 August, A-1.

Newsweek. 1988. 7 November, 66–68.

Nisbet, Robert. 1988. *The Present Age.* New York: Harper/Collins.

Norris, Floyd. 1997. "Supreme Court Upholds S.E.C.'s Theory of Insider Trading." *New York Times,* 26 June, C1.

"NYC's Mollen Commission Paints Grim Corruption Picture." 1993. *Law Enforcement News* 19 (30 November), 11.

O'Conner, J. 1973. *The Fiscal Crisis of the State.* New York: St. Martin's Press.

Ojo, Bolaji. 1997. "Inside the Letter-Scam Industry." *Asia, Inc. Online,* May 20, http://www.asia-inc.com.

Olsen, M., and M. Marger, eds. 1993. *Power in Modern Societies.* Boulder, CO: Westview Press.

"Options Scam in Boston." 1978. *Time,* 30 January, 49–50.

"An Option to Run." 1978. *Newsweek,* 30 January, 64–66.

Packard, V. 1960. *The Wastemakers.* New York: MacKay.

Parenti, M. 1989. *The Sword and the Dollar.* New York: St. Martin's Press.

———. 1995. *Democracy for the Few.* 7th ed. New York: St. Martin's Press.

Passas, Nikos. 1994. "I Cheat, Therefore I Exist: The BCCI Scandal in Context." In *International Perspectives on Business Ethics,* edited by W. M. Hoffman et al. New York: Quorum Books.

Passas, Nikos, and David Nelken. 1993. "The Thin Line between Legitimate and Criminal Enterprises, Subsidy Frauds in the European Community." *Crime, Law and Social Change* 19, 223–243.

Payton, Jack R. 1997. "Gangsterism Plagues Russia." *St. Petersburg Times,* 11 May, A1.

Pearce, F. 1976. *Crimes of the Powerful.* London: Pluto Press.

Pearlstein, S. 1992. "This Time, A Different Kind of Downturn." In *Society in Crisis,* edited by Washington Post Writers Group. Needham Heights, MA: Allyn & Bacon, 2–7.

Pennsylvania Securities Commission. 1983a. "Gold and Silver." *Investor Alert* by NASAA/CBBB, July.

———. 1983b. "Oil and Gas Lease Lottery Investments." *Investor Alert* by NASAA/CBB, April.

———. 1983c. "Tax Shelters." *Investor Alert* by NASAA/CBBB, November.

———. 1984a. "Business Opportunity and Franchise Fraud." *Investor Alert* by NASAA/CBBB, November.

———. 1984b. "Commodity Investments." *Investor Alert* by NASAA/CBBB, April.

———. 1984c. "Penny Stock Frauds." *Investor Alert* by NASAA/CBBB, August.

———. 1984d. "Vacation Timesharing." *Investor Alert* by NASAA/CBBB, January.

———. 1985. "The Renaissance of Ponzi Schemes." *Investor Alert* by NASAA/CBBB, May.

———. 1986a. "Oil and Gas Investment Frauds." *Investor Alert* by NASAA/CBBB, February.

———. 1986b. "Pyramid Scheme Frauds." *Investor Alert* by NASAA/CBBB, July.

———. 1987a. "Precious Metals Bank Financing Programs." *Investor Alert* by NASAA/CBBB, August.

———. 1987b. "Investing in Coins." *Investor Alert* by NASAA/CBBB, December.

———. 1988a. "'Dirt Pile' Gold Swindles." *Investor Alert* by NASAA/CBBB, September.

———. 1988b. "Fraud and Abuse in the Financial Planning Industry." *Investor Alert* by NASAAA/CBBB, August.

Perdue, W. D., ed. 1993. *Systematic Crises, Problems in Society, Politics, and World Order.* Ft. Worth, TX: Harcourt, Brace.

Perot, R. 1993. *Not for Sale at Any Price.* New York: Hyperion.

Perot, R., and Choate. 1993. *Save Your Job, Save Our Country.* New York: Hyperion.

Pilzer, Paul Z., and Robert Deitz. 1989. *Other People's Money, The Inside Story of the S&L Mess.* New York: Simon and Schuster.

Pizzo, Stephen, Mary Fricker, and Paul Muolo. 1989. *Inside Job, The Looting of America's Savings and Loans.* New York: McGraw-Hill.

Pizzo, S., et al. 1993. *Inside Job, The Looting of America's Savings and Loans.* Updated edition. New York: HarperCollins, 466–471.

Plasek, W. 1974. "Marxist and Sociological Concepts of Alienation, Implications for Social Problems Theory." *Social Problems* 21 (February), 21–38.

Plagens, Peter, Mark Starr, and Kate Robins. 1990. "To Catch an Art Thief." *Newsweek,* 2 April, 52–53.

Pontell, Henry, Kitty Calavita, and Robert Tillman. 1994. *Fraud in the Savings and Loan Industry: White-Collar Crime and Government Response.* Washington, DC: National Institute of Justice.

Potter, Gary, and Larry Gaines. 1992. "Underworlds and Upperworlds, the Convergence of Organized and White Collar Crime." In *Proceedings of the Academic Workshop, White Collar Crime,* edited by James Helmkamp, Richard Ball, and Kitty Townsend. Morgantown, WV: National White Collar Crime Center, 35–36.

Pound, Edward T. 1990. "House Operations Panel Assails Former HUD Secretary Pierce." *Wall Street Journal,* 2 November, B8.

Power, William. 1991. "Broker's Case Shows Justice Can Be Slow." *Wall Street Journal,* 12 April, C1-C17.

Press, Aric, Elaine Shannon, and Pamela E. Simons. 1979. "RICO the Enforcer." *Newsweek,* 20 August, 82–83.

Presthus, R. 1978. *The Organizational Society.* Rev. ed. New York: St. Martin's Press.

Preston, Douglas J. 1986. *Dinosaurs in the Attic, An Excursion into the American Museum of Natural History.* New York: St. Martin's Press.

Punch, Maurice. 1996. *Dirty Business, Exploring Corporate Misconduct, Analysis and Cases.* London: Sage.

Purdy, Penelope. 1990. "A Bank They Called Desperado." *New York Times,* 17 July, A2.

Quinney, Richard C. 1963. "Occupational Structure and Criminal Behavior, Prescription Violations by Retail Pharmacists." *Social Problems* 11 (Fall), 179–185.

———. 1975. *Criminology, Analysis and Critique of Crime in America.* Boston: Little, Brown.

———. 1964. "The Study of White-Collar Crime, Toward a Re-Orientation in Theory and Research." *Journal of Criminal Law, Criminology and Police Science* 55. Reproduced in *White-Collar Crime, Offenses in Business, Politics and the Professions,* edited by Gilbert Geis and Robert F. Meier. New York: The Free Press, 1977, 283–295.

Raab, Selwyn. 1997. "Officials Say Mob Is Shifting Crimes to New Industries." *New York Times,* 10 February, A1.

Reasons, C. 1982. "Crime and the Abuse of Power, Offenses beyond the Reach of the Law." In *White-Collar and Economic Crime,* edited by Wickman and T. Dailey. Lexington, MA: D.C. Heath, 60–61.

Rebovich, D. J. 1992. *Dangerous Ground, The World of Hazardous Waste Crime.* New Brunswick, NJ: Transaction.

Reid, E. 1969. *The Grim Reapers.* New York: Bantam Books.

Richardson, Lynda. "Coded-Pencil Caper, Arrest in Graduate-Test Plot."

Riesman, David. 1950. *The Lonely Crowd.* New Haven: Yale University Press.

Roemer, W. 1996. *Acardo: The Genuine Godfather.* New York: Bantam.

Rosen, Ruth. 1994. "Who Gets Polluted?" *Dissent,* Spring, 223–230.

Rosenthal, Harry F. 1997. "Watergate, Keystone Kops Caper That Brought Down a President." *Erie Times News,* 8 June, 7A.

Ross, E. A. 1907. "The Criminaloid." *Atlantic Monthly* 99, January, 44–50.

Ross, Shelley. 1988. *Fall from Grace, Sex, Scandal and Corruption in American Politics from 1702 to the Present.* New York: Ballantine.

Ruggicro, Vincenzo. 1996. *Organized and Corporate Crime in Europe, Offers That Can't Be Refused.* London: Dartmouth.

Russell, James W. 1992. *Introduction to Macro Sociology.* Englewood Cliffs, NJ: Prentice-Hall.

Salerno, Ralph, and John S. Tompkins. 1969. *The Crime Confederation.* Garden City, NY: Doubleday.

Salwen, Kevin G. 1991. "SEC Charges Firm with Defrauding 40,000 Investors." *Wall Street Journal,* 17 May, B6.

Salwen, Kevin G., and John Conner. 1991. "SEC Reportedly Authorizes Charges against American Continental, Keating." *Wall Street Journal,* 22 March, B8.

San Diego Times Union. 1991. 12 April, A-21.

San Francisco Chronicle. 1994. 17 July, C-1, C-4.

"Satisfied Workers Don't Steal." 1983. *Criminal Justice Newsletter* 14 (July), 6–7.

Savio, N. 1993. "The Business of Government, Clinton's Corporate Cabinet," *Multinational Monitor,* January, 24–26.

Schmitt, Richard B. 1990. "Columbia S&L Deposits Drop $243.3 Million." *Wall Street Journal,* 18 May, A5.

Schrager, Laura S., and James F. Short, Jr. 1978. "Toward a Sociology of Organized Crime." *Social Problems* 25, April, 407–419.

"Scientology Fraud." 1983. *20/20.* American Broadcasting Company, 6 January.

"Security Group Sounds Alarm on Computer Crime." 1997. *Reuters,* 6 March, http://nt.excite.com/reuters/970306/06.NEWS-COMPUTERS.html.

Select Committee . . . use cited in Summers. 1980.

Seeman, M. 1966. "Status and Identity: The Problem of Inauthenticity," *Pacific Sociological Review* 9 (Fall), 67–73.

Shafer, Ronald G. 1997. "The Joke's On You, Mr. President." *Wall Street Journal,* 3 July, C1.

Shaw, Sini-Ming. 1997. "Dealing with the Godfather." *Asia, Inc. Online.* May, *http://www.asia-inc.com,80/archive/1997/9705godfather.html.*

Shenon, Philip. 1988. "Enemy Within: Drug Money is Corrupting the Enforcers," *The New York Times,* 11 April, A1, A12.

Sherrill, Robert. 1997. "A Year in Corporate Crime." *The Nation.* 7 April, http://ww.thenation.com.

Shover, Neal. 1973. "The Social Organization of Burglary." *Social Problems* 20, 499–514.

———. 1998. "White Collar Crime." In *Crime and Justice Handbook,* edited by Michael Tonry. New York: Oxford University Press (forthcoming).

Silver, M., and D. Geller. 1978. "On the Irrelevance of Evil: The Organization and Individuals Action," *Journal of Social Issues* 34 (Fall), 125–136.

Simis, Konstantin. 1982. *USSR, The Corrupt Society.* New York: Simon and Schuster.

Simon, David R. 1999. *Elite Deviance,* 6th ed. Needham Heights, MA: Allyn and Bacon.

Simon, David R., and Joel Henderson. 1997. *Private Troubles & Public Issues: Social Problems in the Postmodern Era.* Fort Worth, TX: Harcourt, Brace.

———. 1996. *Elite Deviance.* 5th ed. Needham Heights, MA: Allyn and Bacon.

———. 1995. *Social Problems and the Sociological Imagination.* New York: McGraw-Hill.

———. 1992. "Watergate & The Nixon Presidency: A Comparative Ideological Analysis." In *Watergate & Afterward: The Legacy of the Nixon Presidency,* edited by L. Friedman, and W. F. Leventrouser, 5–22.

———. 1978. "Watergate as a Social Problem." Paper presented at the Meeting of the Society for the Study of Social Problems, August.

Simon, David R., and Stanley J. Swart. 1984. "The Justice Department's Focus on White Collar Crime, Promises and Pitfalls." *Crime and Delinquency* 30 (January), 91–106.

Simpson, Sally, and Christopher Koper. 1991. "Deterring Corporate Crime." Paper presented at the American Society of Criminology Meetings, San Francisco, November.

60 Minutes. 1994. 10 July. First segment.

Slobodzian, Joseph A. 1997. "New Era Founder Pleads No Contest." *Philadelphia Inquirer,* 27 March, 1.

Smigel, Edwin O. 1956. "Public Attitudes toward Stealing in Relationship to the Size of the Victim Organization," *American Sociological Review* 21 February, 320–347.

Smigel, Erwin O., and H. Laurence Ross, eds. 1970. *Crimes against Bureaucracy.* New York: Van Nostrand Reinhold.

Smith, Adam. 1953. *The Wealth of Nations* [1776]. Cambridge, MA: Harvard University Press.

Smith, Dwight C. 1980. "Paragons, Pariahs, and Pirates, A Spectrum-Based Theory of Enterprise." *Crime and Delinquency* 26 (July), 358–386.

———. 1982. "White Collar Crime, Organized Crime, and the Business Establishment, Resolving a Crisis in Criminological Theory." In *White-Collar and Economic Crime,* edited by Wickman and T. Dailey. Lexington, MA: D.C. Heath, 23–38.

Spernow, Bill. 1995. Videoconference. Presented by the National White Collar Crime Center, Morgantown, WV, November.

Spitzer, Stephen. 1975. "Toward a Marxian Theory of Deviance," *Social Problems* 22 (February), 640–653.

Staats, Gregory R. 1977. "Changing Conceptualization of Professional Criminals." *Criminology* 15, 49–65.

Sterling, Claire. 1994. *Thieves World, The Threat of the New Global Network of Organized Crime.* New York: Simon and Schuster.

Stewart, James. 1991a. *Den of Thieves.* New York: Simon and Schuster.

———. 1991b. "Scenes from a Scandal." *Wall Street Journal,* 2 October, B1, B6.

Stieg, Bill. 1990. "A Philly Favorite, Faking Injuries." *Erie Times News,* 4 November, 16A.

Summers, Anthony. 1980. *Conspiracy.* New York: Paragon House.

Sun-tzu. 1963. *The Art of War.* Translated by Samuel B. Griffith. New York: Oxford University Press.

"Super Sleuths." 1991. *In Sync* (Erie Insurance Group), Summer, 2–5.

Sutherland, Edwin H., and Donald Cressey. 1978. *Criminology.* 10th ed. Philadelphia: Lippincott.

Sutherland, Edwin H. 1937. *The Professional Thief.* Chicago: University of Chicago Press.

———. 1940. "White Collar Criminality." *American Sociological Review* 5 (February), 1–12.

———. 1949. *White Collar Crime.* New York: Holt, Rinehart and Winston.

———. 1956. "Crime of Corporations." In *The Sutherland Papers,* edited by Albert Cohen, Alfred Lindesmith, and Karl Schuessler. Bloomington: Indiana University Press, 78–96.

Sykes G., and D. Matza. 1957. "Techniques of Neutralization: A Theory of Delinquency," *American Sociological Review* 22 (May), 664–670.

Szockji, Elizabeth, and James G. Fox, eds. 1996. *Corporate Victimization of Women.* Boston: Northeastern University Press.

Tabor, M. 1971. "The Plague, Capitalism and Dope Genocide." In *The Triple Revolution Emerging,* edited by R. Perrucci and M. Pilisuk. Boston: Little, Brown, 241–249.

Tagliabue, John. 1997. "Fakes Blot a Nation's Good Names." *New York Times,* 3 July, C1, C3.

Tanouye, Elyse. 1991. "Rare Coin Peddlers Are Losing a Survey Some Used for Scams." *Wall Street Journal,* 11 June, C3.

Taylor, Stuart, Jr. 1985. "U.S. Defends Disputed Hutton Decision." *New York Times,* 16 May, D5.

Teresa, Vincent, with Thomas Renner. 1973. *My Life in the Mafia.* Greenwhich, CT: Fawcett Publications.

Terreberry, S. 1968. "The Evolution of Organizational Environments," *Administrative Science Quarterly* 12 (March), 590–613.

"There's a New Sheriff in Town." 1995. *New York Times,* 10 November, C1, C7.

Thio, A. 1988. *Deviant Behavior.* 3rd ed. New York: Harper & Row.

Thomas, R. 1990. "Feast of the S & L Vultures." *Newsweek,* 30 July, 40.

Thompson, Marilyn W. 1990. *Feeding the Beast, How Wedtech Became the Most Corrupt Little Company in America.* New York: Charles Scribner's.

Turk, Austin. 1981. "Organizational Deviance and Political Policing," *Criminology* 19 (February), 231–250.

———. 1982. *Political Criminality, The Defiance and Defense of Authority.* Beverly Hills: Sage.

Twain, Mark. 1899. *Following the Equator: A Journey Around the World.* New York: Harper.

"21 Brokers Charged in Price-rigging Scheme." 1991. *Erie Morning News,* 24 January, 5A.

U.S. House of Representatives. 1979. *Select Committee on Assassinations Hearings.* 95th Congress, 2nd Session.

Vaughn, D. 1980. "Crime between Organizations, Implications for Victimology." In *White-Collar Crime, Theory and Research,* edited by G. Geis and E. Stotland. Beverly Hills: Sage.

Vidal, Gore. 1993. *The United States: Essays, 1952–1992.* New York: Random House.

Viviano, Frank. 1995. "The New Mafia Order." *Mother Jones,* May/June, 17–23.

Waldman, Michael, and Pamela Gilbert. 1989. "RICO Goes to Congress." *New York Times,* 12 March, 4E.

Waldman, Steven. 1989. "The Revolving Door." *Newsweek,* 6 February, 16–19.

The Wall Street Journal. 1996. 11 June, A-3.

———. 1996. 25 March, B-7.

Waller, Douglas. 1992. "The Open Bar Door." *Newsweek,* 4 May, 58–60.

Walton, J. 1993. *Sociology and Critical Inquiry.* 3rd ed. Belmont, CA: Wadsworth.

The Washington Post. 1992a. 25 January, A-18.

———. 1992b. 28 February, A-18.

———. 1992c. 27 September, A-24.

Weber, M. 1946. "Bureaucracy." In *Images of Man, The Classic Tradition in Sociological Thinking,* edited by C. Wright Mills. New York: Braziller, 149–191.

Webster's International Dictionary. 1986. New York: Meridian.

Weiner, Tim. 1994. "Blowback from the Afghan Battlefield." *New York Times Magazine,* 13 March, 53.

Weinberg, S. 1990. "The Mob, The CIA, and The S&L Scandal, Does Pete Brewton's Story Check Out?" *Columbia Journalism Review,* November/December, 33–36.

Weisburd, David, and Kip Schlegel. 1992. "Returning to the Mainstream, Reflections on Past and Future White-Collar Crime Study." In *White-Collar Crime Reconsidered,* edited by Kip Schlegel and David Weisburd. Boston: Northeastern University Press, 352–366.

Williams, Phil. 1997. "Money Laundering." *Criminal Organizations* 10 (Spring), 18–27.

Winters, L. 1988. "Does It Pay to Advertise to Hostile Groups with Corporate Advertising?" *Journal of Advertising Research* 3 (June), 1–15.

Wolf, L. 1993. "Victim, 84, Testifies She Prayed for Attacker during Rape Ordeal," *San Diego Times-Union,* 17 March, B-1.

Wolkimir, R. 1994. "Hot on the Trail of Toxic Dumpers and Other Eco-Outlaws." *Smithsonian,* May, 26–37.

The World Almanac and Book of Facts. 1993. New York: Pharos.

World Almanac and Book of Facts. 1994. Mahwah, NJ: Funk & Wagnalls, 52.

The World Almanac of U.S. Politics, 1993–1995 Edition. Mahwah, NJ: Funk & Wagnalls.

Wright, J., ed. 1997. *The New York Times World Almanac, 1998.* New York: Penguin.

Wyatt, Edward. 1997. "Small Investors and Big Money Taken by Tale of Jungle Gold." *New York Times,* 6 May, A1, C21.

Yin, Tung. 1992. "Sears Is Accused of Billing Fraud at Auto Centers." *Wall Street Journal,* 12 June, B1.

Zepezauer, M., and A. Naima. 1996. *Take the Rich off Welfare.* Tucson, AZ: Odonian.

Name Index

Subject Index